D1505471

Political Parties in a New Nation

Political Parties
in a New Nation

The American Experience, 1776-1809

WILLIAM   NISBET   CHAMBERS

New York
OXFORD UNIVERSITY PRESS

TO

S
M D C
C

Party is a body of men united for promoting by their joint endeavors the national interest upon some particular principle in which they are all agreed. . . Public life is a situation of power and energy. . . . The medium of [a] just connexion with their constituents . . . will not suffer that last of evils to predominate in the country: men without popular confidence, public opinion, natural connexion, or mutual trust, invested with all the powers of government.

EDMUND BURKE
The Cause of the Present Discontents (1770)

The process by which the parties move to a point between the extremes is erratic, jerky, disorderly, and accompanied by no little friction and commotion. . . In short, a conception of the party system must take into account its dimension of time. It may even be more useful to think of the party system as an historical process than as patterned institutional behavior. . . If the party process is viewed through time, additional aspects of the workings of party dualism may be identified.

V. O. KEY, JR.
Politics, Parties, and Pressure Groups (FOURTH EDITION, 1958)

The active leadership and their freely recruited following are the necessary elements in the life of any party. . . But the structure of parties varies.

MAX WEBER
"Politics as a Vocation" (1918-1919)

Foreword

This essay tells the story of the genesis of the first modern political parties in the United States as the first modern new nation. Drawing on the American experience as an example, it also explores general problems in the development of political parties as an aspect of nation building, and examines the general nature, functions, and behavior of political parties in a democracy. It is addressed not only to American readers or those who are concerned with the American scene as such, but also to men of democratic aspirations in nations that are new today as the United States was new in the decades that immediately followed its Declaration of Independence in 1776. With this in mind, it undertakes to compare various aspects of the American development with the experience of contemporary emerging nations.

For American readers, the story is an account of the shaping of parties in their own country as a struggling republic, when it was groping toward the political stability and democratic methods it now takes for granted. This recounting may give Americans today a deeper understanding of the trials of contemporary emerging nations and shed some light on the fundamental nature of American political parties as they have evolved in the past and as they function in the twentieth century.

Our first national parties represented the conflicting forces of pluralism in American politics, while at the same time they worked to harness them. They provided vehicles for political participation, fulfilled to a remarkable extent the capacity of parties for offering effective choices to the electorate, and brought new order into the conduct of government. Yet American parties today are often pictured as the supine victims of pluralism or as pliable agents for the decentralization of power, rather than as instruments for coherence on the national scene. If party politics are contrasted with the near chaos of faction politics that preceded the formation of parties, however, it becomes apparent that even a loose party system brings substantial advantages in both democratic responsibility and coherence. Early American experience also suggests that our parties today may possess a greater potentiality for responsibility than they often bring about, although the question always hangs in balance from era to era.

In any case, the story of the origins of American parties reveals the basic role they play in the dialogue of democratic government.

While I have not sought to draw designs for today's new nations based on the American experience, I have assumed that some knowledge of that experience may be useful. As such nations in our own times have worked their ways out of colonialism, quasi-feudalism, or tribalism, their guiding belief has often been the notion that economic development and perhaps social progress are sufficient to establish national well-being and stability. Political development is also basic, however, and workable solutions for political problems do not follow automatically from economic or social advance. Nor can those who desire a stable democratic system expect it to emerge simply from strong government, a few great leaders, and elections. Democracy requires, in addition, the representation and interplay of interests, the active involvement of a broad public and electorate, the building of political parties that can bridge the gap between the people and government, and the training of innumerable lesser leaders who can give the whole system life and strength. In this connection, comparisons with the American experience may assist today's new nations in the search for creative answers to the problems of political development.

Reverses, tribulations, and failures attended the original process of party formation in America in the 1790's. Neither there nor elsewhere could the work be carried through overnight, and for America the task of party building had to be done a second time within a generation. Knowledge of such facts may serve as an antidote to undue discouragement for men in contemporary new nations who look toward the ways of political democracy. Moreover, the American case suggests that every nation must eventually find its own way to its own political and party systems, whether it turns for inspiration to a Thomas Jefferson or a Karl Marx, a Nehru or a Nkrumah; and perhaps the first lesson of the American precedent for any new nation in the twentieth century is the importance of developing political structures that fit its own history and needs, rather than copying alien models. Yet, in their general if not in their specifically American form, many of the problems the United States faced in its formative years are similar to those faced by contemporary new nations. Again, a comparison of parallels as well as contrasts might provide much in the way of understanding.

The approach of this study is a conjunction of the analytical concern of political science and the narrative address of history. It looks beyond particular events to generic factors; not only to personalities but also to political regularities or structures; beyond the immediacies of the American story to broader questions. Thus, for example, such secondary party figures as a Fisher Ames, a John Beckley, or a Benjamin Franklin Bache, today all but forgotten, were as representative of important general trends in party development as the party heroes of the time, like Thomas Jefferson, Alexander Hamilton, or James Madison. Many lesser leaders contributed to the total result, particularly in devising new ways of doing political work which became characteristic of modern parties, and their part in the whole is given full weight. Yet the American endeavor depended also on certain remarkable leaders, and they too have their place.

Throughout this book I have sought to derive generalizations from the American story and test them by the facts of that story. By tracing the development of party politics out of faction politics, for example, it is possible to arrive at concepts of the basic nature of modern parties and of democratic party systems. Comparison of American experience with English experience provides the foundations for a theoretical scheme to explain why modern parties should have appeared first in a country like the United States. Similarly, the disintegration of the first American parties by the 1820's offers materials for an analysis of disruptive forces within parties which may prove fatal. The conceptual and theoretical formulations are suggested, moreover, as statements applicable not only to parties in America in its early years but also to modern parties in other places and other times. They are of course subject to further testing, especially by the methods of comparative or analytical history or by research techniques which draw on contemporary data. In a sense, the analysis undertaken here consists of test borings which may indicate useful possibilities for further exploration.

Modern political parties are viewed in this study as broadly based social structures that perform crucial political functions in a regularized manner. Thus I have assumed that modern parties transcend the personal alliances of old-style politics; that they are something more than mere aggregations of men who share certain points of view, such as the Whig and Tory persuasions of eighteenth-century England were; but that they may still be parties even though they may not exhibit full-scale organization of the sort the Democrats and Whigs evolved in the United States in the nineteenth century. The moot questions of just when American parties first appeared and of whether these formations were indeed the first modern political parties depend in part on what one means by a party. If the conception that is advanced here is accepted, such parties did indeed emerge first in America in the 1790's, and they were the earliest examples of their kind.

Inevitably, I have contracted more debts in writing this book than I can ever repay. For ideas or encouragement I am particularly grateful to Stephen K. Bailey of Syracuse University, who first suggested that I attempt this particular essay as part of a larger inquiry on which I am embarked, and to Samuel H. Beer of Harvard University and David B. Truman of Columbia University. For reading the manuscript in whole or in part and for highly useful suggestions, I am deeply indebted to friends and colleagues, some of whom are specialists in American politics or history and others in the politics of emerging nations: V. O. Key, Jr., of Harvard University; William E. Leuchtenburg of Columbia University; and John H. Kautsky, Barry Karl, and Victor Le Vine, all of Washington University; and I am also indebted to Keith B. Berwick of the University of California, Los Angeles, for a careful reading and useful criticisms. Six former students at Washington University have worked with me as research assistants: I should like to thank Norma Schilling who also offered many valuable ideas at the beginning of the study, Stephen Ellenburg, Judith Ann Laws who criticized portions of early drafts of the materials, Robert R. Rothweiler, Marianne Susman Karsh, and Charles Scolare. In addition, I thank another former student, Judith Burbank, for carefully reviewing the manuscript and for preparing the index. For grants to support the research and writing, for hospitality, or for other aid, I express my appreciation to the American Philosophical Society; to the American Council of Learned Societies; to the Social Science Research Council for a Senior Research Award in Governmental Affairs and to Pendleton Herring; to the Center for Advanced Study in the Behavioral Sciences at Palo Alto, California, and to Ralph W. Tyler, Preston Cutler, and Jane A. Kielsmeier; and to

Washington University for assistance from a Ford Foundation Grant for Research in Public Affairs and for aid through the Social Science Institute. For cheerful industry in preparing the manuscript, I should like to thank Dorothy B. Conard, Lynda Clement, Suzanne D. Fleming, and Natalie Sekuler. Finally, I am deeply grateful to Sheldon Meyer of Oxford University Press for his editorial criticisms and suggestions, and for his patience. Throughout the task of research and writing, I have had the support and patient understanding of the quartet to whom this book is dedicated.

Any extended essay about politics is likely to touch on value judgments. This study assumes that democracy constitutes on the whole a useful and beneficent way to conduct the business of government and arrive at acceptable public policy. Although I have tried to avoid taking sides between the two great contending parties of America's early years or the men who led them, the story is often more Jefferson's than Hamilton's, if only because Jefferson's party became the archetype of a modern popular party. On both historical and analytical grounds, however, the study does develop the argument that political parties are essential instruments for the functioning of a modern democratic polity. It also suggests that, by and large, competition between parties in an orderly system will ultimately serve democratic values better than control by a single party will, despite the vaunted efficiency of one-party politics for the initial labors of nation building.

Throughout this essay, however, I have also recognized the inevitability of discordances or weaknesses within the relative order of parties in complex political systems. Parties as institutions are human, all too human, and must be recognized as such if we are not to fall victim to self-induced disillusionment about parties and democracy itself; and there is no denial here of the less inspired, less inspiring, grosser activities of party politicians and party politics. Perhaps in some better world, politics and parties may be altogether democratic and responsible and truly hygienic. In the American reality, however, the value of parties for democracy and coherence has often proved to depend on what leaders and voters wish to make or are able to make of their parties in given historical situations. It seems likely that this will turn out to be the case for other nations as well.

William Nisbet Chambers

Saint Louis, Missouri
December 1962

Contents

Contents

List of Figures

Political Parties in a New Nation

The Genesis
of Modern Parties

In 1790 Alexander Hamilton, as Secretary of the Treasury in the new government of the United States, proposed to Congress the first in a long series of measures aimed at the economic development of the new nation. Before he was finished he had brought into being a powerful political engine to advance his program, to support his determined effort to shape the destiny of the infant republic. In effect, he had founded the Federalist party. He began this task fourteen years after the declaration of American independence, seven years after the treaty of peace which followed the Revolutionary War.

In 1797 Thomas Jefferson boarded a coach at Monticello, the gracious home he had built on a Virginia hilltop. After three years of retirement devoted mainly to agricultural experiments and to country life, he was on his way to the nation's capital to assume fresh duties as Vice-President. Yet the trip of a week or so was more than just a return to the chores of office. It was a crucial stage in a political odyssey which was to bring him at last to full acceptance of active leadership in the opposition Republican party, a political force which was unique for its time.

The two events symbolize the genesis and ultimate establishment of national political parties on the American scene. These political engines were not only the first parties to adventure on the precarious ground of politics in an emerging nation but also the first true parties of modern times, appearing well before such formations de-

1

veloped in England or other European countries. They were shaped slowly and painstakingly, as part of a general progress in which the American states moved from colonial dependence and revolutionary uncertainties to become a stable, democratic, modern republic. Like the nation itself, parties were the work not only of Hamilton and Jefferson, and of other great leaders like George Washington, the industrious James Madison, and the conscientious John Adams, but of nameless lesser workers as well. The final result was not only parties but a system of competing parties in interaction. Yet no man could have said in advance just what the outcome would be.

Indeed, the whole national and party progress was beset by the difficulties and hesitations of exploration. It was fortunate that most of the new nation's leaders were men not only of high public faith and national vision, but of a profoundly pragmatic ability to learn and invent as they went along.

2.

If parties were to act as unifying forces in the diversity of the nation, they had to prevail over thorny obstacles in the social and political structure itself.

The most obvious difficulty lay in the fact that the "nation" at the outset was actually a loose assemblage of thirteen states. Each had its own history, sense of identity, and political climate; and neighboring states were often engaged in intense rivalries. One of the aims of the Constitution of 1789 was to reduce such rivalries and join the states into a nation. Yet, even after the adoption of the new frame of government, localisms persisted and a tangle of conflicting interests and attitudes remained within the states and across the country. Here were small-freehold farmers and great planters owning platoons of slaves; domestic merchants, shipowners looking to the trade of the ocean seas, and shipbuilders on the coastal streams; struggling manufacturers seeking home markets, and importers and exporters; and artisans or "mechanics." Here also were varieties of ethnic shoots and religious flowerings; divisions between sober "Anglomen" who adhered to English ways as the measure of stability, or sanguine "Gallomen" who saw the

2

French Revolution as the millennium for the rights of man; and cleavage between men who wanted an "aristocratic," consolidated republic, and others who looked toward a "democratic" regime and state rights. In short, the nation was the scene of an indigenous, deeply rooted, conflicting pluralism. In the early American states, the multiform interests, sentiments, and opinions of this pluralism had produced a highly uncertain faction politics of hybrid combinations and perishable alliances. Furthermore, each state had its own taproots of power and its own government offices to fill, and thus its different leaders "ambitiously contending," as Madison put it, for preferment.

To bring the order of national parties out of such diversity was obviously no moment's task. This was particularly the case when scattered settlement, great distances, and poor roads impeded assembly and communication. In view of the fact that a truly national political arena first opened with the joining of the several states into the national government under the new Constitution in 1789, the political task looms as even more formidable. The surprising thing was not that America's political founders took so long to evolve parties, but that they managed to bring any order into the nation's politics at all. The process by which they did so was inevitably erratic and halting. It was also inevitably accompanied by much groping, by fumbling invention as well as brilliant innovation, and by doubts and reversals.

Indeed, American party founders scarcely realized at the outset that they were building parties. They did not see themselves as a set of political contractors who had undertaken to create a modern party system, and in any case they had no earlier plans or models to go by. In England, the mother country and chief source of early American practices, politics in the eighteenth century was still a helter-skelter of personal maneuvering and personal "connexions" —in the old spelling and the old style—of ties based on family, narrow bonds of special interest, or friendship. Public affairs were managed by a few aristocrats, great magnates, eminent families, dependent agents of the Crown, or occasional freebooters. The right to vote was limited to a thin layer of the population; it was common talk that many voting districts were in some Lord's or magnate's

3

"pocket"; the mass of the people counted for little in political calculations; and governments could be made or unmade without regard to broad popular opinion. Despite the persistence of loosely applied labels like Whig or Tory, which actually denoted general persuasions rather than distinct political formations, there were no parties in the proper or modern sense. Furthermore, American politics in colonial times duplicated English modes in many ways. Thus, neither the English experience nor early American politics offered blueprints for the eventual development of parties.

Yet new forces were beginning to appear on the American scene, forces which as time passed stimulated new methods. Most American leaders of the Revolutionary era did want to establish a stable republic, more or less based on the popular consent which the Declaration of Independence in 1776 had promised. During the colonial years the right to vote had been accorded to many men who held a parcel of land; and the suffrage was extended during the Revolution or in the decade that followed to the point where American, as contrasted with English, political leaders were beginning to have a substantial electorate to deal with. Thus even in colonial times, Washington as a candidate for the House of Burgesses in Virginia had found it necessary to arrange for an appetizing outlay of rum, punch, wine, cider-royal, and beer to please the varied tastes and win the votes of electors in his district. The high-minded Madison, who had lost one election because he disdained to "treat," turned to more principled appeals in another contest in the late 1780's, traveling in mid-winter over frozen roads to state his views at a meeting in the snow outside a country church: "I then had to ride in the night twelve miles to quarters," he noted afterwards, "and got my nose frostbitten, of which I bear the marks now." Early in the 1760's, stirred by his Puritan conscience, John Adams had commented self-righteously on the procedures of the Boston "caucus":

This day learned that the Caucus club meets at certain times in the garret of Tom Dawes, the Adjutant of the Boston regiment. He has a large house, and he has a moveable partition in his garret which he takes down, and the whole club meets in one room. There they smoke tobacco till you cannot see from one end of the garret to the other.

There they drink flip, I suppose, and they choose a moderator who puts questions to the vote regularly; and selectmen, assessors, collectors, fire-wards, and representatives are regularly chosen before they are chosen in the town.

In short, leaders faced with new ranks of voters had for some time been groping toward effective methods of popular appeal and toward native patterns of co-ordination.

By and large, however, such methods had remained fairly primitive and were in any case not employed by parties as such. In state after state in the American republic until the 1790's, politics remained a gamble of individual endeavor, or of shifting factions; of family cliques in New York, which virtually duplicated the patterns of old-Whig "connexions" in England, or of intermittent caucuses in New England; of social elites like the ruling "Fifty Families" in Maryland, or of exclusive "juntos" in much of the South. The slow evolution of political methods to deal with an expanding electorate was merely a foreshadowing of party practices, not the advent of true party action.

Additional obstacles to party development came from doubts about the wisdom of parties. For men like Washington or Hamilton, such doubts were concentrated around the question of the legitimacy of an opposition party. A man of forceful presence, a balancing and unifying force in politics, and the supreme hero of the Revolutionary War, Washington was convinced that once the new national government had been put in his hands, it was up to him and his chosen aids to manage it. Filled with determination to join the struggling states into a great and powerful nation, a far-seeing leader of determined purpose, Hamilton also was impatient with criticism, intolerant of democratic demands or the very idea of opposition. Many other leaders held similar views. Uncertainties as to the wisdom of party went beyond fear of opposition, however, and were particularly apparent in the course of Jefferson himself. As easy and amiable as Hamilton was intense, Jefferson had won undying fame as the chief author of the Declaration of Independence and was also something of a practical visionary in politics, and his democratic vision of the national destiny usually ran contrary to Hamilton's view. Yet, although he has been hailed as the founder of the Republican party, he was in fact long unconvinced of the advisability of party action. In Washington's cabinet as Secretary of State, he found himself in increasing disagreement with Hamilton over great issues of economic and foreign policy as well as political philosophy; conflict between the two men was one reason for Jefferson's retirement at the end of 1793. At the same time an opposition to Hamilton's Federalist party and its policies had begun to form, but its early leadership lay less in Jefferson's gentle hands than it did in the hands of other men. Pre-eminent among them was Madison, whose trained intelligence and unflagging industry belied his quiet manner and diminutive stature; and he was soon joined by leaders less well known, like the adept political manager John Beckley of Virginia and Pennsylvania, the poet-journalist Philip Freneau of New Jersey, and other half-remembered activists in the states, counties, and towns. Meanwhile, even as he sympathized with Madison's views, Jefferson held to his early faith in a pristine conception of an unstructured, almost automatic democracy, and persisted in the belief than an aroused public opinion would be sufficient to put government policy on a proper course. In consequence, he was slow to make the transition from republican prophet to Republican party chief. Even when the election of 1796 revealed sharp party cleavage, he remained well disposed toward Adams as president-elect despite party differences and hoped to co-operate with him in office. When a man as shrewd as Jefferson continued so long unconvinced of the need of party, it is hardly surprising that the development of parties was erratic.

Such uncertainties reflected even deeper general uncertainties in the political perspectives of the nascent democracy. Urging the adoption of the new Constitution in the *Federalist* essays he wrote with Hamilton in 1787, Madison himself had warned explicitly against "the violence of faction," particularly against the dangers of a majority faction which might tyrannize over minorities—though he was ready to accept broad coalitions which, as they grew out of compromise among a variety of interests, might rest on principles of "justice and the general good." As late as 1797, the magisterial Washington in his Farewell Address voiced a still significant (if by then declining) view when he warned against "the baneful effects

6

of the spirit of party generally," which he saw as serving "always to distract the public councils and enfeeble the public administration" —it was "a spirit not to be encouraged." The conception that an "in" party of those who held government authority should accept a stable party of opposition was slow to take hold. To many Americans, efforts toward an articulate "out" party of criticism vying for power seemed to portend fires of disruption, if not the flames of sedition.

In short, the very idea of party rivalry was long suspect. In the retrospect of peaceful American party development it is easy to argue that the fear of party rivalry was exaggerated in the years of party formation, but it was widespread at the time.

3.

Other conditions, however, were more favorable for the development of parties. In large part these followed from the special nature of the American Revolution, the way in which the new nation found its identity and established its character thereafter, and the political tradition and political system it began to evolve in consequence.

The American Revolution was a genuinely anti-colonial movement. It threw off, by violence, the ties of imperial control from London and ultimately established the thirteen colonies as legally independent entities joined in a new confederation. Many later emerging nations, however, have tended to look for inspiration more to the French Revolution of 1789 or the Russian Revolution of 1917 than to the American experience. For them, the striving for nationhood has been a long and bitter experience, a rebellion against foreign economic exploitation and foreign cultural domination as well as against foreign political control. For them, the national revolution has tended also to be a social revolution, as the French and Russian revolutions were. Like these revolutions, it has tended to bring sharp social cleavages, ideological animosities in an intense and sweeping anti-colonialism, and the hatreds toward old masters which accompany such overturns. The American rebellion was not a profound social revolution in this sense, although local "Loyalist" elites were displaced from power by American

"Patriots," and the Revolution did inspire a decade of moderate reform. In this respect, the first great colonial revolt of modern times differed from many twentieth-century national movements.

Such movements have brought their own kinds of consequences. When national revolutions become also social revolutions, particularly in underdeveloped areas previously subject to substantial exploitation, the nations that emerge are likely to face difficulties in achieving a sense of national identity. Alienated from the way of life typified by their colonial "oppressors," they cannot readily build a national unity and character out of this culture, even though they aspire to the modernity the imperial power has achieved, even as they employ techniques their colonial experience has left with them. On the other hand, as leaders try to change the society "whole" into a new, advanced nation, indigenous cultural materials are likely to be still more difficult to mold into patterns of national identity and unity keyed to aspirations toward economic and social modernization. Such materials, if not primitive, are far too often pre-modern, traditionalistic, and hostile to the highly rationalized concepts of modern nationhood and an industrialized society. Also, they are often scattered by deep-reaching ethnic, regional, or tribal differences and animosities. Thus, as many national movements of the nineteenth century and later looked to the French Revolution for a model, so have many twentieth-century national movements turned to at least some aspects of the Russian experience. Often the result has been an attempt to force an idealized and still alien concept of national identity on refractory native materials. At the same time the bitterness of the colonial experience has combined with such concepts to intensify attitudes of intolerance or intransigence in politics.

In its time, the American experience and Revolution left a different kind of heritage. The English colonies in America had not in fact been subject to long or severe exploitation, despite the tightening of imperial economic policy and increasing harassments in the years from 1763 to 1775. Furthermore, even the revolutionary leaders thought of themselves as true Englishmen in America, fighting for ancient English rights, the ancient English tradition of equable law, and English liberties. The resistance to imperial power began with the argument that the colonists were being denied their English heritage by a misguided Parliament; and it was some time before Americans brought themselves to sever the ties of loyalty and obedience to the Crown and attack the King himself. Even when they did so, they did not reject their English patrimony totally, but rather built on some parts of it (such as English law and English liberal philosophy), while they sloughed off others (such as monarchy, aristocracy, and the idea of royal prerogative). Thus, they began nationhood with familiar elements that could be shaped into an indigenous and workable national outlook. They did not have to try to build national identity and unity entirely anew, out of bitter residues of conflict, chaotic or intractable native materials, or an idealism imported from a contemporaneous France or Russia, with all of its rigidities. Instead, they reshaped what they found best in their old tradition, evolved new ways as they seemed necessary, and generated ideals of their own. They were at once the heirs of a useable past, and able to be flexible as they looked to the future.

Whatever their differences, a Washington or a Jefferson, a John Adams or a Madison, or a Hamilton—with some reservations—and countless others, all worked by and large to solve the new republic's political problems in this fashion; and Washington lent his prestige to smooth the transition to new patterns of national loyalty.

The result was helpful, not only for the development of political parties as such, but ultimately also for the acceptance of opposition. In part because their Revolution was not a social revolution setting system against system, class against class, or modern against fixed and traditionalist ways on the domestic scene, Americans were able to arrive more readily than many other new nations at basic understandings on political structure, at the same time that they were arriving at a consensus on political means. Much of the emerging national outlook was summarized in the Declaration of 1776 and the Constitution of 1789, and this outlook eventually became a tradition. It countenanced substantial freedom of action in the political as well as in other realms, and over the years this basic liberal view did much to reduce the fear of parties and even of opposition parties. The first amendment to the national Constitution pro-

vided clearly for freedom of speech, assembly, publication, and petition, and the rule won ultimate acceptance. The national tradition,
growing in a favorable soil in which most citizens owned at least
some measure of property and in which distinctions of rich and
poor were minimized, also promoted an increasing degree of social
equality and political democracy, along with attitudes that kept
political conflict generally within a moderate range and subject to
peaceful resolution. Fear of opposition or an opposition party remained for some time, but a counter-tradition could be invoked
against it. Furthermore, intolerance of opposition reinforced by an
official ideology could not be invoked as a revolutionary virtue.

Still, modern parties and the party system in the United States
were indeed products of a labor of Hercules, and not "natural," un-
tended flowerings from the soil of independence and popular government. Rather, parties were ingeniously shaped "artifacts," in the
sense of structures built up over years by the industrious, if often
groping, activities of men. To assume that a democratic political
party system in the United States in the 1790's—or in any new nation—could grow overnight from independence and a democratic
constitution, or be struck off at a blow by one or two great leaders,
is to underestimate the problems involved. Revolution on Monday,
independence on Tuesday, a constitution on Wednesday, political
parties on Thursday, orderly elections on Friday, stable democratic
government by Saturday, and rest on Sunday—any such conception
of political creation is the stuff of dreams. If parties and democratic
party systems are the products of human ingenuity, time and energy
in abundance must go into their making.

4.

In the process of party building, American founders confronted
and effectively solved a long series of political problems. Some
were foreseen and some unforeseen, some were at hand from the
outset and some emerged only in the course of the work. It was
throughout an endeavor of pragmatic adaptation and inventiveness
under necessity, guided at the beginning by immediate purposes or
a general desire to prove the republican experiment, informed only
later by a conception of party as a goal. The problems of establish-

ing the republic and of establishing party overlapped, and in a sense they all involved the practical fulfillment of the national and democratic promise of the Declaration of Independence.

The first task was to fix workable patterns of legitimacy and authority in the new polity, under which the conflict of interests and opinions could go on within a larger national unity. The solution to this problem ultimately drew on elements as disparate as Washington's personal appeal and Jefferson's rationalist philosophy.

As any emerging nation must, young America faced the issue of shaping national economic development and policy, with all of its payoffs and costs for different interests. As a new national power, it also faced the trying problem of establishing national identity and effective independence in an often threatening and sometimes contemptuous world. The first great, controversial steps in economic policy were taken by Hamilton, whose party found its origins in the ties of interest and action his program brought forth. Contention over world politics and foreign policy followed, pitting Madison against Washington as well as Hamilton, and Jefferson against Adams; and full-scale party division ensued. Yet policy was evolved, and the nation survived.

To man the posts of government and the new force of party, new recruits for leadership were necessary; and the nation was fortunate in the skill and imagination of the political lieutenants, cadremen and foot soldiers who came forward to administer public affairs and develop party formations.

One task such men confronted was devising stable methods which could link a hitherto unprecedented mass public and electorate to hitherto unprecedented party structures. Another was forging sufficient unity within parties in government to enable them to govern coherently and bridge the gap between the constitutionally separated executive and legislative branches in the American system. The first great essay at governmental management was Hamilton's, and he accomplished much toward coherent policy. Within a decade, however, Jefferson and his co-workers had gone even further and achieved a near model of responsible democratic party government in office.

Given the pluralism and state-by-state fragmentation of power in

11

the American federal system, party builders had to assemble national parties out of varied and widely scattered state and local materials. Indeed, the interplay (and often conflict) between disparate state and local elements on one hand, and national structures and concerns on the other, has been a continuing theme of American party development and action. After some years, the Republicans also developed modern organization to reinforce party strength, but the Federalists never arrived at this device.

With the establishment of parties, Americans faced the intricate problems of conducting a system of parties in competition and the delicate questions of accord in the idea of opposition and of the peaceful transfer of power from one party to another.

The eventual solution of these various problems was to become the story of America's formative political years.

American party development also touched another issue of fundamental concern. This was the question of the practical functioning of a democratic political system as a whole. Various processes have been proposed as the criteria of democracy: free entry to the political arena; widespread participation in the political system; effective representation for and balancing of varied interests in the society; open discussion and debate; free elections; government that is somehow responsive or responsible to the demands or judgments of the public or electorate; or the right to criticize government decisions. It is easy to speak broadly, as Jefferson did in the Declaration of 1776, of governments "deriving their just powers from the consent of the governed." It is more difficult in practice to realize such consent and to assure the faithfulness of governments to the governed, to meet significant criteria of democratic functioning. In practical terms, some sort of party system has proved necessary to the operation of modern democratic politics.

In the American case, the machinery of democratic functioning came to comprise three major elements. The first two developed as popular participation and the representation of varied interests. The great practical fulcrum of American democracy in a large complex society, however, became popular choice: the presentation to the public or electorate of alternatives concerning policies and leaders, and choices by the public or electorate among such alternatives, primarily in elections. It is here that parties and party competition came to play their great role, in shaping and clarifying options for popular choice or decision, and in giving such choices some effect in the conduct of government. If such choices are to be effective, they imply the operation of other crucial processes of democracy. Different patterns of democratic practice are conceivable, including the mechanisms of representative single-party systems which some later new nations have evolved. In the developing American system, however, the party Hamilton founded and the rival party Jefferson came to lead offered a remarkably useful set of political instruments.

In 1788, a Republican-to-be with a properly protesting first name, Melancton Smith of New York, expressed his fear that the new national government would come under the control of the well-to-do and the eminent. Their "influence," he argued,

will generally enable them to succeed in elections. [Those of] conspicuous military, popular, civil, or legal talents . . . easily form associations; the poor and middling classes form them with difficulty. . . . A substantial yeoman, of sense and discernment, will hardly ever be chosen. From these remarks, it appears that the government will fall into the hands of the few and the great. This will be a government of oppression.

A dozen years later another Jeffersonian leader, Charles Pinckney of South Carolina, spoke of his long battle in the old-style faction politics of the state against domination by "the Weight of Talent, Wealth, and personal and family interest." From its very beginnings American democracy has been threatened by the power exerted by established wealth, status, or influence, but parties were to prove that they could do much to offset these advantages. In particular, the party of Jefferson was to emerge as a new kind of broadly-based, "popular" party which was conspicuously effective to this end.

In the process of nation building, the American founders explored many problems generic to new nations. Their experience cannot provide literal lessons for other peoples today, who face different conditions and must devise political procedures that are appropriate to their own circumstances, as their American predecessors did. Yet there are important parallels. The American instance revealed the significance of a concern for political as well as economic development in the progress of a new nation, as it also showed that political construction is bound to be difficult and disappointing to utopian hopes, and proved the value of moderate and pragmatic approaches to political problems. It brought to light important factors which may make for national stability, underscored the role of economic development as a foundation for democracy, and underscored the crucial role of broad as well as specialized education for promoting democracy and training leaders. It also provided an early example of parties as vehicles to contain the forces of pluralism and bring coherence into public policy. It demonstrated the eventual utility of a two-party system as an instrument of democracy and a device to redress imbalances of privilege and power. Finally, the American experience set a pattern for a responsible opposition which avoided the intransigence that may disrupt a nation. In short, it uncovered viable democratic ways to conduct the conflict of politics and manage government within national unity.

Yet at the time, no one could foresee the result. Only after they had taken long steps toward the solution of the political problems they faced, only after the tasks of party development had been accomplished, could American leaders and the American public look back and see what they had achieved.

5.

As the American founders resolved problem after problem in the shaping of the republic, they not only established the first modern political parties. They were also involved, if mostly unknowingly, in a general process of political modernization in which parties were at once an element and a catalyst in a broader change from older to newer things.

Such modernization, particularly as it showed itself first in the West, has typically revealed a variety of political developments. The tendency has been for traditionalized, highly personalized, and often parochial patterns of authority to break down, whether they have been patterns of simple custom or more complex systems of feudal hierarchy, monarchy, or social deference. Thus the sway of

14

kings and barons, nobles and retainers, or magnates and "connexions" becomes outmoded. Authority tends to become based on rational-legal foundations in a regularized form which is expressed in constitutions or general law—although often the process may involve a transitional stage of personal foundations for authority built around an early unifying leader. The modes of conducting politics become rationalized also, in several ways. For example, the claims of political interests must be advanced more and more on allegedly rational, rather than prescriptive, grounds. The very procedures of politics and administration become more orderly, methodical, and efficient. Political formations and political action come to stand on a less personalized basis, although within the more rational politics ample opportunity may remain for new-style personal influence, as it has in much "inside" party politics. The new political culture permits innovation as against fixed, traditional ways. There is an increase in rational discussion of political values and goals, and of political methods as means to such goals. Birth and family become less important than work and achievement as keys to political success, and politics becomes more and more a matter of competition. Parties, active interest groups, press, and propaganda appear in the political arena—and often revolutionary organizations also appear. Taken over all, a new energy or *élan* comes to characterize political life.

In America, party development was caught up in such an unfolding, energizing process. Parties could emerge as political formations which were "modern" or even "popular," because the nation was becoming "modern" and "democratic." At the same time, they could help it on its way.

Modern parties must be sustained by human energies after they have been set going, and sustenance has not always been sufficient. The United States advanced toward a party system in the 1790's and the sway of party was strengthened in the years that immediately followed. The decade from about 1809 to 1819, however, brought the disintegration of the first American parties as the acids of pluralism ate away at party bonds and leadership faltered. After a brief try at virtual one-party government, it appeared that the American experiment in modern parties in competition had failed.

Political Parties in a New Nation

Yet the succeeding dozen years brought new beginnings toward a second system of popular parties, which stirred a mass public even more fully than the prototype Federalists and Republicans had done. The man who shaped these later parties had to grope less than their predecessors, for they could foresee what they wanted. Because the first parties had been built upon a modern and rationalized basis rather than on traditional or merely personal foundations, later leaders had examples to work from.

The new party framework Hamilton had begun had cast a long shadow. The coach that took Jefferson from retirement to active political labors in 1797 had carried more than he or his contemporaries could know. The work of the two men, who were so different and so often in conflict, had set precepts for modern party action from which later generations could learn and upon which they could build. It had marked one new nation's progress from political confusion to comparative order, from colonial dependency to a viable democratic system.

1

The Confusion
of Faction

Early American politics was, almost without exception, non-party or faction politics. In the decades of winning independence and establishing the nation, Americans proved as ingenious in political procedures as they were in other realms of practical life: they were remarkably prompt, for example, in devising state constitutions to provide orderly governmental structure. They were slower, however, in arriving at political parties as a means of bringing greater coherence into politics as a whole.

The revolution against British rule brought sharp cleavages. Men divided into "Patriots," who demanded independence and supported the Revolutionary War of 1775-1783, and "Loyalists," who sought to maintain the British allegiance. The Patriots caucused, launched local societies like the Sons of Liberty or sponsored committees of correspondence, produced publicists from the legalistic John Adams to the apocalyptic Thomas Paine, and sent delegates to a co-ordinating Continental Congress. Yet even when men in Congress subscribed their "sacred Honor" to the Declaration of Independence, the Patriot force remained fundamentally a comradeship of arms among Revolutionary leaders against English rule, a body of opinion in the populace, and an uncertain net of interstate communication among state caucuses and factions. The Patriot alliance evolved patterns of parallel action and loose co-ordination up and down the seaboard and obtained a mass following, but, despite its strength and activity, did not constitute a party

17

in the full sense. Thus the American Patriots did not generate a stable nationalist political party—as many later national revolutionaries have done. In consequence, party development remained to be accomplished "from scratch."

Within the American states in the 1770's and 1780's, party was even less discernible than it was in the Revolutionary struggle. Certain common elements existed, with variations. At the outset the new commonwealths tended to be patrician or elitist with their constitutions embracing only hesitant or limited democratic reforms. The long-range trend, however, was toward democracy in the sense of popular activity in politics, a trend which was to continue through the popular-republican era of Thomas Jefferson into the *hoi polloi*-democratic age of Andrew Jackson. Its first impact came in the extension of voting rights in nearly all of the states through the reduction of property or tax qualifications; and widespread ownership of property in freehold farms meant that the vote was at least legally open to the majority of white, adult males. To be sure, suffrage was not always exercised. Nonetheless, the 1770's and 1780's saw the emergence of a rough native American populism as well as a moderate-liberal impulse that called on government for the satisfaction of the interests of the many as well as of the few and that worked against dominance by social elites. Such pressures were often frustrated in the early years, and a patrician style of politics persisted for some time. Yet the impulse toward democratization was to triumph in the end.

In day-to-day politics, old turmoils of the colonial years bubbled into new conflicts. In most of the states, pressures for broader voting rights or for proportionate representation in the legislatures for rural and western counties as against the richer or more urbanized seaboard marked the early appearance of what was to become a standard American political theme: the impulse toward equalitarianism. In some states loose "country" factions stirred attacks on what Adams in colonial days had called "court" factions, or the elites of entrenched officialdom in state capital and courthouse, thereby expressing another emerging American attitude: the suspicion of governmental power.

Such broad currents of division were mixed, however, with a

bewildering variety of crosscurrents. Thus, in Massachusetts animosities between dominant Congregationalists and underdog Baptists simmered along with economic or town-and-country conflicts. In Maryland and South Carolina, preponderant power for planter-slaveholding factions or juntos withstood pressures from merchants or town "commoners" in Baltimore and Charleston, although in South Carolina the planter-"Nabob" group had to win support from the British mercantile agents to fight off a potential "Republican" or "Radical" alliance of native merchants, town artisans, and back-country farmers. Yet, in Virginia, Jefferson as governor in 1779-1781 was able to introduce moderate social reforms without stirring intense conflict, and over the years a relatively open, free-style politics developed around leaders who were already prominent figures in Commonwealth or county. National economic distress in the late 1780's precipitated new cleavages between debtors and creditor-investor groups, often extremely involved as in Connecticut or South Carolina. In Massachusetts a struggle of debtor-farmers against merchant-creditors boiled in a brief agrarian rebellion led by a former Revolutionary War captain, Daniel Shays—but a curious rebellion it was, a movement for the protection of mortgaged lands against the claims of creditors rather than a *Jacquerie* of propertyless peasants to despoil propertied aristocrats. In Rhode Island a complex alignment of urban and rural interests managed to secure power and carry through a program of paper-money inflation.

Yet, despite all these bubblings of the political pot, only one of the thirteen states managed to brew something like a party system. The exception was Pennsylvania, where in the 1770's and 1780's two parties had developed out of the clash of interests, particularly as they touched the question of the state constitution of 1776. One formation was generally called "Constitutionalist," while the other was known as "Anti-Constitutionalist" or "Republican." Under such notable leaders as Benjamin Franklin, Robert Morris, General Thomas Mifflin, and James Wilson, flanked by lesser, semi-professional politicians, the two parties even managed to generate substantial early organization. They remained sufficiently stable so that the issue of ratifying the new national Constitution was fought out

19

mainly between them—in a reversal of symbols, the Pennsylvania Constitutionalists opposed and the local Anti-Constitutionalists, or Republicans, supported the new national charter. By the early 1790's, however, the state parties had practically disintegrated, and a new alignment on national-party terms was in the making.

In neighboring New York, meanwhile, an old, familiar gruel of highly personal politics remained. A few powerful families provided centers for political cliques which made and broke alliances as convenience dictated, and politics was largely a potpourri of the De-Lanceys, the Livingstons, the Schuylers, the Clintons, the Van Cortlandts, and other prominent clans. Men, far more than measures, were the determining factors in formations strongly reminiscent of the old-Whig "connexions" of English politics. New style politicians like the upstarts Hamilton or Aaron Burr brought more modern ingredients to the brew, but even they had to depend on old-style personal ties, at least at the outset. At the center by the 1780's stood the Clintonians, who managed again and again to elect their leader George Clinton to the governorship. From 1777 on, "His Excellency" held together a series of alliances which withstood all opposition until the ratification controversy of 1788, when his anti-ratification forces lost out to a pro-Constitution combination of Schuylerites, Livingstons, Hamiltonians, and New York City elements. Yet, although New York in the 1780's has sometimes been described as a state with parties, not even the Clintonians were a true party. Not until old personal "connexions" were blended into new national alignments did New York have a party system.

On the national scene, there were also no comprehensive political formations that could be called parties. The central Congress of the Confederation, composed of state delegates under the original Articles of Confederation, did not really constitute a national legislature or national political arena: voting was by state delegations with one vote for each state, and the delegates were chosen by the state legislatures. Thus there was no national electorate to mobilize, not even a set of state electorates to canvas in terms of national politics.

In short, American politics in the 1770's and 1780's, with the

20

exception of Pennsylvania politics, remained a swirling confusion of interests, issues, leaders, opinions, shifting factions or factionlike formations, and loose alignments, marked by extremes of particularism and localism. The swirl of pluralism might well have kept American politics in continuing confusion and disorder, had it not been modified over the years by nationalizing currents, and partially subdued by the order national parties were to provide.

2.

Political practices in the early states were also generally loose and subject to change without notice. Like any people undertaking self-government, Americans faced three crucial problems of political functioning. These were the conduct of nominations for office; the conduct of elections; and management in government or policy-making—and in the early states with their circumscribed executives, policy was made largely by legislation. These tasks were performed in a medley of non-party ways.

Nominating procedures, by narrowing the range of candidates for any given office, may provide manageable choices for voters. Most rudimentary among early American practices was the procedure of self-announced candidacies or, less directly, "nominations" by letters in local newspapers. This latter practice was followed particularly in the South, where announcements or letters frequently came after private discussions or tacit agreements among leading planters in the locality. In the Middle Atlantic and to some degree in the New England sections, the absence or more rapid decline of cohesive social elites prompted more advanced procedures. In colonial times a common method was selection by secret "parlor caucuses," or "garret caucuses" like the ones Tom Dawes arranged in Boston. During the Revolution, nominations often came from larger caucuses, societies like the Sons of Liberty, or the committees of correspondence; and by the 1780's local caucuses lost their secret, private character and became public, with local nominations also often falling into the hands of ward or township meetings open to all voters. Presumably a gain for emergent democracy, this latter practice may also have marked a setback for order. In a few states, the mid-1780's also saw the emergence of ephemeral county conventions. These early conventions, another step toward democratization, were, however, very irregular in their operation and in drawing representatives from townships or election districts. Called *ad hoc* by caucuses, town meetings, or coteries of leaders, they had no continuing life from election to election. Leaders would often revise the slates named by the conventions, putting forth carefully devised "mixed tickets," which included popular nominees of rival conventions; and convention decisions were not binding on anyone. Frequently, rejected hopefuls would offer themselves as candidates on their own. By and large, the flaccidity of the early, non-party conventions was due to the fact that they generally had no continuing machinery available to mobilize voters for their selections. In this respect they were weaker than many caucuses.

In comparison with nominations for local office, nominations of candidates for governor or other statewide offices posed a thornier problem. Efforts toward state meetings or conventions foundered on the difficulties of distance, rough roads, and expense. The issue was thus often left to correspondence among local leaders or semi-regularized local committees, or (particularly in the South) in the hands of courthouse juntos. Eventually, well after the end of the Revolutionary War, a partial solution was found in caucuses of like-minded members of the state legislatures. Yet at the beginning such caucuses remained loose and uncertain. They were often attended by leaders who were not legislative members as well as those who were, and were called before some elections and not before others.

The conduct of elections, critical in giving voters a voice in public policy, was also variable. In many cases in the early years there was little campaigning, and candidates were local "notables," prestigious and well-known figures in their communities, who simply "stood" for election more often than they "ran." Efforts to woo voters did lead to "treating," however, and Washington was not the only candidate to indulge in it, despite criticism of the practice. Addresses to meetings of voters, or "speakings," were also occasionally resorted to, though few candidates went so far as Madison did when his nose got frostbitten. In Pennsylvania, prompt naturalization of immigrants who could then be herded to the polls, and the practice of "repeating," or voting the same individual several times in an election, gave evidence of an early sophisticated (if seamy) style in politics. In New York, early rival houses set a pattern for later cliques by simply marching their tenants to the polls and by seeking to mobilize the less dependent voters of New York City by public appeals. Mobilization in rougher wards was often reinforced by local "bruisers." More in accord with democratic ideals, freely formed but short-lived organized groups, like the Associators in Pennsylvania in the mid-1770's or the grandly-named Society for the Preservation of Liberty in Virginia in the mid-1780's, resolved to support only candidates whose views they approved. The political press also stepped up appeals to public opinion on behalf of candidates.

Early American political leaders clearly showed far more ingenuity than naïveté. They had seen the need for concentrating votes on a single candidate or slate if they were to win, grasped the tool of association, invented devices of backdoor politicking—which offered lessons for later bosses and machines—and developed engines of propaganda. Yet as candidates were cast up and stood or ran for office, they presented no party or other labels to clarify their identity to the voters, for, in a personal politics, candidacies were also personal or sponsored by cliques or factions, and methods were irregular and erratic. Furthermore, clique or factional associations were often partially hidden or subject to change from election to election, and there was little or no machinery to polarize, mobilize, or stabilize public opinion over the years. In short, the new nation still lacked the rudimentary co-ordination that political parties can bring to provide clarity and continuity in nominations and elections.

Considering American experience down to the adoption of the new Constitution in 1789, it is possible to note several immediate reasons why this was so. By and large they lay in certain conditions which came out of the colonial past, conditions whose effects still persisted in some degree through the 1780's even though the acids of the Revolutionary era were gradually dissolving them. Not only was there no national political crucible in colonial times to precipitate a national politics, but in the long years of colonial rule there had been few elective offices to fill in the provinces, little patronage to stimulate party development, and comparatively few voters, despite early grants of suffrage—and what voters there were often had to travel to distant polling places, where their vote was not secret, to participate in infrequent elections. Furthermore, despite the emerging fluidity and free individualism of the new American society, colonial gradations of social dominance and subordination remained at certain points, and men at the higher levels of social position were accustomed to winning compliance from men at lower levels. Different regions exhibited different patterns of such notables and deference to them: in New England, the Congregational clergy and old families; in New York, the Hudson River magnates, frequently with New York City mercantile connections; in the South, the great planters. Whatever their basis, however, such patterns had a limiting effect on the development of parties as a product of mass or popular politics. The liberal effervescence that followed the Revolution ate away at social hierarchy and habits of deference to "the few and the great," as it also promoted the extension of voting rights. Yet even in this situation the formation of parties required new skills in popular leadership, and such skills necessarily emerged slowly. Finally, there were continuing obstacles to the minimal necessities of association: communication and assembly. In western Pennsylvania, for example, poor roads and postal facilities, the absence of newspapers in the earliest years, and a paucity of natural social gatherings worked against political association; and these disadvantages were only gradually offset by increases in the number and popularity of churches, taverns, court sessions, and militia musters as opportunities for meeting or assembly. Communication and face-to-face meeting between people living in different states were still more difficult when, for example, a trip from Philadelphia to Charleston, South Carolina, might take two weeks.

Yet probably the greatest obstacles to party development remained the refractory individualism and pluralism of the society and general attitudes which were inimical to party alignment. Many individuals resisted being herded; states and state leaders stressed their special identities and interests; and heterogeneities, from regionalism to economic variety to religion, tossed up a multiplicity of opinions and interests. Although this very individualism and pluralism were eventually to stimulate the resort to party coordination, it was no easy matter to harness them at the outset. The bonds of party support could be established only by devising intricate agreements which would join together broad pluralistic combinations—all in the face of doubts about the legitimacy of party combinations as such.

In the legislative process, where the outcome of policy decisions was determined, politics also proceeded in pre-party ways. Central control at some times or in some states contrasted with free-style fragmentation in others. In Massachusetts after 1776, close association in the Boston caucus under the adept organizer and propagandist Sam Adams marked early paths to control by the caucus; but this power was limited and soon balanced by Shaysites and the varied thrusts of free-lance individual members of the assembly. In Maryland, legislative control remained in the hands of the planter junto, with members drawn from the state's leading "Fifty Families" repeatedly returned to office while mercantile Baltimore was nearly unrepresented. Continuing power for the Tidewater planter faction in South Carolina depended on gross under-representation in the assembly for middle- and back-country elements. In Rhode Island, where the dominant force in the late 1780's was a so-called country faction—which actually enlisted as many or more merchant investors in state-debt securities as it did plain farmers—a caucus of this faction met nights, reviewed proposed legislation, and the next day marshalled its assembly members accordingly. In New York, the Clinton clique cozened allies and watchfully served a sufficient diversity of interests by special legislation to undercut rivals. In Connecticut, an involved combination of four factions was held together by shared interests and loose personal ties among a few leaders, who parceled out the benefits of politics. In Pennsylvania, the infant state parties jockeyed in the assembly, but the helter-skelter of interests between and within parties became more and more difficult to sort out. In Virginia, a politics of notables and personal followings was given some direction by the influence of Patrick Henry as governor, but legislative decision-making remained individualistic, sometimes sectionally influenced, and fluid. In New Jersey, fragmented representation of diverse interests prompted an extremely free-style, unstructured politics, with few significant or divisive issues.

In early American state politics as a whole it is possible to distinguish four types of political formation: factions, cliques, juntos, and caucuses. Generally a faction appeared as a portion of an electorate, political elite, or legislature whose adherents were engaged in parallel action or co-ordination of some consistency but limited durability in conflict with other portions. A clique, most readily seen in the notable-family "connexions" in New York, was a factional group whose relationships depended upon a family, a commanding individual, or a close coterie of personal associates: generally the demise or retirement of the focal person led to the collapse of the clique. A junto, as the term was used most commonly in the South to apply to statehouse or courthouse groups, was a small, often secret, dominant factional formation at a center of government, which might or might not act for a larger social stratum. A caucus was generally the co-ordinating nucleus of a larger faction or alignment of interests, or sometimes merely a temporary, *ad hoc* assemblage. None of these formations took on the stature of parties. It is in this sense of hinging on factionlike formations that we may speak of early American politics as "faction politics," using the term "faction" to include lesser but similar groups such as cliques, juntos, and caucuses. Such politics depended heavily on personalities and personal ties, and was subject to abrupt, kaleidoscopic change.

From the point of view of clarity or order of democratic functioning, faction politics had little to offer to the new American nation. Control by social elites or hidden juntos tended, by its very nature, to thwart popular participation or influence over policy. The confusion of individualistic, factional, or clique patterns of legislative policy-making, on the other hand, made the realities of the legislative process virtually invisible or nearly incomprehensible to the voters. Even when the process was visible, the absence of stable party or factional designations in elections made it extremely difficult for voters to hold representatives responsible for their acts.

26

Legislative decision-making was often only tenuously oriented to divisions outside the assemblies, while blocs, alliances, or cabals formed and dissolved almost independently in the assemblies themselves; and thus, voters were baffled by frequent discontinuities from election to election or by the smudging of choice on issues in a given election. Links between the electorate on the one hand and government policy on the other remained uncertain. Insofar as democracy may hinge on an orderly choice in elections which has some effect in government, faction politics failed. It was inherently unable to provide voters with reasonably clear, continuing, and effective alternatives.

The result, even in a nation that was broadly "republican" in character and generating a "democratic" climate, was an advantage in power for certain elements in the society. Thus planter, mercantile, or similar groups with access to influence, inside information, and the levers of authority were able to "work" the system more advantageously than plain men or less favored groups, such as the nation's broad ranks of small-freehold farmers. The common run of men were thwarted by the looseness, semi-invisibility, disorder, personal ties, and confusion of faction, and popular impact on policy-making was limited accordingly. Compared to the faction politics of the 1770's and 1780's, party action in the 1790's was to mark a giant step toward political order and democratic influence.

3.

Further exhibits of pre-party politics may be found in the struggle over the adoption of the new Federal Constitution in 1787-1789. The result made a national political arena, established basic rules for government and politics, and thus provided both symbol and substance for the development of national consensus on the conduct of politics. The controversy in the states, where elected conventions were called to pass on the new charter, was marked by adroit propaganda, careful timing by the pro-Constitution forces, and at some points by deception or pressure. In New York, for example, adoptionist factions threatened the secession of New York City if the state convention refused to ratify.

Once again, however, sophisticated methods operated in a pluralistic context of non-party alignments. The issue has been pictured as a struggle between national "Federalist" and "Anti-Federalist" parties, the former favoring and the latter opposing ratification, each representing sets of economic interest groups locked in continental combat. The developing American economy was in fact creating economic undertakings which were to produce common interests across the nation, and this trend was portentous for national politics. Yet the ratification issue was fought not primarily by national interest groups or parties, but in multigroup variety in thirteen state arenas.

Different interests and perspectives provided different alignments from state to state. In New Jersey, Delaware, and Georgia, for example, easy ratification came with nearly unanimous convictions that these states (for different reasons in each case) could hardly "go it alone." The planter elite in Maryland carried the day there (though not without opposition) in the interest of a strong central authority which they thought necessary to protect social order. In South Carolina the bulk of planters led a congeries of local interests each of which would be served by adoption, although in different ways, and won a favorable vote. Ratification in Connecticut depended on a conjunction of interests and personal purposes among factional groups, and on the obvious relief the Constitution would bring for difficulties which the state as a whole faced. In Pennsylvania and New York, sharp controversy was played out between established party or clique alliances; an adoptionist coalition in New York, led chiefly by Hamilton, finally won a bitter uphill battle in the ratifying convention over Clintonian anti-adoptionist forces. In Massachusetts and New Hampshire, alignments of economic interests dominated, and a complicated coalition carried ratification in the Bay State. With Patrick Henry and a number of other notables in opposition in Virginia, and planter-slaveholders divided, ratification faced a close contest and won largely by virtue of the prestige and strategy of leaders who favored the Constitution and by the support of small farmers, particularly in the interior of the state. Two states, Rhode Island and North Carolina, each stirred by a complex of anti-adoptionist interests and sentiments, accepted the Constitution only after ratification by all other states left them in an untenably lonely position.

Adoption of the national Constitution thus emerged from a diversity of local forces, divisions, and decisions. Though "Federalists" from state to state co-operated to some degree, they did not constitute a national party. The so-called "Anti-Federalists," far from being a single national formation, can be thought of only as a conglomeration of more or less like-minded elements from state to state. Nor was the contest a clear, two-way battle between conservative, investing, or "business" groups on the one side and radical, agrarian, or "populist" masses on the other: the actual group foundations of interest and opinion on both sides varied in different areas and were often contradictory as between states. The issue was dualistic, to adopt or not to adopt; but the lines of forces involved were pluralistic and loose. Nor were the alignments on the Constitution the roots from which later national parties grew, as has sometimes been contended.

4.

The elections of 1788-1789 under the new Constitution were the first national electoral expressions of the American republic. Yet elections, in plural, is the proper term. A president and vice-president were to be chosen by electors named in the several states—in about half by popular vote, in the others by state legislatures. Two members of the national Senate were to be named in each state by the legislatures; and members of the House of Representatives, in proportion to state populations, were to be elected by popular vote. Voting methods varied from state to state, and polling places were scattered, in some areas no more than one to a county.

In such a situation it is easy to postulate a "need" for national party structure. Certain potential party functions are obvious: to represent, and find some accommodation among, the variety of interests in the newly extended political arena, and to shape opinion; to work the complicated machinery of national elections; to undertake management of the agencies of government, separated as they were into the executive, the Senate, the House, and the appointive judiciary, each with power to check the others; and to interpret the work of the new government to the public. Indeed, putative "Federalist" and "Anti-Federalist" alignments persisted in New York and Pennsylvania, based on old clique or state party divisions, and in other forms in such important states as Virginia, Maryland, and South Carolina. Yet national parties to bring coherence into the far-flung electoral machinery were not forthcoming. In New York, indeed, maneuver for local political advantage actually dominated the contests, with the "Federalist" Hamilton shrewdly advancing the erstwhile "Anti-Federalist" Robert Yates as his faction's gubernatorial candidate in order further to weaken the Clinton forces—a maneuver in which Aaron Burr joined for his own reasons, and which Clinton barely survived in a close and nearly hollow victory, while "Federalists" won out for Congress. In Pennsylvania, eight representatives and ten presidential electors were to be chosen at large throughout the state by popular vote. An "Anti-Federalist" (formerly Constitutionalist) conference was held at Harrisburg, and a "Federalist" (formerly Republican) convention of delegates chosen by public meetings in the counties met at Lancaster, each to draw up slates of nominees for representative and elector. Yet in the end, top leaders on both sides revised the slates to present mixed tickets, the better to lure uncommitted voters in the persisting state-party rivalry. In Virginia, Patrick Henry managed to block James Madison's election by the legislature as a senator, and secured the choice of two men who were at least reserved toward the new Constitution. Thereupon Madison, going directly to the voters, ran successfully for the House, traveling from county to county to debate with his opponent at that time, Henry's choice, James Monroe. In many other states, including Massachusetts and South Carolina, pro-Constitution men swept the day. In still others, contests revolved almost entirely around local, factional, or personal connections. In short, the confusion of faction persisted.

Flashes of excitement were generated in Maryland, but when the shouting was over the outcry had accomplished little. Opposing tickets were drawn up, and public meetings and published addresses rang with rhetoric as dissident elements in Baltimore, An-

napolis, and certain other areas frightened the forces of the dominant planters. A German farmer in the unfriendly western horn of
the state described the intensity of "Federal" electioneering efforts
there. On the last day, "you would wonder to see so much people
together, two or three thousand, maybe, and not one 'anti.' An ox
roasted whole, hoof and horn, was divided into morsels, and every
one would taste a bit. How foolish people are when so many are
together and all good natured! They were so happy to get a piece of
Federal ox as ever superstitious Christians or anti-Christians were to
get relics from Jerusalem." Ox-treating "Federal" candidates won
over the opposition by more than five to two. In years to come,
however, Baltimore, the western horn, and other less "superstitious" and less deferential forces were to break the control of
Maryland's planter junto.

The great potential focus for the first elections was the choice of
president and vice-president. Here were the high prizes of politics,
and the only offices that could be looked upon as representing a
national constituency. For the presidency, however, there was only
one obvious choice, George Washington, whose halo as the hero of
the Revolutionary War and whose solid competence brought him
substantially unanimous support. For the vice-presidency friends of
the new Constitution looked largely to John Adams of Massachusetts, and there was at least a tacit understanding among some pro-
Constitution leaders in various states that Adams should be supported along with Washington. Proponents of George Clinton in
New York offered him as a candidate also, dispatching a circular
letter to leaders in other states in his behalf, and Henry in Virginia
took up Clinton as an item in his personal anti-Constitution cause.
A factional standoff between the two houses of the New York legislature, however, led to a failure even to choose electors in the state
and destroyed any chance Clinton had. Voting by the electors gave
Washington 69, Adams 34 and election as vice-president, with 35
remaining votes scattered among 10 other candidates. How little
national or "party" co-ordination there was with reference to the
two great national offices is revealed by the wide scattering of the
votes for vice-president, and the fact that even electors from the
same state were often not united in their preferences.

Political Parties in a New Nation

There was little popular interest in the elections over-all, a fact which suggests significant consequences for democratic functioning in faction politics as compared with party politics. Estimates place the total vote for members of the House of Representatives at 75,000 to 125,000, or from 5 per cent to 8 per cent of the white male population—slaves, Indians, women, and of course minors under twenty-one, were denied suffrage. In part the explanation for such limited participation lies in remaining suffrage restrictions which, moderate as they were, blocked off some portion of the population; and many who were legally entitled to vote had not developed the habit or found it difficult to get to polling places. Yet the diffused, unstructured character of faction politics and of the elections, in the absence of party alignments and efforts by competing parties to mobilize voters, was perhaps a more important factor—and one which touches the matter of popular participation as a crucial aspect of democracy.

Certain comparisons support the point. Thus, in Pennsylvania, where state parties did contend, estimates of voting turnout run up to 25 per cent of those eligible—well above the national mark. Other calculations of participation, summarizing turnouts in federal and local elections in states other than the southern tier of Virginia, North Carolina, South Carolina, and Georgia, show the following progression: for the period 1788-1791, about 23 per cent of the white adult male population; for 1792-1798, 24.4 per cent; and 1799-1802, which covered the year of Thomas Jefferson's partisan campaign for the presidency, 39 per cent. These figures show voting participation increasing as party development and rivalry advanced, although other factors probably were also operative. A second series of data on voter turnout for later presidential elections in states where electors were chosen by popular vote (as they were in eighteen out of twenty-four in 1824 and in all but one in later years) also reveals similar results: for 1824, 26.5 per cent of white adult males; for 1828, 56.3 per cent (which was also approximately the figure for 1832 and 1836); and for 1840, 78 per cent. The election of 1824 actually yielded a substantially lower turnout than had been achieved by 1799-1802 and in many state elections in the first decades of the 1800's. Significantly, this low point occurred in a period of party breakdown and the confusions of a multifactional scramble. By contrast, an upturn in 1828 marked the appearance of a vigorous new party around Andrew Jackson, and a further spurt in 1840 accompanied a keenly drawn contest between well-established Democratic and Whig party rivals. Again an instance of faction politics is associated with a low point in voting participation, while instances of party action and particularly of sharp party rivalry are associated with high points of voter turnout. Of course other factors were again probably involved, such as some enlargement of suffrage and the *hoi-polloi* democratic thrust, or the personal appeal of candidates. Viewing the two series of voting data together, however, and noting the similar voting trends for similar spans of years in two different eras, suggests once again a significant role for party and party competition in relation to democratic participation. Democracy as popular participation in the national arena, weak in American faction politics at the end of the 1780's, showed healthy growth as parties gave it strength.

In general, the balloting of 1788–1789 stands as only barely or formally a national election. The total picture is again one of eddies of localism and pluralism. In the absence of parties, or of strong currents of national popular concern, channels of special advantage for favored groups still lay open; and the elections meant little as a democratic flow of power or approval from people to government. They did, however, designate a president, vice-president, and Congress. National political attention was soon turned to the new government these and other men formed.

Toward a Party Force:
The Federalists

As a general marches at the head of his troops," wrote Alexander Hamilton in his Memorandum Book, "so ought wise politicians, if I dare use the expression, to march at the head of affairs: insomuch that they ought not to wait the event, to know what measures to take; but the measures which they have taken, ought to produce the event." The maxim was copied from Demosthenes. It admirably expressed the political style of the arrogant but brilliant gentleman from New York who became the young nation's first Treasury secretary, promptly stepped forth as a bold, innovative policy advocate, and drew new issues.

Yet he did not confine himself to advocacy. In the Massachusetts ratifying convention of 1788, an over-excited delegate named Amos Singletary had looked darkly to the future. "These lawyers, and men of learning, and moneyed men," he declaimed, "expect to be *the managers of this Constitution*, and get all the power and all the money into their own hands." Of humble origins, born out of wedlock in the West Indies, Hamilton had achieved eminence as an able lawyer. He was also learned, had attended King's College in New York (renamed Columbia after the Revolution), and was reasonably well-off by his marriage to the daughter of wealthy Philip Schuyler and by his own efforts. He now turned the energies of his slender, graceful frame toward playing "manager," and the passion of his deep-set eyes toward power, although he was more interested in public purposes than in personal gain. He aimed to make the new government work toward fixing the character of the commonwealth as he envisioned it. He also understood that management in government was an effective means toward such larger objectives.

The endeavor was complex, in effect an essay in nation building. At the constitutional convention in 1787 Hamilton had set forth his idea of "the great and essential principles necessary for the support of Government," and of course it was the infant government of the United States that he had in mind. He argued that government must draw on "an active and constant *interest* in supporting it," by serving, presumably, the wishes or interests of different men or groups in the society who could give it strength. It must also tap another common human impulse, "the love of power," or the prestige of strength, and add to this "an habitual attachment of the people," by bringing them to think of government as the source of justice and public good. Where such resources were not sufficient, government must have at hand the sanction of "*force,* by which may be understood a *coercion of laws* or *coercion of arms.*" Finally, there was "*influence*"—"he did not mean corruption, but a dispensation of those regular honors and emoluments, which produce an attachment to the Government." It was perhaps a somewhat cynical set of specifications, but not unrealistic; and at the Treasury Department in 1790 Hamilton bent his efforts to put them into effect. Measure after measure that he proposed was aimed at establishing a strong and stable nation and polity.

Fortunately, some of the resources of authority necessary to Hamilton's hopes were already provided by the very presence of Washington. His imposing character, his standing as a wealthy and respected Virginia planter, and above all the glory he had won as the steadfast leader of Patriot troops against English Redcoats in the darkest days of the Revolutionary War, had given him a commanding prestige. In personality Washington was solid, reserved, even remote—a colleague who once, on a dare, familiarly clapped him on the back reported that he was frozen in his tracks by the icy stare Washington turned on him. Yet his reserve as well as his strength and integrity all contributed to the respect and popularity he won, to his standing in his own lifetime as "first in war, first in

35

peace and first in the hearts of his countrymen," as a contemporary put it. In short he was a figure of charisma, of the aura of extraordinary powers which raise a man slightly above his fellows, and give him the status of a providential agent. In the difficult first years of testing for the new national structure, he served as a focus for emotional loyalty or "attachment to the Government," in Hamilton's words, as a foundation for legitimacy and obedience. The long-range American trend, which Washington encouraged, was toward a rational, legal basis for authority built on the Constitution. In the period of transition to the ultimate acceptance of the new charter, however, the Revolutionary hero played an essential role.

During the Revolution Hamilton had worked closely with Washington, and he now collaborated with him again. Indeed, Hamilton as cabinet innovator virtually played prime minister to Washington as president. On the other hand, just as Washington's prestige buttressed the government itself, so did his confidence in Hamilton and the endorsement he gave to most of the younger man's policies strengthen the Secretary's position in that government. Years later Hamilton himself commented somewhat condescendingly on the President's role in the success of his measures: he was, Hamilton said, "an *Aegis very essential to me!*" He certainly provided Hamilton with resources of power which he would not otherwise have enjoyed.

In his advocacy, political management, and nation building, Hamilton brought together the elements that came to constitute the Federalist party. He did not consciously set out to do so, but such was the ultimate result.

2.

It took some time to set the government going, first briefly in New York and then after 1790 in Philadelphia as temporary capitals. The first session of Congress was devoted mainly to establishing the executive departments and the judicial branch, and to other housewarming chores. It was not until 1790 and 1791 that Hamilton presented his proposals, and a new political era opened.

His recommendations drew consistency from his basic politico-economic perspectives. They constituted what amounted to a comprehensive plan for the economic advancement of the new America, but one which was founded on the fact that the nation was already relatively developed economically, and which looked to powerful groups that development had brought forward. In brief, Hamilton sought a happy and fruitful marriage between the special interests of "moneyed men," and the larger interests of orderly national government, from which the one might derive strength and authority, and the other gain. An Anglophile, he admired the hierarchical political order he saw in Great Britain, and its elitist, ministerial style of government; to foster the marriage of wealth and government in America, he would copy the English model as far as he could. At the outset he called for the "funding" and "assumption" of the Revolutionary debts. By "funding," securities of the old Confederation which had depreciated sharply in the market would be exchanged at face value for interest-bearing bonds of the new government. By "assumption," the Federal government would make itself responsible for debts incurred by the states during the Revolutionary War. Next Hamilton urged Congress to charter a hybrid public and private Bank of the United States, which would hold federal funds and handle government financial transactions, meanwhile undertaking private banking, credit-extension, and note-issue functions. Finally, he proposed internal excise taxes as a means of raising revenue to sustain his debt policies, and a protective tariff on manufactured goods.

These proposals offered gratification to a wide range of interests, but this was not their only significance. The debt policies, for example, marked an immediate gain estimated at $40,000,000 for holders of public securities or speculators—"stock-jobbers," Jefferson called them at one point. A medley of other groups, from merchants or "infant" manufacturers to certain segments of agriculture or working men, could take satisfaction in other measures. Yet the farseeing Hamilton was not merely responding to group demands or playing broker to various interests. In particular, his fiscal proposals were by no means policies that were taken for granted even in the new American business community. As advocate and manager, he was rather staking a course of creative policy-making, and offering

37

a coherent program, a sweeping, intricately devised program, which went well beyond the limited purposes of an old-style faction or the agenda of a caucus or junto. It was something the narrow political formations of previous decades could scarcely have envisioned, the sort of endeavor which has come to characterize parties at their best, as they have presented comprehensive formulations of public policy. Furthermore, Hamilton's policies were designed to have a wide appeal. Besides providing a payoff in economic development for business groups, his program as he saw it would stimulate national growth, increase the flow of goods and services, and raise living standards for the nation as a whole. In short, while Hamilton knew the need to recruit immediate political support from particular groups, he was also concerned that his policies promote a broad conception of the national interest—again, of course, as he saw it. At the same time, he was determined to prove that the new government could be effective, at least in economic rewards.

In this effort, he was favored by an unusual political context. Not only did he move in the protective shadow of Washington's prestige. He was also able to "produce the event" so brilliantly at the outset—only in the tariff did he fall much short of his goals—largely because he could "march at the head of affairs" along comparatively open ways. In a new governmental system still being formed and in an unstructured national politics, he found ready opportunity for his purposes.

At the outset, the legislative branch Hamilton addressed was a leaderless herd. Composed almost entirely of "Federalists," in the sense of men who had supported the Constitution of 1787, Congress set no direction of its own for the new government. During the first session of April-September 1789, in a nearly free flow of legislative individualism, members had agreed or disagreed as issues came and went. There was sharp cleavage over proposals by Vice-President Adams to establish a "high-toned" government by giving grandiose titles to the president and other such devices, but alignments on the issue disappeared with the defeat of Adams's proposals. The choleric "Billy" Maclay of Pennsylvania, an Ishmael in the Senate who smelled conspiracy in any alliance however temporary, noted periodic instances of "caballing and meeting of members in knots." Yet even he could find little consistency beyond certain joint exertions by the "mercantile interest," or the support that Pennsylvania, New Jersey, Maryland, and Delaware members gave proposals for imports to encourage manufactures, or the tendency of "the New England men" to join together in opposing molasses duties. The ramblings of individual views and shifting relationships were only occasionally joined into blocs representing particular interests or sections. Otherwise, there were not even clear factional divisions. A summary comment by Maclay on early Congressional behavior was not far from the mark: "The mariner's compass has thirty-two points; the political one, perhaps as many hundreds."

The sessions of 1790 and 1791, however, revealed the stamp of Hamilton's firm leadership. The law creating the Treasury Department had sketched unusual ties between the head of that department and Congress in the reports and interchange of information it required. Beginning with the debt-assumption issue, Hamilton elaborated these formal ties into the bonds of informal executive-legislative leadership, utilizing, in Maclay's phrase, "every kind of management." His "reports" were calls to action, and he and his assistants provided arguments and statistics for Congressional debates. He followed legislative affairs with the utmost care, keeping a sharp eye on timing, favorable committee appointments, and chances for maneuver. He met privately with members, and discreetly arranged informal conferences to draw his followers together. Everything "is prearranged by Hamilton and his group," Maclay cried in the anguish of opposition.

Although Maclay exaggerated, he was right in perceiving that the debt and bank issues, with the prestige of Washington's "name," had produced a "court faction." Its genesis in Hamilton's executive or "ministerial" leadership marked the beginnings of coherence and order in politics in the new nation's capital.

3.

The emergence of management at the capital brought strong responses across the country. In the process, what began as a capital faction soon became a national faction and then, finally, the new Federalist party.

From the national center, ties of common interest and action were extended into the states, counties, and towns. Again Hamilton played a prominent role, weaving a web of correspondents out of his wartime associates, his business connections and friends, and the many individuals whom, as Secretary, he was able to oblige. His personal contacts and personal influence were used to draw together a new political formation, which eventually became less personal. The Federalists also drew on the first American veteran's association, the Society of the Cincinnati, a strongly knit organization of Revolutionary War officers and their descendants. Such notable figures as Fisher Ames and Theodore Sedgwick in Massachusetts, John Jay and Rufus King in New York, John Marshall in Virginia, or Robert Goodloe Harper in South Carolina joined the cause, along with many others. Thus Hamilton's original faction reached out into the countryside and developed into a national political structure which could support its capital leadership by undertaking the labors of propaganda, electioneering, and other political tasks. Its key local leaders were men of position and high respectability in their communities: former military officers everywhere, or mercantile magnates in New York; the Congregational divines in Massachusetts and Connecticut, or Episcopalian ministers in the Middle Atlantic region and in the coastal plains of the South; captains of finance in Philadelphia, or great planters in Maryland or South Carolina. From the Federalists' center at the capital to their periphery in the counties and towns, relationships among established notables provided the strong strands of the emerging Federalist structure. Such notables drew in other participants, and together they soon formed the ranks of the active workers or "cadre" of the emerging party.

Yet the party-in-the-making also rested on a broad combination of interests and opinions. Like any open major party in a pluralistic society, it came to include in its following a substantial range and significant density of groups and individuals. Domestic merchants, men in the shipping trade and shipbuilders, holders of public debt securities, bankers, investors and financiers generally, owners of struggling manufactories, great Tidewater planters, dependent business and professional men—all could look happily to Hamilton's promotion of enterprise under the protection of government action. Furthermore, most of these groups had already enjoyed sufficient economic development to enable them to support their interests with significant political power. Yet the Federalist appeal was not limited to capitalist or proprietary interests. Many wage earners, particularly in shipbuilding along the coastal rivers, where a man might farm part of the time and work in the shipyards another part, could see employment and higher wages in Hamilton's proposals. Modest farmers who looked to the export market could also anticipate prosperity and higher prices as a result of Federalist policy, although ultimately the great weakness in the Federalist fabric proved to be an insensitivity to the concerns of agriculture as a whole. The assumption scheme had a strong appeal in states that had incurred heavy Revolutionary debts and failed to pay them off. This special issue operated in Hamilton's favor in debt-ridden South Carolina as well as in mercantile New England. Indeed, Massachusetts and South Carolina became the early Northern and Southern foundations of Federalist strength.

Their emerging structure and broad base gave the Federalists a position of effective influence in the electoral arena. Working through their network of notables and lesser leaders, and through Hamilton's web of correspondents, beneficiaries, and officeholders, the Federalists were able to put forward candidates and mobilize voters for them. Though they tended to look upon elections largely as opportunities for the public to ratify their policies, Federalist managers knew that co-ordinated action in election contests was essential to maintaining power.

The Federalists also drew support from an imposing propaganda array. In 1789 Hamilton and Senator Rufus King of New York raised funds to enable John Fenno to establish the *Gazette of the United States*, which became the semi-official national Federalist organ, published first in New York and then in Philadelphia. In 1790 the *Columbian Centinel* in Boston, under the editorship of Benjamin Russell, began a long career as polemical spokesman for New England partisans. In 1793 gifts from Federalist merchants in

New York launched the *American Minerva*, under the great grammarian and lexicographer Noah Webster, as the city's first daily. These and other major presses gave the lead to lesser sheets, and the Federalists could soon count a majority of the nation's editors on their side. Early newspapers were overwhelmingly political in character; and taken together they constituted a major force for factional or party cohesion, communicating partisan information and views from the centers of power to the outlying communities. Thus the Federalists undertook another key function of parties: influencing or polarizing national opinion, on particular issues as they arose or around their program as a whole. In the process, they brought additional measures of order into national politics.

The Federalists' achievement of full party status came with the development of emotional attachment to the party as such. The concerns of interest, economic as in Hamilton's proposals or otherwise, provided critical strands for party formation; but something more was also necessary. This was the emergence of unifying faiths and loyalties, of exclusive and distinctive "in-group" attitudes, of emotional commitments, of at least the beginnings of an ideology. Here again the charisma of Washington, his aura as a providential agent of national independence and national identity, supplied "an *Aegis very essential*" to Federalist party development. At the outset of his Administration the President gave an ear to the divergent views of a cabinet which included Jefferson as well as Hamilton and played a chairman-of-the board role, deliberating and deciding among alternative policy suggestions. As time passed, however, Washington himself and his Administration as a whole became more and more partisan; and by 1793 he was seeking advice almost entirely from a limited number of Federalist-minded leaders. Meanwhile, his portentous name was increasingly used as a distinctively Federalist symbol. Thus the Father of His Country became also the father figure of Federalist propaganda, a focus for partisan faiths, sentiments, and loyalties.

Reactions to new issues furthered the development of ideological ties. The French Revolution, at first widely hailed in America, ran its course toward regicide, radical republicanism, and (in Feburary 1793) war with Great Britain. Determined to avoid involvement,

Washington proclaimed a policy of official neutrality, a course Jefferson at the State Department accepted reluctantly in the face of treaties of commerce and alliance with France which had been signed in America's own hour of revolutionary trial. Yet to most Federalists the issue had become one of sanity against madness, stability against chaos, and their sentiments lay with the established order they thought England represented. The whole controversy prompted a war of words in which, as it intensified over the years, Federalist "Anglomen" came to stigmatize opponents with the cry of "Jacobin!" while opposition "Gallomen" responded with "Monocrat!" Though group or economic interests were not absent from the French-British issue in America, the controversy once again brought an emotionalized, philosophical, or symbolic cleavage of deeper faiths, convictions, and loyalties. In the ideological controversy the Federalists could perceive their party as a knightly band of saviors, the true champions of society, stability, and the nation. Irrational as attachment to Washington as father figure may have been, exaggerated as the logomachy over the French-British question was, these symbolic reactions and emotional ties completed the great transition from a Federalist faction to a Federalist party, as part of a general transition from old-style faction politics to modern party politics. They did so by reinforcing the seams of structure with crucial threads of emotional *élan*, of Federalist party spirit.

Throughout the long shaping of the Federalist formation, Hamilton played a curious though commanding role. In effect he had initiated the whole effort with his vision and advocacy, and throughout its early years he stood forth as the party's unquestioned spokesman and leader. Yet at no time, apparently, despite his energy and brilliance, did he see himself in full consciousness as a man who was building a party. Like his colleagues, he had no pattern of party in mind to go by, and had to devise what amounted to party practices as party structure took form. His purposes, as he saw them, were to point the new nation in the "right" direction, place its new government on firm foundations, mobilize support for his management in that government, and thwart such political foes as might appear. Furthermore, even while these goals brought him to act as a bold party leader, he could condemn the very idea of party. To be sure, what he usually had in mind by the term was a "factious opposition"; it was as much the idea of a co-ordinated opposition as the idea of party that he feared, and he and other Federalists tended to use the terms "party" and "party spirit" more and more as stigmas to damage their opponents. Nonetheless, the labors of Hamilton and his allies did make a party also—the first modern party of Western history, and a remarkably effective one at that.

Indeed, its early achievements in structure, following, and ideology made the Federalist formation a powerful political phalanx, and marked it for initial success. Yet certain characteristics that grew out of its origins also marked it for ultimate failure in the American context. It began as, and remained, a "party of notables," in Max Weber's phrase, despite its wide early following. It was such because it was led by and found its center among men of established property, position, and power; and the attitudes of such men gave the Federalist outlook a particular cast. Hamilton himself had remarked, "The mass of the people are turbulent and changing— they seldom judge or determine right." Such attitudes of elitist condescension, which became typical of the Federalists, ultimately offended the mass of voters. These attitudes also led the Federalists themselves to resist the development of broad, public organization as a means to mobilize mass support. Such organization as the Federalists did achieve was largely oligarchic and more than half clandestine.

Thus, to their chronic weakness of appeal to the bulk of the nation's small farmers, the Federalists added an elitist structure, corresponding attitudes of condescension, and disdain of popular organization. As time strengthened the new democratic impulse in American society, such characteristics were to prove fatal flaws. For some years, however, their party remained dominant.

4.

Viewed in historical analysis and against the retrospect of American faction politics in the 1770's and 1780's, the emergence of the Federalists reveals a transition from the older "connexions" of fluid factions, family cliques, or juntos to the newer, modern connection of party. Four key distinctions between party on the one hand and faction on the other may be noted.

First, there is the matter of structure. "Active leadership" and a "freely recruited following," as Max Weber has pointed out, "are necessary elements in the life of any party." Structure as the mark of party exists as a relatively durable or regularized relationship between leaders and followers. In America it has developed as a pattern of stable connections or relations between leaders at the center of government and lesser leaders, party workers or cadremen, and active participants at the outposts in states, counties, and towns. At the outposts, structure has extended to relations between local loaders, cadremen, or actives on the one hand, and the members of the public or electorate who support the party, and who constitute the party's following, on the other. By contrast, as early American experience reveals, factions lacked such stable relationships, consisting of *ad hoc* or shifting alignments as they generally did, limited to personal followings or capital coteries as they often were. Structure may or may not eventuate in full-scale organization, strictly construed as a regularized division of labor and co-ordination of activity toward a common set of goals. Nor does structure necessarily imply formal, mass membership in a party. American parties have been from the outset "cadre" parties in which active leaders and workers constitute the party as such, which in turn appeals to and mobilizes a freely attached following. The "mass" party of members ranged in local units was an invention of later times and other places, and has never been characteristic of American major party structure.

Next, parties contribute continuing procedures for performing certain key political functions. At a minimum, these functions include nominating candidates and campaigning in the electoral arena, and readiness to undertake management or the general conduct of public business in the governmental arena. In order to win elections or maintain power, however, and to win support for the policies they may espouse, parties also find it necessary in modern or mass politics to appeal to public opinion. In addition, if they are to succeed at management in government, they must establish some connection between decision-makers in various agencies of

45

government—as, for example, the Federalist phalanx succeeded in doing between the executive branch and Congress. Finally, in order to maintain a power base, parties in a society with any significant measure of pluralism must find formulas of agreement that will bring disparate groups together, or play broker in gratifying, adjusting, or compromising conflicting interests. Thus parties move toward the performance of six critical functions: nominating; electioneering; shaping opinion; mediating among groups, "brokerage," or finding formulas of agreement; managing government; and supplying connections between the branches of government. Many of these functions were performed, though generally in hit-or-miss fashion, by early American cliques, factions, and juntos. In party politics as contrasted with faction politics, however, the functions are undertaken in a relatively more continuous, co-ordinated, and visible fashion, as they were by the Federalists. In party politics, furthermore, functions are typically inter-related in party action. The first purpose of party may be "to elect," to get its men into office; and American parties have usually shown more cohesion and greater activity in elections than in government management. Yet the very visibility and accountability of party in a free republic generates pressures for at least some success in government management, if the party is to succeed in later elections. If a party embarks, as Hamilton and the Federalists did, on a course of innovative management, it must also turn to opinion formulation and electioneering to sustain that course.

In performing its functions, a party may develop a broad program, as a means of mobilizing group interests and public opinion and of strengthening its appeal in elections. This was the path Hamilton and the Federalists explored; and in years to come Madison, Jefferson, and the Republicans were to evolve a counter-program of their own. Indeed, the formulation of comprehensive statements of issues, positions, and policies has become almost a defining characteristic of modern parties. In pluralistic societies, such formulations must inevitably be designed to appeal to or accommodate the demands of various groups in the population. Thus they may often be somewhat contradictory in their terms, or more *pro forma* than meaningful in their substance. Yet, if only formally, they also represent a conception of public policy broader than the claims of particular groups, and in two-party systems they offer options for electoral choice not only on particular issues but on wide ranges of policy. When party programs are cogent for the times, reasonably coherent in their content, and meaningful, as was the Federalist program in the 1790's, they may serve as nationalizing forces, put some limits on the crosscurrents of localism and pluralism by polarizing opinion, and provide significant instruments for democratic functioning. In short, they may act as creative forces for coherence in the interplay of democratic politics.

To the two aspects of party as structure and functions, a third aspect may be added: range, density, and stability of support. Here is the idea of the interest-group foundations of parties stressed by such students of the American scene as Charles A. Beard, David B. Truman, and Wilfred E. Binkley. Generally parties, as contrasted with factions, encompass a wider range of groups in their power base; a greater density of the number of individuals enlisted in their followings as a ratio of all possible supporters; and a greater stability of alignments in the public. In a pluralistic democracy with a substantial electorate, party success inevitably entails a broad combination of groups, and a considerable ingathering of persons who identify with the party, not just in a given election or on a single issue, but over a period of years. Such, in Edmund Burke's language, are the links parties develop in a "just connexion with their constituents," in "public life [as] a situation of power and energy." By contrast, as the pre-party politics of the 1770's and 1780's reveals, cliques, juntos, and even substantial public factions generally are associated with a narrower range of group support, less dense followings, or greater fluidity of alignments in the electorate. A party combination may be built in Hamiltonian style, by joining parallel interests behind advocacy of a bold policy. More typically, it depends heavily on the brokerage function and on compromise to bind disparate interests and individuals into a working coalition. In any case, some measure of agreement, or what may be called concordance on outlook and policy, is an essential ingredient of ultimate party stability.

Finally, a party in the full sense entails a distinguishable set of perspectives, or ideology, with emotional overtones. As perspectives take on emotional or moral impact, beliefs develop into faiths, identifications emerge as loyalties, ideas of right and wrong become moral commitments. If the men are available, attachments to revered leaders may reach charismatic intensity. As opposition appears, attitudes take on the cast of "in-group" as opposed to "out-group." Party outlooks are drawn in terms of "we" and "they"—our rightness and their wrongness, the goodness of having our leaders in office and the danger of having theirs, the "truth" of our doctrines and the "error" of theirs. The limited range of clique, faction, or junto politics rarely develops such broadly shared attitudes or highly emotional overtones. Certainly faction politics seldom generates the kind of emotional symbolism the Federalists attached to George Washington, or the broad ideological views they associated with European conflicts. Carried to extremes, the "we-they" perspectives of parties or ideological cleavages may disrupt a polity. Operating in moderation within a larger national agreement or emerging consensus, as they did on the American scene, they may advance party development or buttress party stability and cohesion. This can be so even in periods of party fatigue or comparatively empty politics-as-usual, when sentiments become increasingly vague, detached from immediately relevant issues, or flaccid. Even in such epochs, party loyalties and symbolism remain among the most tenacious of the ties that bind.

The concept of party sketched here—as structure, functions, substantial following, and in-group perspectives—is an analytical model. Thus stated in abstract form and related to the particular Federalist experience, the model may suggest a clearer consciousness in party building than America's political founders possessed, or greater order and clarity than the actualities of political hurly-burly ever reveal. This is the way of types or models, which are nevertheless useful as abstractions for purposes of inquiry. Parties are indeed instances of "an historical process," as V. O. Key has put it, and any model of their character must be elaborated as one traces their often disorderly development in different historical contexts. Nonetheless, the four criteria for party as contrasted with faction provide a basis for continuing analysis.

Toward a Party Force: The Federalists

Thus, if party is interpreted according to the model, it follows that party as such is a product of human ingenuity and not simply a natural growth. It must be built by the efforts of skilled political craftsmen, including major leaders at the center and hundreds or thousands of lesser leaders in outlying localities, who must at least know that they are devising co-ordinated means to their immediate ends, although they may not be wholly aware of the fact that they are shaping a party in the process.

The model underscores the ways in which party formations of the sort the Federalists generated are characteristically modern phenomena. Seen against the background of its time, the Federalist phalanx marked an important advance from the narrow, heavily personalized, tradition-bound, shifting "connexions" of eighteenth-century English or early American politics. The Federalist party was modern in that it was a relatively open, regularized political structure built around the free association of men from various walks of life, who evolved rationalized methods as efficient means to political goals and, in the era of emerging popular participation in politics, turned to propaganda and campaign tactics aimed at the mass of voters. It was modern also in the way in which its leaders and cadre workers devised orderly procedures to meet the claims of the plurality of interest groups thrown up by a developing economy, undertook to perform key political functions in a co-ordinated, regularized, consistent manner, and offered a generalized ideology and program. As the first formation of its kind, the Federalist party lacked the organization attained by parties in the Jacksonian era and in the twentieth century, and it never achieved the sweep of popular appeal which later parties were to enjoy. Organization, however, is not a necessary criterion of modern parties in the sense in which the term is used here, and the quality of popular response to parties varies even today. In one aspect after another, the Federalists in their time represented a distinctively new kind of political engine and realized in practice the major themes of political modernization.

The criteria of the model also enable us to say, not precisely when, but how faction politics ends and party politics begins. Thus the Federalist formation began as a capital faction, extended its lines into the states and communities, evolved a structure that proved durable, took on essential political functions, united a significant combination of interests, and developed an ideology and *élan*. We may speak of a Federalist party proper by the late months of 1793 and the early months of 1794—the period marked by Washington's adherence to Federalist advisers and attitudes, the ideological clash over foreign policy after the neutrality proclamation of April 1793, the final departure of Jefferson from the Cabinet, and a substantial consolidation of the Federalist voting alignment in Congress. Though a clique or faction here or there may exhibit one or more of the characteristics of party, it will not exhibit all of them together. When all four of the criteria "fit," a party is at hand.

The model also points to the crucial role of parties and a party system in a democratic polity. Faction politics tend to remain murky for the voter, prone to *ad hoc* combinations or majorities in decision-making which shift uncertainly from issue to issue, and thus ill-equipped to provide clarity of electoral choice or democratic accountability. While some of these characteristics may continue to lurk in multiparty politics, or in two-party politics characterized by loose multigroup formations or riven by intraparty factionalism, they are not likely to be so pronounced. Parties generally provide enlarged opportunities for popular participation and representation and for open and meaningful electoral choices, and thereby for democratic accountability. In a democracy, parties constitute the great stable links between public, electorate, and interest groups on the one hand, and governmental decision-making on the other. The utility of a party system for democratic functioning—even a loose, heterogeneous party system—can be seen most clearly if it is compared with the ways of faction politics.

American experience in the 1790's was experienced in the development of a two-party democratic system. Yet the model of party as such applies to modern parties in other systems as well, for parties generally exhibit the basic characteristics which were first fully explored in the American decade of political formation. This remains true even though the particular form of parties, their performance of political roles, or their relations with other parties, if any, will vary with historical circumstances. Thus, for example, many of the nations that are new in the twentieth century as the

United States was new in the eighteenth have at least begun political life with one-party systems, and often with "mass" membership parties rather than with parties based on a cadre who mobilize a following. Where such parties provide popular participation, some effective representation for a significant range of interests within their ranks, and some balance of interests or opportunity for choice, they may claim to perform at least a limited democratic role. Parties in one-party systems will perform this task differently than will parties in a two-party system—generally, within a less-generous spectrum for opposition and with less open opportunity for public choice. Nonetheless, parties they will be, considered in terms of the criteria sketched here.

Indeed, in the world as it is and not as it might be, the democratic role of parties will remain always in the realm of possibility rather than guarantee. At one time parties may perform this role well, at another not so well. How possibility is actualized at a given historic juncture depends on a number of factors: the stage of economic and social development; the political culture and situation; the part played by groups and leaders; the participation, sophistication, and judgment of individuals in the public and the electorate; the particular form of internal party structure, and its relationship to the party following; the nature of party power-base combinations; the relationships between parties, particularly in elections, and their cohesion in power or office; the skill and purpose of party leaders. Patently, all of these factors are also subject to variation from situation to situation, from era to era—and these variations are part of the fascination of party history.

5.

In an open, two-party system, one other thing is needed: the existence of and acceptance of an opposition. In America's great decade of political genesis, opposition to imperious Hamilton and his Federalist phalanx was forthcoming.

Signs of antipathy appeared with Hamilton's fiscal and bank proposals. As early as February 1791, Jefferson noted regretfully the existence of a strong "sect," oriented toward "monarchy." The answer, "the only corrective of what is corrupt in our present [trend] of government," was "the augmentation of the numbers of the lower house, so as to get a more agricultural representation, which may put that interest above that of the stock-jobbers." Sixteen months later, in June 1792, Jefferson complained again that the "sect" espoused the Constitution, "not as a good and sufficient thing in itself, but only as a step to an English constitution, the only thing good and sufficient in itself, in their eye." The answer once again was an enlargement, in the elections of 1792, of the national "representation" to counterbalance the capital "stock-jobbers and king-jobbers."

Such comments signalized an emerging resistance, a resistance led at first by other men who were far more vigorous in opposition than Jefferson himself was yet inclined to be.

3

Voices of Opposition:
The Republicans

As the Federalist party originated with action by Hamilton at the Treasury, so the first clear impetus of opposition came in reactions led by James Madison in Congress. The opposition, however, began not only as a self-styled "Republican" group at the capital, but as a popular Republican movement in the states and communities. Thus, for example, soon after Hamilton had submitted his proposals concerning the public debt in 1790, a jigging polemic appeared in a Philadelphia paper Benjamin Franklin had once edited:

> "Tax on Tax," young Belcour cries,
> "More imposts and a new excise—
> A public debt's a public blessing
> Which 'tis of course a crime to lessen."
>
> Each day a fresh report he broaches
> That spies and nobs may ride in coaches.
> Soldiers and farmers don't despair
> Untax'd as yet—are Earth and Air.

"Young Belcour," of course, was Hamilton; and the attack on his policies was an early register of gathering popular complaints. It was the junction of Madison's Republican faction at the capital with this indigenous opposition that ultimately made the Republican party. Yet the formation of that party was a slow process of discovery and invention for the men who came to lead it, and it was some years before its shape was fully apparent.

No bold innovative protagonist, Madison nonetheless was a dogged antagonist to "Belcour." He was a Virginia planter's son and scholarly graduate of the College of New Jersey, which was later renamed Princeton. Barely five feet, four inches tall, soft-spoken and a bit fussy, he lacked commanding flair, and his leadership depended on the fact that he was shrewd, ready to meet the challenge Hamilton presented, and immensely industrious. He took the floor in the House of Representatives more frequently than any other member; and he was also busy behind the scenes, trying to persuade other members, carrying on a substantial political correspondence, and devising strategy. As early as the second session of Congress in 1790, the philosopher of the Constitution had established himself as the chief spokesman against what Hamilton wanted to make of the national character.

2.

It was a circumspect, slow-forming sort of opposition. Like Jefferson, for example, Madison was willing to compromise on the debt assumption question if he could, even without the bait of establishing the capital on Virginia's border which had been offered by Hamilton to get assumption through. Furthermore, despite Madison's activity in Congress, opposition remained for some time fluid, undisciplined, and scattered. Only by late 1791 and early 1792 were lines discernible between Hamilton's "court faction" on the one hand and a reasonably consistent anti-Administration bloc on the other. Even so, as late as 1794 a fifth or more of the members in the House showed no consistent attachment to any faction or bloc.

On the issues, however, Madison spoke out clearly if moderately. Aware that many of the Revolutionary debt obligations were in the hands of speculators who had bought them at a few cents on the dollar, he objected to paying all holders at par. As a "just" alternative, he proposed "discrimination"—payment at market value to speculators, with "the balance be[ing] applied to solace the original sufferers," many of them former soldiers. He attacked the methods proposed in Hamilton's plan to assume the state debts for imposing burdens on farmer-taxpayers in states like Virginia (which had conscientiously met their debts) in the interest of creditors in states that had been dilatory. He condemned Hamilton's proposal for a Bank of the United States as a precedent "levelling all the barriers which limit the powers of the General Government," and also opening the way through private stock subscriptions to a "scramble for so much public plunder." He supported the excise taxes reluctantly, only because he saw no other feasible means for raising revenue. He attacked Hamilton's report on manufactures vigorously, as another milestone on a path to excessive national powers. By and large, such positions became the positions of the opposition over-all, and provided the outlines of Republican as opposed to Federalist views.

Generally, the Republicans took a negative stand on Hamilton's program for positive action to promote economic development. To the Republicans, the gains from Hamilton's policies for capitalist enterprisers were more than counterbalanced by their cost to agriculturists. On the whole, the opposition in addition saw no pressing need for rapid industrial advances. In their view planters, plain farmers, and many other elements in the population could be happy and prosperous if they were provided the elementary protections of government, not overburdened by taxes, and then left alone. Republican economic policy thus became a policy of "equal rights for all, special privileges for none," as Jefferson put it—of opposition to Hamilton's measures as a panoply of "special privileges," and insistence on a political economy that amounted to "hands off." They were aware that, to succeed, a government must be effective and must provide satisfaction to important interests in the society; but they were convinced that a policy of *laissez faire* could best serve both agricultural interests and the principle of equality, and could also "succeed." Ultimately the forces of industrialization, economic development, and capitalism were to triumph in the sweep of modernization; and the process was to bring new outpourings of goods and services which soon raised American living standards above those of contemporaneous European nations. In the 1790's, however, the ordinary American was already relatively comfortable in comparison with his European counterpart; and thus Americans were not swept so strongly into the current of rising economic expectations which was to characterize later emerging peoples, as they looked to their own contemporaries, the modern industrial nations. In this situation, the new American nation as a whole did not find itself so pressed for the payoff of forced economic development as other new nations have been. In this situation also, the Republican economic outlook could win broad popular support from groups who could see Hamilton's measures as a threat to agrarian ways and to equality.

As the years passed, meanwhile, the Congressional opposition broadened its scope and found increased co-ordination. In 1790 Maclay in the Senate, who could see only "caballing" in Hamilton's "management," was somewhat naïvely startled to discover the peculiar role a Virginian-turned-Pennsylvanian was playing behind the scenes. This was the discreet go-between John Beckley, former mayor of Richmond and now Clerk of the House, who was intimate both with Speaker Frederick Augustus Muhlenberg of Pennsylvania and with Madison, as well as with other members. Thus Billy Maclay found that he could, "through this channel, communicate what I please to Madison." After 1791, Madison was also flanked by other leaders such as, in the Senate, his former opponent Monroe of Virginia and Burr of New York, and, in the House, the bold polemicist William Branch Giles of Virginia and the gentle, simple-republican Nathaniel Macon of North Carolina. Again and again, Giles in particular was effective as a critic of Federalist policies, from the national bank to lesser measures such as the "favoritism" of bounties to aid cod fisheries. Early in 1793 he offered a set of nine resolutions censuring virtually all of Hamilton's official conduct, and aimed at forcing him out of office. For the moment, Federalist fire was directed less against Madison and his faction than against "Giles and his junto."

The bitter Federalist orator of the House, Fisher Ames (of Massachusetts and Harvard) cried out against the new force of opposition. Writing at the beginning of 1793 to a fellow ultra-Federalist, Timothy Dwight (of Connecticut, and President of Yale), he protested: "Virginia moves in a solid column, and the discipline of party is as severe as the Prussian. Deserters are not spared. Madison is become a desperate party leader." Intolerant of any opposition, particularly opposition tinged with democratic "evil," he was exaggerating. But an anti-Administration Congressional faction existed by 1792 and 1793, and Virginia men composed its core.

Changes in relationships between major figures in the national government also exacerbated political cleavage. Quite early Madison had concluded that Adams was hopelessly embroiled in an "antirepublican" (meaning Federalist) course and had written him off. More important, as Washington himself was drawn ever more deeply into the Federalist cause, his trust in Hamilton was strengthened and his ties with Madison and Jefferson were weakened. Late in 1791 Madison's role in establishing Philip Freneau—"that rascal Freneau," Washington called him—as an anti-Hamilton editor had caused a severe chill in relations between the President and the Congressman. Finally, when by 1793 Madison's opposition role became fixed, confidential exchanges with Washington came to an end. At the same time Jefferson, slow to oppose as he was, found it increasingly difficult to get along with Hamilton; and the years brought cankers of difference which even Washington's continued tactful efforts could not heal. In 1791 both men gave the President opinions on the national bank proposal, Hamilton defending his brain child, Jefferson raising doubts on strict-constructionist constitutional grounds. Other questions sharpened the animosity: patronage contentions; differences on financial policy, with Jefferson listing for Washington in 1792 a bill of twenty-one objections to Hamilton's views; and a personal condemnation of Jefferson by Hamilton in 1792. When Jefferson left the cabinet at the end of 1793, rupture at the executive as well as the legislative centers of government was complete.

Meanwhile, events brought increasing collaboration between Jefferson and Madison. In 1791 Jefferson was inadvertently drawn into a press-and-pamphlet controversy in which John Adams was accused of being the author of an anonymous attack on Thomas Paine's pamphlet defending the French Revolution, *The Rights of Man*. Having written a letter praising the pamphlet, Jefferson could condemn (as did Paine) "the doctrine of king, lords & commons," and see Adams as its sponsor. Yet he also regretted that he had been brought into the controversy with his old friend of Revolutionary days, and proclaimed "my love of silence & quiet, & my abhorrence of dispute." By mid-1793, however, Jefferson was aghast at the pro-British, anti-French, executive-prerogative doctrines Hamilton, as "Pacificus," was expounding in a series of articles defending Washington's neutrality proclamation. He urged Madison: "For God's sake, my dear Sir, take up your pen, select the most striking heresies and cut him to pieces in the face of the public." As "Helvidius," Madison did so, urging the role of Congress in the treaty and war powers against Hamilton's penchant for executive authority. In a dramatic Congressional debate on a report Jefferson had submitted at a propitious moment concerning commercial relations with Great Britain and France, Madison directly echoed Jefferson's views. On the other side William Loughton Smith of South Carolina, working from a document Hamilton had put into his hands, took the floor as the Federalist voice. The emergence of Madison as Jefferson's spokesman, balancing Smith as Hamilton's agent, represented a significant crystallization of factional ties between executive and legislative leaders. Although the actual debate had to wait until 1794, just after Jefferson's retirement, the Madisonian Congressional faction was becoming a general capital faction—and turning to foreign as well as domestic issues.

It would be hard to find within the American spectrum two more contrasting major figures than the early cabinet antagonists. The great Federalist, Hamilton, ever distrustful of "the mass of the people," ever seeing "power upon power" (in Hobbes's phrase) as the only reliable instrument of government, was all drive, innovation, force. The great Republican-to-be, Jefferson, ever confident of the judgment of The People—"I am not among those who fear the people; they, and not the rich, are our dependence for continued freedom"—was all humanity, serene faith, hope. Once, as Secretary of State, Jefferson had invited Adams, Hamilton, and other secretaries to dine with him in his rooms. Looking at portraits of Francis Bacon, Isaac Newton, and John Locke on the walls, Hamilton asked who they were; Jefferson named these prophets of

58

the Enlightenment as "my trinity of the three greatest men the world has ever produced." After a moment's pause Hamilton replied portentously: "The greatest man that ever lived . . . was Julius Caesar." The remark, Jefferson thought, rvealed Hamilton's inveterate belief "in the necessity of either force or corruption to govern men."

By contrast, Jefferson—the son of a modest farmer who had married well—placed his faith in the conviction that popular opinion would tell in government. In considerable part, this was the reason he refrained from the direct pursuit of power and from party action. For four years he stayed at his post in the cabinet, assuaged only by Washington's tact, despite repeated "discussions [in which] Hamilton and myself were daily pitted in the cabinet like two cocks." While Jefferson could be forceful when occasion demanded, he faced such necessities with reluctance.

There was as little of drama and urgency in Jefferson's personality as there was in his political style, and yet he possessed a curious magic. A Congressional observer, noting the Virginian's tall, slender figure, lounging manner, and face of "sunny aspect," thought he was characterized on the whole by "a loose, shackling air"—hardly a personality to compel crowds. Yet, as Jefferson sat to talk, "on one hip commonly, and with one of his shoulders elevated much above the other," his conversation was informed and "some brilliant sentiments sparkled from him." Always something of the detached intellectual in politics—he had been an outstanding student at the College of William and Mary—he was at his best in private conversation, where his intelligence, intimate tact, and quiet charm came forth. In writing at his desk, where he proved a graceful and often evocative stylist, he made up with his pen what he lacked in oratory. In short, despite his placid temperament, he was a man of strong personal appeal.

This characteristic, plus what Jefferson had come to stand for as chief author of the Declaration of Independence, as a moderate liberal-reform governor in Virginia, and as the informal philosopher of democratic-republican convictions, inevitably made him a reference point and symbol for the opposition to Hamilton's doctrines. Even in his retirement to his Monticello home in Virginia he was, willy-nilly, the focus of the republican cause and its potential gentle hero. As factional lines drew tighter, he necessarily began to assume a qualified role of leadership, although the main direction of affairs remained with men like Madison or Beckley.

Another landmark in the emergence of resistance at the capital was the establishment of an opposition press. It began with "that rascal Freneau" in October 1791. A poet, a Princeton man also who was friendly there with such future Republicans as Madison and Burr, Philip Freneau was also an effective journalist. Largely at Madison's instigation, but with Jefferson's approval and aid, he was brought to Philadelphia to establish the *National Gazette*. He also served as printer for official State Department papers, just as John Fenno of the earlier *Gazette of the United States* acted as printer for Treasury papers. The *National Gazette* joined the bank fray with a series of essays by Madison. On the issues of world politics and ideology it was strongly pro-French, full of praises for Paine and brickbats for Burke, as champion and critic respectively of the French Revolution. Generally more "radical" and inclined to ideological blacks and whites than either Jefferson or Madison, Freneau was a vigorous catalyst for opposition reactions. He was also an early example of the use of patronage for political purposes, serving not only as printer for Jefferson's State Department but also as a clerk-translator with almost a sinecure in the department itself.

Politically, the *National Gazette* was an instrument of Republican cohesion. It communicated the words and deeds of factional leaders at the center of government to emerging local leaders and followers across the country, thus promoting a national tone. It did this in part directly, in part by playing oracle to local editors, who clipped generously from it. Never so blessed with presses as the Federalists, the inchoate Republican impulse could count on only a few large papers like the *American Advertizer* in Philadelphia and the *Independent Chronicle* in Boston, but numerous country weeklies followed Freneau's lead. The *National Gazette* remained a factional rather than a party organ, however; and it was short-lived, yielding in 1793 to the Philadelphia *Aurora* under Benjamin Franklin Bache. When Jefferson withdrew from the cabinet cockpit, Freneau withdrew from national prominence to lesser journalism in New Jersey and to composing nature lyrics.

3.

In the states, counties, and towns, meanwhile, forces of interest and opinion that could be combined into a complex political entity were beginning to gather.

In Virginia, for example, wily old Patrick Henry, during the movement for a new Constitution, had "smelled a rat." Near the end of 1790, convinced that his fears had been confirmed, he carried a series of strong resolutions through the Virginia legislature at Richmond. They condemned Federalist policies for spawning a "moneyed interest" inimical to agriculture and proper commerce, and as an excessive exercise of national power at the expense of the states. Privately, Hamilton grumbled, "This is the first symptom of a spirit which must either be killed, or it will kill the Constitution." The Federalists might act and assemble for their purposes, but it was presumably not fitting for an opposition to do so.

Again, at Pittsburgh, in western Pennsylvania: "The cause of France is the cause of man, and neutrality is desertion." These stirring words appeared in a public letter sent to President Washington by H. H. Brackenridge in May 1793, after the manifesto of neutrality between warring England and France.

Such expressions revealed a humus of national sentiment that promoted the growth of a popular Republican opposition, a ferment not only of immediate issues but also of larger moral and political questions.

Before long, the opposition had achieved some organization which revealed a strong ideological bent. In 1793 eleven popular political associations calling themselves Democratic Societies or Republican Societies were formed, and by 1794 another two dozen were established. Ten flourished in Pennsylvania, seventeen grew up in the hospitable soil of the South, and in every state but one the Societies flowered. Their political hue was vibrantly anti-Federalist. Though other interests were also intertwined in the movement— merchants looking to the French trade, or some speculators in

61

western lands who saw Hamilton's excise tax as an obstacle to settlement, or dissident sugar or tobacco planters—the appeal of the Democratic or Republican clubs was particularly directed to the mass of "farmers" in the countryside and to "mechanics" in the towns. The latter term included such diverse callings as self-employed craftsmen, ship-carpenters, and mariners. Indeed, one ultra-populist outburst was a printed "Feast of Merriment," in which hearty mariners were heroized in pornographic anecdote while figures of Federalist respectability were subjected to salacious jibes. Yet the Societies had respectable leaders of their own, particularly urban and urbane doctors, editor-"printers," and teachers —intellectuals who gave the Society movement much of its ideological coloration. Several, like James Hutchinson and Benjamin Rush (founder of the Philadelphia Dispensary) in medicine, or Freneau and Benjamin Franklin Bache in letters or journalism, were eminent in their fields. Few lawyers, however, and only a negligible number of ministers joined the movement. Its broad liberal character was less appealing than Federalism to traditionalist-oriented men.

In their brief period of growth and decline, the Societies achieved exemplary early-day organization and articulation. A pattern of formal association which included by-laws and officers was established, first in the "Mother Society" at Philadelphia and then in new groups elsewhere. Circulars were sent from the sponsoring clubs; correspondence grew up between the new clubs and their sponsors; and statements of principles were passed from group to group. Exchange was further strengthened informally by innkeepers, who offered a mixed fare of sociability, a "drap of whiskey," and political talk, and more formally by travelers from Society to Society in a system of "inter-visitation." The Societies also brought forth or promoted effective leaders. In New York, for example, there were Melancton Smith and Edward Livingston, who was elected to Congress in 1794; in Pennsylvania the *éminence grise* Alexander J. Dallas, together with able Albert Gallatin from the western back country and the firebrand Blair McClenachan from Philadelphia, both later members of Congress; and in Delaware, Caesar A. Rodney, who was also to go to Congress and eventually become a cabinet officer. For these, and countless other lesser men, the association growth provided opportunities for activity or for training in politics.

Even at full bloom, however, the Societies were early pressure groups rather than local party elements. They discussed and debated, they issued manifestoes to the public, they doled out blessings or censure to Congressmen, they proposed candidates, they publicized the positions of candidates before elections, and they sent watchers to the polls. Across the country such efforts were probably effective, and the clubs were in themselves a new blossoming of popular political participation and initiative; while at the same time they spread the seeds of still further participation, particularly in voting. Nonetheless, their labors—from propaganda to campaigning, from candidate-proposing (they did not technically "nominate") to pressure—were not performed in a mode typical of parties properly speaking. Nor were the Societies co-ordinate branches of the anti-Administration faction at the capital. It is significant that men like Madison, Jefferson, and Beckley were not members. In short, the clubs were not the early Republican party, nor even the spring shoots of that party.

The Societies did, of course, further the growth of Republican sentiments. In doing so they worked against the widespread conception that opposition was improper. The task was hard, however, marked by bitter attacks and by President Washington's condemnation of the clubs in 1794 as "certain self-created societies." It was ironic, Jefferson thought, particularly in view of the fact that the Federalist-bent Society of the Cincinnati with its secret meetings was apparently above reproach, "that the President should have permitted himself to be the organ of such an attack on the freedom of discussion." Yet by 1796 these and other factors virtually destroyed the club movement.

The most dramatic evidence of anti-Federalist opposition came, meanwhile, in an agrarian insurrection. Almost from the time "young Belcour" had proposed his "new excise" on distilled liquors, protests had come from backwoods areas lying long roads from larger market centers. The tax of 25 per cent on the value of a gallon was a heavy burden to thousands of farmers who distilled their grain into whiskey as a means of producing the greatest value

63

for transportation and sale in the smallest size and weight. Resistance was concentrated in the hill country around the confluences of the Allegheny, Monongahela, and Youghiogheny Rivers near Pittsburgh, in western Pennsylvania, where some 1,200 stills comprised a fourth of the nation's total. As early as 1791, though urging moderation, Albert Gallatin had participated in meetings to protest the distillery tax. A petition called the excise "unequal in its operation," "falls as heavy on the poorest class as on the rich," "a duty laid on the common drink of a nation." Petitions failing, the farmer-distillers armed themselves and threatened to attack Pittsburgh in the summer of 1794. The insurrection was overawed by a force of nearly 13,000 men dispatched by Washington, troops accompanied by Hamilton himself.

The so-called Whiskey Rebellion had complex political implications. Most obviously, of course, it pointed up the strong protest against Hamilton's policies. Yet in its threat of violence the insurrection itself was, in Madison's words, "universally and deservedly odious." To Jefferson it was a gloomy omen of possible separation of parts of the new nation from the central government. There was, in addition, the possibility that disaffection would spread, since agrarian discontent ran high also in parts of Maryland, the Carolinas, and Georgia. Furthermore, some of the Democratic Societies (like the Mingo Creek and Youghiogheny groups) were involved in the insurrection, and thus the whole Society movement could be stained with the Whiskey Rebellion stigma—"a dangerous game," Madison complained, but one that damaged the clubs. In the immediate area, the effect of the controversy was to make western Pennsylvania firm Republican ground.

Meanwhile, the opposition had found a leading ideologist of some quality. He was John Taylor of Caroline County, Virginia, planter and agrarian doctrinaire. Convinced that the mass of the world's peoples had repeatedly been exploited through "loyalty to the throne or altar," he believed Hamilton's economic policies would raise a new, speculative class to dominance in America. After consulting with Madison and Monroe and through them with Jefferson, Taylor wrote in 1793 (and published in 1794) a fat polemical pamphlet, which he called *A Definition of Parties, or the*

Political Effect of the Paper System Considered. His loose definition of "parties" included divisions of interest advantaged or disad-
vantaged by Federalist policies, and alignments of opinion, as well
as Congressional formations. Certainly, he argued, "the existence
of two parties in Congress, is apparent. The fact is disclosed almost
upon every important question." The cleavage ran through all issues: "whether the subject be foreign or domestic—relative to war
or peace—navigation or commerce—the magnetism of opposite
views draws them wide as the poles asunder." "The magnetism of
opposite views"—here, however overexcited, was language transcend-
ing immediate questions, the symbolism of contrasting group perspectives, although they were not yet party perspectives in any full
sense. In years to come Taylor kept his pen busy, and his home was
a rendezvous and fountainhead of ideology for Southern Congressmen and political leaders.

From the Societies or insurrection to philosophical flowerings,
the humus of popular antagonism was producing a lusty growth,
despite bitter counterattacks evoking the magic of Washington's
name. A new movement was at hand.

The whole development brought to the fore the difficult question of an opposition faction or party. Under Hamilton's leadership, the Federalists were building a "government" party, a party
of stability, dedicated to the idea that the first imperative for government in a new nation was that it must govern and sustain itself.
By contrast, the rising Republican movement was maintaining, in
effect, that the new polity should also provide room for counter-
action, for effective representation of interests and opinions that
were slighted or discountenanced in the government party. In addition, the emerging Republicans were "going to the people," in a
virtually unprecedented attempt not only to represent popular interests and concerns but also to mobilize popular opposition to
those who held power. If they had their way, if their appeal
to planters, farmers, and "mechanics" was broadened sufficiently
to succeed, it would end by displacing the Federalists in power and
substituting a new set of governors. It would do so, however, not by
intrigue or violence but by peaceful means, by the weight of votes
in elections, by popular choice or decision. In its notion of opposi-

65

tion and the possibility of a peaceful transfer of power, effected by peaceful democratic action, the emerging Republican movement represented a radically new outlook in political history.

Despite its commitment to peaceful means, opposition brought strains in national unity. It was perhaps fortunate as well as inevitable that the Federalists, with their emphasis on stability and consolidation, came first on the scene and held power first; that the Republicans appeared later and were slower to gain the strength that made them contenders for public power; and that both formations still reached only limited numbers of voters, instead of achieving immediately the full mobilization of popular masses in party competition. If the new polity had begun its political life with two full-blown parties, both stirring broad mass action in their behalf, the frictions of party combat might have proved unmanageable. It was also certainly fortunate that the opposition which looked to Madison or Jefferson was moderate rather than extreme, able to work within a developing national tradition rather than bound to deep social cleavages or to intransigent positions. In fact, the views of Republicans and Federalists were not "wide as the poles asunder." If they had been, or if the methods of the Whiskey Rebellion had been commonly employed, the nation might have been disrupted or opposition might have been snuffed out long before a two-party system could develop. Even as it was, it was years before the nation as a whole came to full acceptance of the idea of a governing party on the one hand and an opposition on the other.

At the outset, meanwhile, the opposition did not yet constitute a party. The Republicans were at most a capital faction that was beginning to find sympathy and support in the countryside in a congeries of dissenting elements, bodies of opinion, associations, and groups. Even more than with Hamilton and the Federalists, the ultimate Republican formation was the end result of a long and halting process of searching and of experimentation in workable ways to meet immediate problems. Although Madison and others spoke of a "Republican party" from time to time in the early years of opposition, the term at first meant little to them beyond sympathy and some co-ordination among like-minded men;

and Jefferson remained unconvinced of the wisdom or necessity of party. What the Republican leaders wanted to do at the beginning was to oppose what they took to be wrong measures and win sufficient support to block them. It was some time before they advanced to the point where they arrived at some conception of a popularly-based party in a full sense and began to fill the new roles it called for. When they did so, they brought about a new kind of political formation or institution—but it was not to spring forth in a day.

4.

Any emerging nation, having cut its colonial ties, must find fresh leaders to further its political development. Often they turn out to be very young men, most of them intellectuals.

There are, of course, variations in the recruitment and character of a national intelligentsia. In new nations that have achieved little economic, social, or educational advance, young intellectuals often have absorbed the values and skills of an advanced but alien society, and are thus estranged to some degree from the traditional ways of their own culture. In America, however, years of colonial development had brought widespread literacy. Furthermore, local centers of higher education had transmitted a common Western culture which was at once English or European, and American, consisting as it did of Western values and skills already integrated into the American context. Thus American intellectuals of the 1790's were generally not alienated from their society. Nonetheless, in a mode that was to characterize other new nations in later eras, much of the innovative work of America's politically formative decade was undertaken by men who were young; and, by and large, the new nation's early leaders were also its intellectuals. In years to come, such leaders were to be replaced by men who showed less intellectual concern or were even anti-intellectual in their outlook. At the beginning, however, the youth, the intellectual prowess, and also the practical skill of the men who were shaping America's first political parties were remarkable.

On the Federalist side, the paterfamilias Washington and his understudy Adams were respectively 57 and 54 years old when they

67

took over the new government in 1789. Yet the brilliant Hamilton, the chief initiator in domestic policy, was only 34 when, as Secretary of the Treasury, he began to lay the foundations of his new economic policy and the Federalist party. By 1792, the year national elections were first contested in a manner that approached party competition, the hard-hitting John Fenno of the *Gazette of the United States* was 41; the suave, polished Rufus King, Hamilton's chief ally in the Senate, was 37; the bitter oratorical leader in the House of Representatives, Fisher Ames, was 34; and his Massachusetts colleague there, Theodore Sedgwick, was 46. A major Federalist figure in New York, John Jay, in the same year was just 47. The early Federalist partisan in Virginia, John Marshall, was 37.

Including even Washington and Adams, the average age of the nine major Federalist leaders in 1792 was barely 44. Omitting the President and Vice-President, the average was a little more than 39.

Youthful leadership is still more pronounced in the opposition ranks. The industrious Madison was just 39 when he first took the floor in Congress in 1790 against Hamilton's policies, and was 41 in 1792. His friend Jefferson, who had played the leading role in writing the Declaration of Independence in 1776 as a stripling of 33 and who had become the nation's first Secretary of State at 46, was a comparatively ripe 49 during the electoral contest of 1792. By contrast the adroit Beckley was only 35 in 1792. Other young national opposition leaders in 1792 included the 40-year-old Freneau of the *National Gazette* and his successor at the *Aurora*, Bache, who was a youth of 24; Monroe in the Senate was 34, the slashing orator William Branch Giles in the House was 30, and his mild-mannered colleague Nathaniel Macon was 34. Opposition leaders in the key states were also generally young. In New York, the Republican recruit George Clinton was by 1792 an old political hand at 53, but his age was balanced by the rising young democrat from another notable family, Edward Livingston, who was 28, and Aaron Burr was only 46. In Pennsylvania, the orator-turned-organizer Alexander J. Dallas was 33 and the quiet, competent Gallatin was 31.

These thirteen opposition leaders in 1792 represent an average age of only 36, including the comparatively elderly Jefferson, Clinton, and Burr. For both Federalists and Republicans the names of other leaders might be added, but they would not alter the picture of youth.

Times of challenge seem often to call forth youthful leadership. In America such leadership in the 1790's was undoubtedly in part a product of the Revolutionary break, which had tended to displace older guiding figures and bring forth new. Yet it may also be that the thorny problems of learning how to build new political structures are often best met not by old hands but by young men who are not bound to traditional ways or to dogma, men who are thus quicker to seize on new insights and devise new tools. Formidable obstacles may, in addition, be most readily overcome by leaders who possess other traits of youth, such as strong purpose, bountiful energy, fresh enthusiasm—or by leaders who have, as intellectuals, a creative flair and the capacity for innovation. This was in large part the story of American party-building in the 1790's.

Practical men, nearly all of America's political founders were also intellectuals by inclination and interest. At a time when college attendance was uncommon, their *alma maters* were a roster of America's first great centers of learning. From conservative Harvard came three: Adams, Fisher Ames, and King; from Yale one: Sedgwick. The College of New Jersey at Princeton provided six: Madison, Freneau, Giles, Macon, Livingston, and Burr. King's College in New York, patriotically renamed Columbia, contributed Hamilton and Jay. From William and Mary in Virginia came one Federalist and three opposition spokesmen: Marshall, Jefferson, Beckley (who was one of the founders of the scholastic honorary society, Phi Beta Kappa), and Monroe. Three others received all or part of their education abroad. The immigrant Gallatin was trained at the College of Geneva in Switzerland; Dallas attended Edinburgh University in Scotland; and Bache absorbed a mixed higher education in Philadelphia, in France, and in Geneva. All of them were serious writers, and some like Madison or Hamilton were writers of brilliance and depth. The omniverous Jefferson applied himself not only to law and politics, but to agricultural experiments, literature, mechanical invention, and architecture, and Freneau wrote lyrics that hold an important place in early American verse. Of the

69

Pennsylvanians, Dallas was a patron of the arts and Gallatin a part-time ethnologist who taught briefly at Harvard. Each of these busy political workers had other intellectual interests and talents as well.

One of the strongest assets most of them held was a concern for ideas and principles as well as for action. Even the jaundiced Maclay was awed by "the wisdom and learning" of his fellows in Congress: "their reputation for knowledge, either legal, political, mercantile, historical, etc." Yet these men also knew how to act, and none feared to be politicians in the best sense of that much abused term. While they held sway, they supplied a quality of leadership which has seldom been matched since in America.

5.

The developing Republican movement was soon to be tried in political combat. In the fall of 1792, John Beckley rode from Philadelphia to New York carrying a letter from Dr. Benjamin Rush to Aaron Burr, urging Burr "to take an active part in removing the monarchical rubbish of our government"—by which Rush meant Vice-President John Adams. The trip marked an early instance of interstate co-ordination among what Madison still often called the "Republican interests"—of action linking national leaders, local leaders, and followings. It was one of a series of steps toward solving the problem of joining state and local Republican elements into a national force.

For a party, working connections are particularly important in the electoral arena. For Federalists and Republicans alike, movement in this direction appeared early in the two states that represented the front ranks of sophistication in politics, Pennsylvania and New York, and appeared more generally in the national elections of 1792. Yet generally such efforts still fell short of full-scale party action.

In the Keystone State, Pennsylvania, the early division of Constitutionalists and state Republicans was giving way. In the gubernatorial election of 1790, the popular Thomas Mifflin drew support from both groups in an overwhelming victory. This personal victory was followed by Mifflin's appointment of Alexander J. Dallas as Secretary of the Commonwealth, and Dallas used his growing power to reorient state alignments in rough accord with developing national cleavages. He worked particularly with leaders of the old state Constitutionalist party, with new men in the Democratic or Republican Societies, and with the future congressmen Blair Mc-Clenachan, William Findley, and Gallatin. This statewide formation gradually developed ties with the voters, and a second Mifflin victory in 1793 foretold a continuance and enlargement of Dallas's effective power. Thus, a state outpost of the gathering national Republican forces emerged. In a reversal of terms, most of the erstwhile state Republicans became adherents of the new national Federalist party.

In the Empire State, New York, a complex reshuffling of old elements also pointed to new conjunctions. An oft-repeated Federalist legend asserts that Jefferson and Madison precipitated the realignment during a trip to New York in 1791 for intimate political conferences with Clinton and Burr; but in truth the journey was not a political journey, and the Virginians spent their time "botanizing," admiring the beauty and wit of the New York belles, and visiting with friends.

The realignments in New York actually followed largely from local causes linked to general national developments. The old Clintonians, shaken by defeats, needed new allies to recoup their position. The powerful Livingston family had been generally allied with Philip Schuyler and Hamilton, but after 1790 the Livingstons were denied recognition or patronage by the Federalists and became disgruntled. In 1789 Schuyler was named to the national Senate, where he acted "the supple-jack of his son-in-law Hamilton," as Maclay put it, thereby further alienating Livingstonites and other moderates. As the Senatorial election of 1791 approached, Clinton saw his opportunity to strike back at Hamilton while at the same time Burr saw his opportunity for advancement: working with a new combination of Clinton men and Livingston men in the legislature, Burr wrested Schuyler's Senate seat from him. In the contest, the Livingstons had been irretrievably severed from the Federalists and joined with Clintonians and Burrites in a new proto-Republican state alliance. In 1792 the coalition was tested when Clinton decided to strike for the governorship again against

Hamilton's candidate, John Jay. In a close and acrimonious contest, Clinton won only by the rejection of votes from certain pro-Jay counties on dubious grounds of technical irregularities. The Federalists were furious, Jefferson commented privately that the maneuver would damage the cause of "republicanism," and the way was opened to a Jay-Federalist triumph three years later. Yet the combat marked a coalescence of local elements in line with national divisions, and it established the beginnings of structural foundations for an alignment of Federalists against Republicans in the crucial Empire State. The brouhaha that followed Clinton's tarnished "victory" futher exacerbated local animosities in accord with national trends.

In other states cleavages were not so sharp, lines of development not so clear. Even in Virginia the Republican movement in the early 1790's had made little progress toward party status. Opposition leaders were hesitant to draw lines of conflict with the Administration too sharply for fear of alienating moderate planters; and Monroe thought the Virginia Republicans were prevented from vigorous attack because they had no clear alternative to Hamilton's program. Structurally, they had not yet established firm connections between leadership on the one hand and a popular base on the other: substantial support in the public they had, but partylike connections with a stable popular following were lacking. In several other states in North and South, such as New Jersey, a formless politics of individual action and shifting liaisons persisted. Generally, the process of party formation in the states groped forward slowly, where it moved at all.

Yet in the national arena, some progress was made toward the co-ordination that marked the ultimate Republican institution. With substantial unanimity that Washington should continue as president, the great electoral contest of 1792 focused on the vice-presidency. The Federalists had early settled on the incumbent Adams as their man and had begun the work of concentrating their votes on him, while Hamilton dispatched warnings across the country against Clinton or Burr, or possibly Jefferson, as potential rivals. For the opposition it was not so easy to unite on a candidate. Before the issue was resolved, the "Republican interests" had in effect gone through an informal nominating process.

In the absence of established machinery, the steps toward a decision were protracted and erratic. The ambitious Burr had important support, not only from his own following in New York but from Dallas and other leaders in Pennsylvania, but many leading Virginians thought Burr a dubious and untried agent—Jefferson, at least privately, preferred Adams to Burr. At the same time, other New York and some Pennsylvania leaders stuck by their original support of Clinton. Despite the efforts of an emissary from Burr to Monroe in Virginia, Monroe and Madison joined in letters to Melancton Smith and others in New York urging Clinton instead of Burr. Other trips for consultation followed, including Beckley's journey to New York, and there were additional informal local conferences and letters back and forth. At last Melancton Smith, as the "specially deputed" agent of the New Yorkers, came to Philadelphia to meet with Beckley, the Pennsylvanians, Pierce Butler of South Carolina, and a few others. There it was decided *"finally* and *definitively"* (in Beckley's words) that "the republican party" was "to exert every endeavor for Mr. Clinton, and to drop all thoughts of Mr. Burr." Promptly, Madison and Monroe were asked to hold Virginia in line, and in North Carolina Nathaniel Macon lent his efforts to the Clinton candidacy. In a loose, halting fashion, still some distance from the regularized procedures of party, the opposition had made a national nomination.

The electoral vote showed the results of co-ordinated efforts. The scattering of 1789 was avoided: Adams received the entire pro-Administration vote of 77, while Clinton garnered all but five of the 55 opposition votes, carrying New York and Virginia (an early intimation of the New York–Virginia alliance that was to become the axis of Republican electoral strength), North Carolina and Georgia. What Dr. Rush had called "the monarchical rubbish of our government" had not been "removed," but a first step toward national electoral mobilization had been taken.

The Congressional elections of 1792 developed more nearly as a series of local contests. Yet national issues were widely discussed, and something approaching party spirit was apparent in many races. A series of anonymous statements in the *National Gazette* (written by Madison) had defined the issues largely in terms of an "aristocratic" few against a "republican" many, and stood in effect as a proto-platform for the Republicans. Some means toward co-ordinated electioneering activity were found in Pennsylvania at least, and when the results were in, Jefferson could note that men of his persuasion had taken nine of the thirteen seats in the Keystone State which "generally turned the balance in the House." Indeed, men of Hamiltonian and Madisonian persuasions were to be in close "balance" in the Third Congress, and each bloc had to appeal to moderate, uncommitted, or wavering members to form majorities on measures as these came up. After Hamilton announced his intention to resign as Secretary of the Treasury late in 1794 to return to his law practice (and to assume Federalist party leadership from outside the government), the Republicans in particular began to drift. Nonetheless, the Federalists saw them as a continuing threat.

The mid-term Congressional elections of 1794 were keenly contested. More and more members of Congress had taken to dispatching circular letters to their constituents, and the effect of these manifestoes was to align their constituents according to the divisions in the capital. Yet most of the serious, co-ordinated election activity that occurred in 1794 was carried forward on the Republican side not by partisan formations, but by the Democratic and Republican Societies. They played decisive parts in such centers as New York, Philadelphia, and the Allegheny region of Pennsylvania, where meetings were held, candidates were proposed, and voters were canvassed. The defeat of major Federalist figures in Philadelphia, together with the election of Edward Livingston in New York and Gallatin in western Pennsylvania, were encouraging Republican portents. In the end, the nationwide results in 1794 gave the Republican opposition a majority in the House for the first time. At the moment of the election, those chosen could hardly imagine how portentous their Congress would be.

4

The Great
Consolidation

In May 1793 Thomas Jefferson had sketched a succinct description of developing political alignments in the new American nation:

The line is now drawn so clearly as to show on one side: 1. The fashionable circles of Philadelphia, New York, Boston, and Charleston; natural aristocrats. 2. Merchants trading on British capital. 3. Paper [money] men. All the old Tories are found in some one of these three descriptions. On the other side are: 1. Merchants trading on their own capital. 2. Irish merchants. 3. Tradesmen, mechanics, farmers, and every other possible description of our citizens.

In August 1795 James Madison wrote a vigorous letter to Robert R. Livingston in New York in which he scored the treaty the Federalist envoy John Jay had recently negotiated with England, and added some political comment:

. . . the Treaty from one end to the other must be regarded as a demonstration that the Party to which the Envoy belongs & of which he has been more the organ than of the U.S., is a British party systematically aiming at an exclusive connection with the British government & ready to sacrifice to that object as well the dearest interests of our commerce as the most sacred dictates of National honor.

Not long afterward a toast was proposed in one of the surviving Democratic Societies: *"May the patriots of '76 step forward with Jefferson their head and cleanse the country of degeneracy and corruption."*

These expressions suggest both the problems and the progress of

75

the Republican movement as it edged toward becoming a Republican party. The problems were manifold: to join leaders at the capital and across the nation into a durable structure; to fuse groups as diverse as "Irish merchants," great planters, town artisans, and back-country farmers into a dependable party combination; to develop fully partisan ideology and attitudes as an animating force; and to bring the natural captain of the movement from Monticello to active leadership. Progress was evident in the fact that the problems were substantially solved in the years 1795 and 1796.

The catalytic agent was the issue of policy toward monarchical England and republican France. In considerable part, this issue depended for its effect on the ferment of ideology and on questions of American independence, "National honor," and the "Spirit of 'Seventy-six." This fact underscores the general point that America's first national parties arose out of reactions to significant issues and were issue-oriented parties. The original impetus for party formation was debate over economic development, but the crystallizing elements—particularly for the Republicans—were issues of world politics and broad ideology.

2.

The grand ideological antipathy became a raging controversy with the Jay treaty. The President had hoped to win peace at home and abroad by sending Monroe to Paris and Jay to London as friendly envoys, but the agreement Jay negotiated with Lord Grenville stirred new domestic discords and worsened relations with France.

In a sense, earlier controversies had merely set the scene for the Jay treaty showdown. The initial division of Gallomen and Anglomen, reactions to the neutrality proclamation, newspaper duels between Hamilton's "Pacificus" and Madison's "Helvidius," and other events had all had a cumulative effect. When the ostentatiously democratic "Citizen" Genêt had burst on the American scene as ambassador from France in 1793, he had been lionized by the Democratic and Republican clubs. Thus, Caesar A. Rodney of the Delaware Society had proclaimed that the issue was between an English ruling class who warred on France because they hated liberty and the friends of republican liberty everywhere including America, "the country that gave birth to the French revolution." Before long, Edmond Genêt's indiscreet conduct proved an embarrassment to the Republicans, but the line had been drawn again. The Jay treaty brought all the scattered sentiments stirred by issues of world politics to a clear climax. It concretized these issues and threw them dramatically into public and Congressional conflict.

The negotiations for the treaty had begun in 1794 against a backdrop of highly charged questions. One was continued British occupation of military posts on the American northwest frontier, contrary to agreements in the peace treaty of 1783. American spokesmen claimed that these posts had retarded settlement, provided bases for Indian massacres of American citizens, and kept the rich fur trade in British hands. Against these contentions, British spokesmen put forth the pre-Revolutionary debt claims of British exporters against American purchasers, while Americans in return posed the question of redress for slaves carried off by British troops at the close of the Revolutionary War. Finally, the war between France and Great Britain had led to British seizures of American neutral shipping and to impressment of American seamen. Matters were complicated further by the importance of continued British exports to the United States, as a mainstay of American trade and as a source of tariff revenues in the Federalist fiscal system. The makings of a major political drama were present.

Thousands of Americans saw Jay's text as a compound of sins of commission and omission. It did include a promise of evacuation of the northwest forts by Britain and some easing of restrictions on American shipping in certain channels of trade. But the price—too high as critics saw it—was American payment of the British debt claims on a basis to be worked out by a joint commission, and establishment of British trade with the United States on a most-favored-nation basis. On the side of omission, there was no settlement of the question of British seizures of American slaves during the Revolutionary War or of the impressment issue. In a series of letters he dispatched to Chancellor Livingston in New York and to other political correspondents, Madison roundly condemned the agreement. It was offensive to France, our key ally in the Revolution to whom we were still bound by prior treaties, and it fed the forces of "Aristocracy, Anglicism, and Mercantilism" in Federalist New England. In effect, it comprised American independence and our "National honour" in order to provide special benefits for "the banks," "the insurance companies in N.Y.," and a few "mercantile interests." Defense of the treaty was also forthcoming, based on what it did accomplish in the face of Great Britain's position of power vis-à-vis the infant American republic. Yet even Washington was dubious when he first saw the text. He hoped to keep the treaty secret and secure quiet passage for it in Congress.

In the event, the political dialogue was not to be so confined. A Virginia Senator gave a copy of the treaty to the assiduous Bache, who published it in the *Aurora* in 1795, and one Republican press after another took it up. From Philadelphia, Beckley wrote to George Clinton's young nephew and secretary in New York, De-Witt Clinton, "to keep all the republicans in line against the treaty." He also wrote a broadside to local leaders in an effort to build up pressure on wavering members of Congress and to stir anti-treaty meetings in as many communities as possible. Petitions against the treaty were prepared, and pamphlets followed hard on; Dr. Charles Jarvis presided over a protest meeting of 1,500 in Boston, and Beckley and Blair McClenachan were able to count 5,000 at a Philadelphia rally; the unfortunate Jay was burned in effigy in town after town. The Franklin Society in South Carolina decided not to burn the envoy in effigy but added: *"if the original were here . . . !"* More and more toasts called for Jefferson as the inevitable national savior, "for he is incorruptible."

Again and again, two dramatic themes recurred in the hostile chorus. One was the paean to American independence, accomplished politically by the Revolution but yet insecure or unfinished in terms of economic relations, power and recognition in world politics, and a sense of assurance of nationhood at home. The other was the refrain of America at the crossroads of civilization, choosing between the courses set by aristocratic England or by republican France. The sober Washington commented that the public had been agitated over the Jay treaty "in a higher degree than it has been at any period since the Revolution." Of course, many of the reactions were stage thunder; but perhaps recurrence to a sense of crossroads is in the script for any vital new nation. Meanwhile, after their early hesitations, Federalist leaders made the treaty a party measure. Various mercantile and investing groups saw concrete advantages in its terms, as did speculators in western lands and many frontier settlers. Outside of the South, substantially all the forces of Federalist-inclined respectability favored ratification.

In the South, however, the treaty brought the Republicans to new stages in their development toward party standing. Planters found no gains to balance the losses they saw in the treaty's debt-payment provisions and in its failure to meet the issue of British slave seizures. In Virginia the impact of the treaty gave increased confidence to Republican spokesmen, who intensified their appeals to the populace on questions of domestic as well as foreign policy. In Richmond, for example, a protest meeting commanded the services of the eminent Chancellor George Wythe, who had earlier lent his presence to a Federalist-inspired meeting to support Washington's neutrality proclamation. A vote of 100 to 50 in the legislature on resolutions praising Virginia's senators for their stand against the treaty was an approximate measures of the Virginia alignment. In North Carolina also, party attitudes were clarified by the treaty. Only one of the state's twelve senators and representatives favored it, and that one was from the commercial town of Fayetteville which handled trade on the Cape Fear river.

The most striking developments occurred in South Carolina, where Hamilton had won his strongest support below the Potomac. There the treaty brought the redoubtable Charles Pinckney (cousin of the Federalist Pinckneys) to join Senator Pierce Butler in the growing Republican ranks, and these men could count increasingly on other leaders or local cadre-workers like Representative Wade Hampton or Thomas Sumter. Opposition to the treaty also gave them a basis on which to win to the Republican standard such heterogeneous elements as outraged planters, poor whites of the pine flats, and Charleston ideological democrats. By 1796 their strength had increased sufficiently so that South Carolina's combined electoral vote for president and vice-president was divided evenly between Jefferson and a native-son Federalist candidate. The Federalists could no longer count on the Palmetto State as an invincible rampart in the South. By 1800 Charles Pinckney could urge his party's leaders not to plan "any arrangements for this state" concerning patronage without consulting him first. He spoke from strength, for the Jay treaty had opened his way into the national Senate as a Republican.

The sound and fury also beat against the northern Federalist bastion, Massachusetts. Issues of world politics, ideology, and the Jay treaty roused such a man as Dr. Nathaniel Ames from his absorption in medicine and farming to active political participation. The Dedham physician was the younger brother of Fisher Ames, whom Jefferson had called "the Colossus of the Monocrats"; and Nathaniel was as avidly against the treaty on the local ground as Fisher was for it in Congress. In the face of the judgment of those Fisher Ames termed "all the wise, the good, and the rich," opposition to the treaty stirred. Old Patriots of the Revolution, men in the farming district in the middle and western countries, and the followers of Governor Samuel Adams in Boston all protested, in processions which carried effigies of Jay festooned with scurrilous labels. Before long, a Unitarian divine in Salem commented on a developing practice which came with the Jay agitation: a pattern of popular "electioneering," which he saw prophetically as "the commencement of a new career." Yet it was some time before modern methods could wring significant Republican victories from the stony soil of the Northeast, although the Republicans could claim one representative each from Massachusetts and Vermont.

Nationally, the ultimate effect of the Jay treaty dialogue was to transform the Republican movement into a Republican party. The controversy established co-ordination in activity between leaders at the capital, and leaders, actives, and popular followings in the states, counties, and towns. Furthermore, as the drama moved toward its climax, co-ordination was generated between elections, rather than just at the time of an election. It was also generated around what were becoming partisan perspectives on a major national issue.

3.

The vital center of this development was Philadelphia, not only because of its strategic position as the national capital, but also because it was the eye of the vortex of Pennsylvania politics, which had attained an unusual degree of complexity and activity.

Several factors explain the Pennsylvania phenomenon. In New England and to a lesser degree in New York, the clergy, mercantile magnates, family cliques, and other social elites who were tied to English traditions in politics had managed to maintain substantial political leadership. In much of the South, planter dominance, the fact that the population was widely scattered, and limited effective suffrage had also slowed the emergence of popular or clearly partisan political action. Such obstacles had retarded political modernization through party development. By contrast, Pennsylvania was characterized by a relatively highly developed and varied economy and by a remarkably open politics which provided opportunities for the conflict of numerous interests and opinions. The complex interplay of economic, religious, ethnic, regional, and other groups produced strongly divisive crosscurrents; if partylike machinery had not been developed, political chaos might have been complete. Thus Pennsylvania pre-eminently exhibited both the opportunity and the need to devise modern political methods to cope with intricate political problems.

Two groups had played key roles in bringing together the elements which ultimately made the new Pennsylvania Republican party. The first consisted of the family and friends of Benjamin Franklin, whom the Federalists had slighted in recognition and patronage. Here were kinsfolk like his son-in-law Richard Bache, his grandson William Temple Franklin, and the youngster Benjamin Franklin Bache, together with personal associates in the old Pennsylvania government like David Rittenhouse and the Doctors Rush and Hutchinson. The second group may be described as old Revolutionary War rivals of Washington, like General Thomas Mifflin, who brought the able manager Dallas to the fore. Such men found new recruits, and before long a triumvirate of Dallas at the statehouse, the ubiquitous Beckley behind the scenes, and Bache at the *Aurora* formed the nucleus of full Republican party development. By the mid-1790's they had become adept at maintaining discipline among legislators and lesser political activists in the counties and towns, who needed the support of the party for their advancement or survival. They had also learned the uses of continuous propaganda and activity among the voters.

All of these men knew Jefferson and looked to him as their natural leader in the national arena. One, Dallas, could serve as a liaison between the Virginian and Governor Mifflin; another, Beckley, could, in addition to his other chores, spread through the Philadelphia bookshops and coffee houses the hints that Jefferson threw out; a third, Bache, could keep Jefferson's views and name before the public. Thus, in terms of national party development, the members of the triumvirate and others with them may be thought of as crucial party cadre workers—men who might or might not hold government office, but who spoke for, made decisions in the name of, and labored assiduously for the party. As lesser actives in the counties and towns looked to them for direction, they looked for cues to national leaders like Jefferson or Madison.

From the center in Philadelphia, particularly as the Jay treaty controversy raged, lines of national party development were gradually firmed across the country. Here Beckley was again a powerful energizing figure. His indefatigable, widely scattered correspondence had extended not only to men like Clinton and Burr in New York or Monroe and Taylor in Virginia but to innumerable lesser figures. He knew the value of polemics, gossip, and canard as well as policy proclamation. He was, for example, the first to bring to light in 1796—five years after the event—Hamilton's brief *amour* with a Mrs. James Reynolds, with all its sordid overtones of Caesar and Cleopatra, and Hamilton's acquiescence in Mr. Reynolds' blackmail. Well beforehand, Beckley was determined that the reluctant Jefferson should be a Republican standard bearer in 1796 and replace "old Washington" as president, and he bent his correspondence and travels to this end. Meanwhile, other Philadelphia cadre workers followed Beckleyan precepts and began to develop national connections.

Party-building activity by members in Congress also intensified in the Jay treaty years. More and more members of the Republican persuasion began to act not only as legislators, but also as part-time cadre workers, shaping national party directions, maintaining relationships with local figures and potential lieutenants in their districts, or dispatching circulars to their constituents. Though Madison remained in the forefront, new men like Gallatin, Burr, Livingston, Henry Dearborn of Massachusetts, Thomas Blount of North Carolina, Pierce Butler of South Carolina, and Abraham Baldwin of Georgia joined him in an increasingly close-knit group. These men, with Beckley, Giles, and a few others—and with Jefferson's advice or consent when he would vouchsafe it from Monticello—reached the point by 1796 where they could in effect make decisions for the emerging national Republican party. At the center of government, in the stimulating atmosphere of Pennsylvania's highly charged politics, they acted as a kind of informal national committee.

Meanwhile, the mills of central publicity ground faster. Such men as Bache and his aid William Duane, the rough-and-tumble pamphleteer James Thomson Callender (who published the Hamilton-Reynolds exposé), and Beckley, under pseudonyms like "Valerius" and "Calm Observer," threw off reams of printed information and polemic. Their attacks on Federalists were often virulent or vulgar, dealing scabrously with personalities as well as with issues, and they finally pilloried even the hitherto sacrosanct Washington. Yet by 1798 the circulation of the Aurora had surpassed that of Freneau's Gazette at 1,790, a substantial circulation for the time.

In many states, local cadremen and actives were also finding ways to co-ordinate partisan activity. The most important of these outposts were New York and Virginia, the Empire states of North and South. The electoral votes of New York (twelve) and Virginia (twenty-one), together with Pennsylvania (fifteen)—forty-eight all told—constituted more than a third of the total electoral vote in presidential contests in the 1790's. If the Republicans could win the bulk of these votes and add a modicum from the South while conceding New England, they could elect a president.

In New York fresh forces had come to supplement the antique "connexions" of family-clique leadership. The old Clinton faction remained important in Republican calculations and new-style connections, but so were the new recruits. Some were trainees from the Republican Society movement, as was, for example, Edward Livingston. This bright young democrat from an old patrician family had worked his way up as an active in party councils, was a member of the Tammany Society, and based his claim to a Congressional nomination in 1794 not only on his family influence but on his partisan labors. Even more important was the part of Aaron Burr and his associates. From the 1780's Burr had been a lonely free lance among the family alliances that controlled politics, moving among them in search of support but never becoming the agent of any one group. Cool, reserved, little concerned with political principles but remarkably adroit in political methods, something of an upstart yet always urbane, he approached politics as a profession and office as a career. He thus represented a new phenomenon as an early (if extreme) archetype of the self-made cadre politician, the single-minded *homo politicus* who was to play such a large role in American party life. In this he differed both from the old New York family chieftains and from men like Hamilton, Jefferson, and Madison, all of whom were practical enough in politics but who remained (as compared with Burr) semi-professionals with other interests and concerns. In particular, Burr labored to build a power base among the urban masses of New York City and to make the old Tammany Society into a political group. He and his band of lesser professional cadremen and actives soon flanked the Clintonian and Livingston forces as major elements of Republican party structure in the state.

In the seedbed of Virginia, old leaders began to cultivate new shoots of co-ordination and popular action. Since the early 1790's Madison or Jefferson or Monroe had corresponded and counseled with notables across the state. Yet, because the Republican movement had not found deep roots in popular participation, the average Virginian had not been able to claim a firm partisan identity. Rising concern with foreign policy gave the Virginia leaders their opportunity. In 1793, when Federalists at Richmond had called a public meeting to adopt resolutions praising Washington's foreign policy, Madison had pressed Taylor and Edmund Pendleton to prepare counterresolutions and to arrange for similar meetings to adopt them. Within a month, rallies in Caroline, Culpeper, New Kent, Williamsburg, King William, Fredericksburg, Albemarle, and Staunton counties had all spoken out. In the sweep of the Jay treaty excitement in 1795 these procedures were employed again in expanded form in an effort to mobilize a broad public: instigation by national leaders, conferences among local cadremen, arrangements by cadre workers and actives, resolutions by popular voice. The key conferences remained informal, unpublicized, even amateur by the standards of a Beckley, a Dallas, or a Burr, and comparatively few men were involved. Yet in Virginia soil such practices were effective in building a party.

Taken together, developments in Pennsylvania, New York, Virginia, and other states constituted a single process with local variations. Firmer connections than had previously existed were being established between the national center at Philadelphia on the one hand and the states and localities on the other, between leaders at the capital "point" of an emerging party phalanx and lesser leaders or followers at the "tail." At the same time connections were being drawn tighter in the states and localities, and strong new echelons were being developed in popular support and popular action. The Republican movement was coming closer to full national Republican party structure, which extended from the capital through articulations with state formations to the varied state and local party followings. The national Republican party structure was subject to further elaboration in the decade to follow, but its basic lines had been laid down during the struggle over the Jay treaty.

Figure 1

RELATIONSHIPS IN EMERGING PARTY STRUCTURE

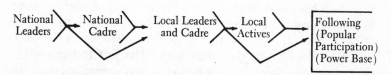

Indeed, by 1795 or 1796 it is possible to discern patterns of structure in reasonably full development in both parties. In each case, party in government at the capital was connected to party formation and following in the states and localities, in a great chain with a series of intermediate links. In the Federalist structure the links were stronger at the outset, but the Republicans were catching up fast and were soon to profit from their more active and durable ties with their popular following. In time, their central party structure was to find its great source of power in this democratic substructure. The end product stood in significant contrast to the factions, cliques, or juntos of earlier years.

4.

At the national center in Philadelphia, meanwhile, the Jay treaty also drew party lines tighter and prompted party innovations among the Republicans. In the Senate, ratification was accomplished in 1795 before publication of the treaty had blown up the storms of national debate—but only with the support of Washington's name, only after Hamilton as a Federalist party leader behind the scenes had exerted his commanding influence, and then only by a vote of 20 to 10 or barely the two-thirds majority required. All of the New England senators but two voted for ratification, while members from the South were nearly unanimous in opposition.

The great equinoctial storms came in the new Congress the next year. The issue, in the House of Representatives in March and April 1796, was an appropriation to carry out the treaty's terms—and in the crisis the Republicans in the House acted in a distinctively partisan manner. Key leaders like Madison, Giles, Livingston of New York and Gallatin of Pennsylvania, Blount of North Carolina, and Dearborn of Massachusetts conferred repeatedly and coordinated their efforts carefully. The Federalists were also stirring, with such leaders as Sedgwick and Fisher Ames of Massachusetts, William Loughton Smith of South Carolina, and Jonathan Dayton of New Jersey. It was clear that when the crossed winds blew, they would blow with unprecedented force. The first test came on a resolution introduced by Livingston which demanded that the President put before the House his instructions to Jay and other relevant documents: adopted, 62 to 37, with every member elected as a Republican (and recorded) voting yea, while all but six members elected as Federalists (and recorded) voted nay. Bluntly, Washington—coached by Hamilton, Madison was convinced—refused to submit executive papers to legislative inspection.

Meanwhile, new pressure areas were building up around the treaty. More and more, the Federalists were stating the issue as the Jay treaty and peace, or war. From the North came rumblings of secession if the appropriation was not passed, and the petition campaign for the treaty was intensified, particularly in areas represented by uncertain members of Congress.

Faced with a climactic issue and the urgings of necessity, the leaders of the emerging Republican party in Congress evolved new devices to strengthen their position. One was a caucus of Republican members to co-ordinate strategy and tactics, the first of two such gatherings to be held in the years 1795-1801. Although Beckley was encouraged by the evening conclave—"there appears a disposition to make a firm stand"—Gallatin noted that members were left free "to vote as they pleased," without fear of proscription. Nonetheless, the Congressional caucus marked an important step toward means to arrive at a party position. Another innovation was the appointment of standing committees in the House, and the initiative toward the eventual system of Congressional committees was a Republican move. The most important committee, Ways and Means, was established at Gallatin's instigation; as chairman he made it an instrument for minute examination of the Administration's financial undertakings, which in a phase of international crisis were mainly military. Before long, the standing committees were to emerge as distinctively partisan instruments.

Despite all efforts, however, the political winds turned against the Republicans on the great question. The crucial appropriation for the treaty was granted on April 30, 1796, by a close vote of 51 to 48. The bulk of the yeas came from Federalist-dominated delegations from New England and New Jersey, the bulk of the nays from predominantly Republican delegations from the South. The Federalist and Republican representatives from Vermont split on party lines, as did the two Federalists and four Republicans from South Carolina. All told, 44 Federalists and 7 Republicans voted yea, 45 Republicans and 3 Federalists (all from Virginia) voted nay. As contrasted with the looseness of factional or party ties in past Congressional voting, cohesion among both Federalists and Republicans was strikingly high, reaching a salutary 93 per cent of members voting among the Federalists and 87 per cent among the Republicans. Yet for the Republicans there was a fatal break, which came in the Middle Atlantic delegations of New York, Pennsylvania, and Maryland. While the Federalist members from these states voted unanimously for the appropriation, all seven of the Republican votes for the treaty were from the three Mid-Atlantic states—and they constituted nearly half of the eighteen Republicans from the area. If only two of the Middle Atlantic defectors had stood with Madison (for a cohesion of 90 per cent), the results would have been reversed and the Republicans would have scored a triumph. At the crucial juncture, party discipline in the House had failed by a hair.

Figure 2

VOTE ON JAY TREATY APPROPRIATION IN HOUSE FROM KEY STATES

	Total Members	Party Fed	Rep	Federalist Yea	Nay	Republican Yea	Nay
New York	10	5	5	5	0	2	3
Pennsylvania	13	4	9	4	0	3	5[b]
Maryland	8	3[a]	4	3	0	2	1[b]

[a] Party affiliation of one representative undetermined; voted yea on Jay treaty appropriation.
[b] One Republican from Pennsylvania not voting, one from Maryland resigned.
Compiled from Manning J. Dauer, *The Adams Federalists* (Baltimore, 1953), 289–92.

No wonder Madison was disappointed and felt overborne by the Federalist pressures built up in the Jay treaty gale. He had counted on the Republican members from New York and Pennsylvania to stand with him—and so they did, with one exception, on most other important measures in both sessions of the Fourth Congress through 1797. He had looked hopefully for a majority of nearly twenty on the treaty appropriation until two weeks before the roll-call, but as the day grew nearer he fretted that his margin had all but blown away. He should not have been too surprised, in view of the men involved and their constituencies, for nearly all of the defectors came from districts where mercantile interests set up strong pressures for the treaty. The two New Yorkers who broke ranks were from commercial New York City or the Hudson river valley immediately to the north, and one was Pierre Van Cortlandt of the wealthy, investing Van Cortlandt political family. Of the three from Pennsylvania who voted for the appropriation, two were from commercial Philadelphia or the Delaware river area above. One of these, who became an all-out deserter to the Federalists, was former-Speaker Frederick Augustus Muhlenberg, who however returned to the Republican standard in 1800. The third Pennsylvanian was Andrew Gregg, from a central district on the Susquehanna river, who was later denounced by Beckley as "Gregg the Trimmer." The two Marylanders were both from the Baltimore–Chesapeake Bay–Susquehanna river commercial area. The important figure was Samuel Smith, a wealthy Baltimore merchant who later became a leading factional marplot in the Republican ranks.

Dissension on issues, based largely on constituency pressures, was to become a recurring feature of internal factional division in the Republican as in other American parties. The immediate result in 1796, however, was a remarkable attempt at party discipline, an attack on some of the chief dissenters in the fall elections—a response which has seldom been duplicated in later American party practice. Three lost out to Federalists; the hapless Muhlenberg was replaced by the Democratic Society stalwart Blair McClenachan; and Van Cortlandt and Gregg, re-elected, stopped their "trimming." Only Samuel Smith pursued his old, eccentric ways.

In terms of party development, however, the salient fact for the Republicans as the Fourth Congress ran its course was not in a few defections. It was rather in the cohesion and discipline which they, as well as the Federalists, were after all able to muster as the political storms blew. In the whole "Jay Treaty Session" from December 1795 to June 1796, party voting on all major issues reached an impressive 93 per cent of Federalists and Republicans in the House, taken together—a representative being classified as a party voter if he voted with the majority of members in his party two-thirds of the time or oftener, in accord with calculations Joseph Charles has made. This figure contrasts sharply with a party-voting level

Political Parties in a New Nation

of 58 per cent (liberally estimated) in the crucial session of 1790, the year of Hamilton's great innovations. While the Republicans lost some roll-calls in addition to the Jay vote through periodic breaks in discipline, they achieved a higher level of voting cohesion than they had shown in previous years. If the winds of Jay treaty contention brought no other good, they blew favorably for party consolidation at the legislative center.

Figure 3

RISE OF PARTY VOTING,[a] HOUSE OF REPRESENTATIVES, 1789–1797

Congress, Session	Dates of Session	Voting as Federalists	Voting as Republicans	Non-Party
I/1	Apr–Sept 1789	25	11	21
I/2–3	Jan–Aug 1790 Dec '90–Mar '91	22	15	27
II/1	Oct '91–May '92	28	23	14
II/2	Nov '92–Mar '93	29	25	11
III/1–2	Dec '93–Jun '94[b] Nov '94–Mar '95	45	38	20
IV/1	Dec '95–Jun '96	40	57	7
IV/2	Dec '96–Mar '97	36	55	12

[a] The criterion of "party voting" is that the member must have voted with others of the party indicated on two-thirds of the measures "of national importance," or involving "some important principle of government," as members saw it, which arose during the session. The measure of party voting is not the same as the measure of party cohesion on a particular roll-call, as given in the text for the Jay treaty appropriation. The latter expresses as a per cent the proportion of the representatives attached to a given party who voted with the majority of the members from that party on a given issue.

[b] Membership in the House increased from 65 to 105.

Adapted from Joseph Charles, *The Origins of the American Party System* (Williamsburg, Virginia, 1956), 93–4. Some data was taken by Charles from Manning J. Dauer, *The Adams Federalists* (Baltimore, 1953).

They did more, however. They marked an issue which was intensely partisan, in which not only members of Congress but leaders outside of Congress and popular followings across the country came to think in partisan terms and to act in party–co-ordinated ways. Republicans as well as Federalists had learned that in purposeful contention, cohesion and concentration of energy was essential. In the process, the ultimate linkages of structure between capital and countryside had at last been established for the Republicans.

5.

The Jay treaty controversy stimulated not only advances in party structure, but also other tangible and intangible consequences which were crucial in Republican party development.

The great intangible result was an intensification of party spirit. The whole deep-reaching ideological and emotional cast of the treaty issue did much to intensify for the Republicans a sense of mission, such as the Federalists had experienced earlier. It took shape, in their eyes, as a cause at once patriotic and partisan: to defend the nation against British domination and against those who would supinely yield to such domination, and to use the Republican party as an instrument in this cause. No longer, in the Republican view, could they be thought of as somehow unpatriotic in their opposition role; in their own eyes, they, not the Federalists, were now the great patriotic party, although of course Federalists could not agree. Such perspectives became linked with earlier views on other questions, in a general party outlook. The result was a sense of forward movement, an *élan*, which provided powerful springs of energy and cohesion.

In the articles he wrote for the *National Gazette* in 1792, Madison had provided an early sketch of the distinctions between Republicans and others. The issue was not only the economic one raised by Hamilton's proposals, he argued, but general questions of government, such as the spirit of republicanism as opposed to the principles of monarchy and aristocracy. The true republicans, or Republicans, were those who loved liberty and despised tyranny, who believed that the people should be enlightened rather than kept in the dark about public affairs or condemned for licentiousness or stupidity, and who thus could trust the people. The "anti-Republicans," on the other hand, disdained a rational view of politics, clinging to the vaunted wisdom of tradition as a sufficient guide for government. They, the Federalists, were:

91

those who from particular interest, from natural temper, or from habits of life, are more partial to the opulent than to the other classes of society; and having debauched themselves into a persuasion that mankind are incapable of governing themselves, it follows with them, of course, that government can be carried on only by the pageantry of rank, the influence of money and emoluments, and the terror of military force.

In the face of such differences, Madison was by 1792 convinced that parties were unavoidable. In a republican society, the great object should be to balance the contending parties, not to try to eliminate the one or the other, or pretend (in the name of national solidarity) that they should not exist. There was no question as to which party he thought was overbalancing the other. The obvious conclusion, in consequence, was that the Republican opposition had to mobilize its forces to fight back.

The lines of political doctrine which Madison distinguished could be traced far back into the nation's English colonial heritage. The Federalist tendency, historicist, legalistic, hierarchical, theistic and Anglican, and aristocratic, ran back to the English feudal tradition. The Republicans' ideological bent, nonconformist or Deistic, individualistic, anti-hierarchical, romantic and anti-historical sometimes even to the point of Utopianism, and democratic, flowed from one aspect of Puritanism and from the Enlightenment. Its great philosopher was John Locke, and its American exemplar was Jefferson far more than Madison. In the long run, what Jefferson saw as "the common sense of the subject," as expressed by Locke and in the Declaration of Independence, became in effect the mood and address of the basic American liberal tradition. In their ascendancy in the 1790's, the Federalists were well served by conservative-traditionalist writ. In the future, when the liberal-Lockian ethos was bound to dominate, traditionalist doctrine was bound to wane and the party that counted on it would decline accordingly.

To Republican true believers all lines of doctrine and interest seemed to be caught up in the Jay treaty drama, and its effect was to fix them in the playbooks of Republican philosophy. In 1795 Jefferson sketched again the groups that adhered to the two parties. On the Rpublican side by that time he saw the whole body of landholders in the nation, and laborers in agriculture and artisanship.

Among the Federalists he listed old refugees of the Revolution, and Tories; the British merchants living in America; the American merchants who traded on British capital; holders of bank and public funds, and speculators; "nervous persons, whose languid fibres have more analogy with a passive than active state of things"; and most officers of the Federal government, and office-seekers. In Jefferson's view, the Republicans composed the creditable and the Federalists the discreditable elements in the political cast of characters. On the last day of 1795 he wrote to William Branch Giles a letter which fairly breathed the new spirit of party and its importance:

> Were parties here divided merely by a greediness for office, as in England, to take a part with either would be unworthy of a reasonable or moral man, but where the principle of difference is as substantial and as strongly pronounced as between the republicans & the Monocrats of our country, I hold it as honorable to take a firm & decided part, and as immoral to pursue a middle line, as between the parties of Honest men, & Rogues, into which every country is divided.

Certainly not Madison, hardly even the resolute Beckley with his canards and cries of "trimmer," not even Bache of the *Aurora* heralding the Republican dawn, could have written more in the spirit of party, more in the sense of mission and *élan* which had come to cue partisan action. For the cool, cautious Jefferson, it was a remarkable fulmination.

In fact, it was a prelude to the great tangible result of the Jay treaty drama for the Republican cause. Motivated far more deeply by symbolic and ideological concerns than he had been by concrete economic interests, Jefferson was nearing the point where he would do as Hamilton had done before him: "march at the head of affairs," in order "to produce the event." It had been a long, slow process; it was not to be completed without further hesitations and expressions of aversion; and even when Jefferson did permit himself to be drawn to the center of the political stage, he persisted in his inclination toward a moderate, conciliatory approach. Yet early in May 1796, stirred by the House vote on the treaty appropriation, he made at least a passive decision to allow himself to be advanced as his party's candidate for president.

A few weeks later he suggested to Monroe that only the regard of the people for Washington kept the Federalists in power. If Washington's successor was a "Monocrat," Jefferson predicted, he would be overborne by the people's republican sense.

5

Modern Politics
and Popular Parties

The establishment of the Republicans as a full-blown party was only one aspect of a general movement in the new republic to solve its basic political problems. These included questions of democracy and national stability, and issues of economic development, as well as the establishment of political parties. Over-all, the national development constituted steps toward political modernization.

Indeed, American development after the Revolution of 1776 was almost a classic instance of political modernization. Thus, we find a constitution on the rationalist model, and Washington serving as a charismatic focus of acceptance and legitimacy in the transition to fully rational, legal foundations of authority; an open politics of conflicting interests; orderly administration, particularly as exhibited by Hamilton; free, formal associations of individuals on a rational basis for political action, as in the Democratic or Republican Societies, and the gradual displacement of family or fluid-faction "connexions" by the open, rationalized, stable connections of party; innovations in policy or inventions in political methods not only by Hamilton, but by men like Madison or Gallatin, and emphasis on rational discussion as typified by Jefferson and practiced by thousands; mass communication and propaganda in the two *Gazettes,* the *Aurora,* and other papers; the rise of "new men" like Beckley and Burr to labor at the "new careers" of methodical politicians as contrasted with notables in politics; and a

95

tendency toward national outlooks and co-ordination as against parochial patterns and localism.

There were special and significant features in the American experience in modernization. As contrasted with European nations, American political shapers were not confronted with a protracted conflict to overthrow a closed, traditionalistic, or hierarchical social and political structure, for such a structure was never firmly fixed in America. Unlike most emerging nations of the twentieth century, where modernization has entailed an intense race from a slow start to bring an underdeveloped society to the level of modernity seen in alien Western societies, the new America worked from an already comparatively favorable position. It was thus able to achieve modernization as a development of existing elements and trends, rather than a forcing of alien patterns. Furthermore, in comparison with both European and latter-day underdeveloped nations, the American republic was fortunate in that it enjoyed crucial preconditions for a democratic polity. Nonetheless, the American experience followed typical paths of modernization, from the rationalization of authority to the development of political parties.

The passage from clique, faction, or junto politics to party politics has, in general, been an important aspect of political modernization. Certainly, it was so in America. As compared with faction-like formations, parties represented rationalized, comparatively ordered, and methodical ways of performing crucial political functions, even when they showed aspects of disorder on their own. Also, their public and continuing character made them less dependent than cliques or factions on particular persons, families, or "connexions," and virtually required leaders and active workers in a modern style. Yet the development of American parties also depended on national political stability and national economic development. Without these, the new America might not have continued as a democratic polity, and the first experiment in modern parties might have died with it.

2.

An infant democracy, if it is to survive, must evolve modes of carrying on political conflict without destroying national order and unity. To Washington or to Hamilton, as to many who shared their views, such national unity was paramount, and opposition was a threat to stability. Unity and order were a delicate web which must not be strained.

To other shapers of American politics, however, democracy implied criticism, free access to politics, real options in elections. Thus Madison, Jefferson, and the Republicans fought for the right to construct open yet peaceful competition between parties for power.

The Federalists had a cogent cause in their concern for stability, a cause which the Republicans in their way shared. An opposition may indeed tear asunder the untried fabric of a new democracy if it runs to conflict over fundamentals of social and political order, or utilizes the methods of violence. If conflict is to go on without disrupting national unity, it must stay within agreement on certain basic values of the society, or at least on certain underlying rules of the political game. Where social cleavage is deep and broad, and political issues are basic and intense, it is difficult to generate shared attitudes or secure agreement on rules for politics. Yet viable democratic politics involves a paradox: at once agreement and disagreement, consensus on fundamentals and cleavage on issues.

In dealing with this vital paradox young America drew heavily on its colonial background and early experience. It had at hand the strong threads of English law, Locke and the eighteenth-century Enlightenment, and republican precepts, or what Louis Hartz has called the "liberal tradition." Furthermore, it wove the central threads of this tradition (with some modification) into the durable republican cloth of the Constitution of 1789. Early conflict over the Constitution gave way to a remarkable acceptance of it, particularly after the addition of the ten amendments called the Bill of Rights in 1789-1791; and acceptance gradually became a strong emotional attachment to the Constitution as symbol and instrument—though patriotic men could still disagree over what particular provisions of the document should mean in operation. Thus the new nation developed a set of central faiths, commitments, and loyalties woven around a concept of individual liberty, and a widespread acceptance of basic republican rules for the conduct of politics. It did so within a society which could readily develop in a liberal direction because it was not bound to a feudal fabric of graded estates, or of aristocracy against bourgeoisie, submerged masses, or peasantry. It arrived, in Tocqueville's phrase, "at a state of democracy without having to endure a democratic revolution," or without having to endure the breaks in the social texture which social revolution may bring.

Conflict generally remained within the moderate borders of the liberal tradition. Even Shays's Rebellion in 1786-1787 and the Whiskey Insurrection of 1794 were movements of small-property owners to protect their property rights, not instances of primitive communism threatening all property, of the sort Babeuf represented during the French Revolution. Cleavages between the Federalist and Republican parties did not really shake the fundamentals of liberty or property, the rules of republican politics, or the social order. Furthermore, early proposals that the nation should take George Washington as a dictator or even as King George I also foundered on the liberal tradition and the developing republican consensus. To be sure, some men favored the interests of one kind of property, others those of another; some men wanted a more elitist, restrictive, "English" republic, others a more democratic, libertarian, "French" republic; some distrusted The People, others relied on them—and consensus was subjected to strains, or questioned, or accepted half-heartedly in certain quarters during its years of formation. Yet, generally, conflict did not become so serious that groups or parties clashed over fundamentals.

The strength of the new national fabric was repeatedly tested. One danger that may threaten a new nation is the possibility that particular conflicts may explode into national disruption. In Shays's Rebellion, the Whiskey Insurrection, the intimations of disunion in the Jay treaty controversy—or in the later Fries Uprising in eastern Pennsylvania in 1799, or proposals for separation by New England in the early 1800's—such threats stained the early American experience. The grave issue in each case was whether partial conflicts would lead to general violence or to secession of part of the nation from the whole. Yet in the event, no national leader or party was ready to extend local dissent to general disruption. Faith in the republic, attachment to orderly decision-making, and abhorrence of violent methods were too strong in the nation's leaders, people, and parties to permit them to indulge in insurrection or in schemes of disunion. In each case, a loyal opposition valued national survival above immediate concerns. In each case, national unity and the emerging national consensus prevailed.

3.

The progress of a nation's economy may both provide support for political modernization and democracy and also be affected by them. In the West, historically, the emergence of democratic politics has been associated with the rise or existence of segments of the population which constitute a substantial middle class, with inclinations toward middle-class modes of life and attitudes among other segments of the society, and with a considerable sharing of economic well-being. In its earliest manifestation at least, the liberal-democratic tradition has been a middle-class tradition, although in certain kinds of social development middle-class groups may not pursue democracy as a goal.

In a more general sense, the emergence of the democratic spirit has been associated with certain preconditions of economic and social advancement. Such conditions do not automatically produce democracy; but they have, in general, constituted prerequisites for full democratic participation and practice. Four such preconditions have been suggested by Seymour Martin Lipset: high or rising levels in national wealth, in economic development, in urbanization, and in education. High indices in these areas have been closely correlated with the rise and continued stability of democracies, low indices with dictatorships or with unstable democracies. National wealth, in an economy which is relatively advanced, can lay foundations for economic well-being and economic security. If economic well-being is widely diffused, the probability increases that the society will escape broad social cleavages between haves and have-nots, and that political conflict and party cleavage will occur within a moderate range. With the increased contacts and communication among men which urban centers bring, and also with the tools of political understanding and administration which widespread education makes available, the chances for democratic development are further increased. The existence of such features in a society means, in effect, the existence of a "modernized," generally middle-class way of life.

All of these preconditions may be discerned in early American history. The new nation was a relatively wealthy one compared to its contemporaries. Property—particularly agricultural property— and economic well-being were unusually broadly diffused among its people. To be sure, its economy was not "advanced" in terms of latter-day industrialization. Out of a total national income of $668 million in 1799, agriculture accounted for an overwhelming $264 million, while manufacturing produced only $32 million; the nation bought most of its manufactured goods abroad. Nor was the United States in the 1790's characterized by the urbanization that accompanies a manufacturing economy. The first census in 1790 showed 3,727,559 rural dwellers out of a total population of 3,929,214; and the 201,655 urban dwellers lived in only two centers larger than 25 thousand (a total of 61,653), and were otherwise dispersed in 22 so-called "urban places" of 2.5 to 25 thousand. Yet, for its time, the United States was no provincial, peasant economy. It was not significantly "backward" by European standards of the eighteenth century, and it was certainly not so in comparison to many markedly underdeveloped new nations of the twentieth century, whose road to democracy is thereby more difficult. Although manufactures remained small, commerce and other kinds of enterprise accounted for much more of the total national product: miscellaneous enterprises and finance for $60 million; transportation, including overseas shipping, for a substantial $160 million; construction, including shipbuilding, for another $53 million; service and service trades for $64 million; and trade for $35 million. Indeed, shipping, shipbuilding, and related commerce made up in considerable part for the infant standing of manufacturing; and, in addition, a significant portion of American agriculture was involved in the market economy. Furthermore, the nation's modest but lively urban centers did produce urban middle-class intellectuals and intellectual ferment and also exerted powerful influences over the countryside. Literacy and educational levels, while not readily measurable, were by all accounts high, and they extended to the great rural population as well as to town dwellers.

In short, many crucial social prerequisites were present for the development of democracy and the parties that depended on it—while at the same time the variety of groups, sections, and regions stimulated modernization in national politics and the emergence of parties. Only the purposes and energies of *homo politicus* remained as necessary to establish democratic institutions, and these had been forthcoming.

The direction the economy of a new nation takes inevitably becomes embroiled in its politics. A common tendency has been positive government action toward industrial growth. In one sense, this was Hamilton's approach to political economy, even though his policy ran counter to the path many later emerging nations have taken—the path to government control, substantial government ownership, or socialism. To Hamilton the proper role of government in the economy was to promote, rather than control, capitalist enterprise. Indeed, his program of a funded national debt as a source of capital, a national bank to provide venture credit, excise and other taxes to service the debt, and high tariff duties to protect native industry, rehearsed the steps which Karl Marx's analysis decades later described as the standard pattern of forced capitalist accumulation. The ultimate result was a long stride toward economic advance for the American nation. One immediate effect, however, was gain for a few special interests through hothouse government sponsorship.

There was of course another possible direction. This was the political economy Jefferson and most Republicans came to represent: a course looking toward a continuing planter's and freeholder's Arcadia, a predominantly agricultural life in which merchandising and manufactures widely diffused among small units would serve as handmaidens to husbandry. The political economy of this direction, as it developed in America, was characterized by a strong equalitarian stress mixed with *laissez faire*. The proper role of government, Jefferson thought, should be to secure property in as many hands as possible. It was time, he wrote in 1795, "to provide by every possible means that as few as possible shall be without a little portion of land. The small land holders are the most precious part of a state." More generally, Jefferson looked to the widest possible diffusion of human well-being as the most favorable soil for maintaining the dignity of the individual personality. Yet, given the conditions of the times, the Republican agrarian economic prescription would, ironically, have entailed a slow pace of economic growth for the new nation and limited standards of living for its population.

There was indeed irony in the positions of both parties. The general ideological theme of the Federalists was conservative and traditionalist, whereas new parties in later emerging nations have been radically innovative and anti-traditionalist. On the other hand Federalist economic policy was highly innovative and modernist, emphasizing government action toward an advanced, industrial, capitalist society—again, however, contrary to the often anti-capitalist attitudes of new nations in the twentieth century. The Republicans were post-Enlightenment and anti-traditionalist in political ideology, but still largely wedded to agrarian economic conceptions in a pre-industrial economy—conceptions that the American nation with its already comparatively prosperous agricultural economy could afford, but which stand in sharp contrast to the intense drives for industrialization in new nations today. Thus in both parties political outlooks ran in some sense in contradiction with economic policy, and in crossed or atypical ways as compared with the course of later emerging nations.

Yet cleavage on economic policy was not total. Both the Federalist program, stressing government innovation and promotion with elitist consequences, and the Republican direction, emphasizing a minimum of government intervention and equalitarian norms, were consistent with the values of individual property ownership and with republican methods. In an ultimate sense, furthermore, the purposeful direction Hamilton espoused and the values Jefferson represented are not necessarily incompatible: planning and promotion need not serve elitist purposes or narrow group interests, and equalitarianism need not be tied to agrarianism, or pay the price of a slow rate of economic development and a modest standard of living.

One virtue of modern political parties is that they can facilitate rational or democratic decisions on such matters, by providing—as Hamilton and the Federalists and Jefferson and the Republicans were doing—reasonably clear choices on policy, including issues of political economy.

4.

The party of Jefferson in the 1790's was a new political engine, the first of its kind in modern history. It exhibited little continuity with antecedent formations, and it developed political relationships which carried it well beyond the Federalists as an archetype of a modern, "popular" party. In the long process of learning and inventing in the face of need and opportunity, it had pioneered in rationalized or modernized political practices, which observers abroad later referred to as "American methods." Such practices, from the caucus to mass electoral appeals, were nonetheless frequently reproduced as democracy made its way in other nations.

Early Republicans were often stigmatized as "Anti-Federalists," a reference to the opposition to the Constitution of 1787. The idea was a plausible one, and it is true that most of those who favored the new Constitution at the convention of 1787 became Federalists in the 1790's, while those who refused to sign became Republicans. It can also be argued that many districts (and thereby presumably interests) which voted against the Constitution in the ratification controversy also stood as Republican bastions in succeeding years. Thus, for example, the argument runs that the districts which opposed the Constitution in New York in 1788 were the same as those which opposed the Federalist Jay for governor in 1792, or that the forces which had fought ratification in western Pennsylvania reappeared in the whiskey tax protests of 1793-1794 and in later Republicanism. Parallels may also be found between the elitist, "energetic"-government ideas of many pro-Constitutionalists and of the Federalists, while beliefs in popular, limited government were shared by many anti-Constitutionalists and Republicans.

103

Figure 4

PARTY ATTACHMENT OF MEMBERS OF
CONSTITUTIONAL CONVENTION LIVING IN 1791

	Party Attachment in 1791		Not
Position on Constitution	Federalist	Republican	Known
Supporters, 43	25	12	6
Opponents, 6	0	6	0

Compiled from Charles A. Beard, *Economic Origins of Jeffersonian Democracy* (New York, 1915), 34–74.

Nevertheless, serious difficulties attend the assumption of clear continuity from anti-Constitutionalists to Republicans. While most leaders who had opposed the Constitution became Republicans, so did many who had favored it, including Madison and Jefferson. At the state ratifying convention in New York, for example, representatives of the powerful Livingston and Van Cortlandt families and even Melancton Smith voted for the Constitution and yet all later supported the Republican cause—as did the anti-ratification Clintonians. Of Pennsylvania's two initial senators, both staunch supporters of the Constitution, one became a Federalist while the other, Billy Maclay, rebelled against the Hamiltonian *"high-flying* Federalists" of 1790-1791. Among Pennsylvania's first delegation to the House, four leading members followed a similar course from support of the Constitution to Republican affiliation, though the later Republican leader Gallatin was an "Anti-Federalist" in 1787, at least in his insistence on the addition of a Bill of Rights to the Constitution as a condition for its adoption. In Virginia the "philosopher of the Constitution," Madison, was joined in the Republican cause by anti-Constitution men like Patrick Henry (at the outset), George Mason, and James Monroe, and also (soon or late) by such pro-Constitutionalists as Wythe and Giles. Indeed, Giles was described by the anti-Constitutionalist Mason at the ratifying convention in Richmond as "a stripling of a lawyer at the Hotel this morning who has as much sense as one-half of us, though he is on the wrong [pro-Constitution] side." Another strong friend of the Constitution, Henry Lee, helped Madison to recruit

Freneau for the *National Gazette* and proselytized for subscribers in Virginia, although he, like Patrick Henry, later turned Federalist. All told, of the twenty-two anti-Constitution members at the Virginia convention whose careers can be traced, thirteen became Republicans and nine became Federalists. Of the leading quartet of South Carolina Republicans in 1795-1796, Pierce Butler and Charles Pinckney had supported the Constitution, Hampton and Sumter had opposed it.

Similar catalogues could be made for other figures in the national or state arenas. Over-all, far too many pro-Constitutionalists became Republican leaders or cadre workers to sustain the notion that the "Anti-Federalists" simply metamorphosed into the Republican body of the next decade.

The point is highlighted in the Congressional divisions over Hamilton's proposals. In the House, where the strongest resistance to Hamilton's measures emerged, not more than a half-dozen members had been active against the new frame of government. Yet, in broaching federal assumption of the state debts, Hamilton touched off a stiff and continuing Congressional resistance which included friends of the Constitution. In so far as there were lines from proponents or opponents of the Constitution to Federalists or Republicans, they were broken or badly bent in the debt assumption controversy. The party conflict Hamilton sparked was a new conflict.

Yet the crucial difficulty lies even beyond such questions as these. The argument of continuity oversimplifies the actual politics of ratification, particularly as it relates to parties. It persists in seeing the controversy as a single national battle, even a battle between "Federalist" and "Anti-Federalist" parties, each based on a broad and continuing cleavage of "business"-mercantile interests on the one side and "populist"-agrarian interests on the other. In fact, however, as we have seen, the question was not fought out on such clear, dualistic, national lines; and certainly the controversy was not fought out between national parties as we have defined parties. It is possible to trace important continuities (as well as discontinuities) between the alignments of interest groups and opinion aggregates for and against the Constitution on the one hand, and the alignments for the Federalists or the Republicans in the 1790's on the

105

other. If parties are distinguished from other, looser political formations in terms of structure, function, and ideology, however, alignments of groups and bodies of opinion are only elements in the followings of parties, while parties as such are the durable structures of national leaders, local leaders or cadre, and actives, who perform the manifold functions of party. These functions, to be sure, include mobilizing followings as the foundations of party power, but the followings which parties mobilize are not the parties themselves. Thus, parties as structures had to be built new in the 1790's.

It is in terms of relationships between structure and following that the Republicans may be thought of as a new kind of political institution. The Federalists achieved party structure earlier and found a substantial popular power base; and yet they never quite transcended their ministerial, English-oriented, elitist origins. They represented interests, shaped opinion, and offered choices to the electorate; but they were not given to encouraging intraparty popular participation. They always depended on a comparatively close nucleus of leaders in government, and their attitude toward the public and electorate was always an uncertain mixture of condescension and fear. The Republicans on the other hand, although slower to form, finally established a close rapport between leaders and followers.

The difference is manifest in various facets of the Republican formation. Like the Federalists, the Republicans built out from a nucleus at the center of government, many of their early leaders also were notables, and Jefferson frequently showed at least a trace of condescension in his attitude toward the people, despite his republican philosophy. Yet the coruscations of republican sentiment in currents of opinion, in the Democratic and Republican Societies, and in the furor over foreign policy, before there was a Republican party, gave the party a broad potential power base in advance. Furthermore, from the outset the Republican leaders, cadres, and actives included a large number of "politicians," of men who made their careers and achieved prominence in politics, as contrasted with notables; and the Republicans were very nearly a "party of politicians," in Max Weber's term. In this situation, the party's leaders came to look to public opinion and to the electorate as vital powers to which the party should be responsive or responsible. Thus the Republican outlook developed in terms of leaders not only acting on their following but also interacting with it. The Republican founders were the first modern party-builders to conceive of a party in a distinctively democratic role, and thus the first to create a genuinely "popular" party.

The distinction between popular and other parties raises the important question of relationships between leaders and followers which facilitate intraparty democracy. A popular party may be thought of as an open modern party which combines substantial stability in structure with responsiveness to an extended popular following and with encouragement of popular participation or initiative in party action. Not all modern or successful parties are popular parties. Thus the Federalist formation remained a semi-elitist party in a democratic context. It never developed strong ties of popular participation or responsiveness to popular opinion, and it continued to look upon elections as referendums or plebiscites on its established policies rather than as expressions of popular influence. In short, it operated as a plebiscitarian rather than as a democratic or popular party, as many parties in other new nations were to operate in later years. As a plebiscitarian party, the Federalists were less concerned with popular participation or initiative than with popular mobilization or manipulation, less sensitive to popular opinion than determined to mold it.

The character of the Republican formation as a popular party may be seen in its tripodal foundations. At the center of government was the party "point," exercising or seeking to exercise governmental power and providing national leadership and co-ordination. In the localities were ranged the component units of party structure proper, composed of local leaders, local cadres, and local actives, together with such local organization as they may have achieved. Also in the localities were the varied elements of the party following. Between men at the point and local leaders, and also between local party workers and their followings, there were strong lines of direct, often face-to-face, or primary interaction. Between point and following, there was a more distant, secondary relationship of action, by leaders impinging on or influencing fol-

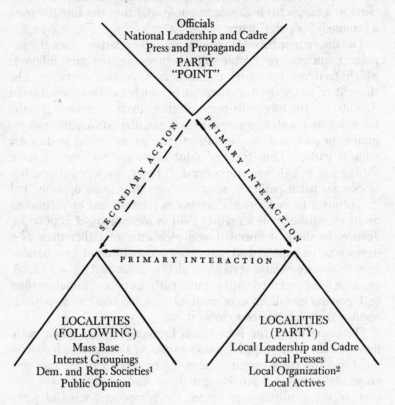

Figure 5

TRIPODAL FOUNDATIONS OF DEVELOPING
REPUBLICAN PARTY STRUCTURE

Officials
National Leadership and Cadre
Press and Propaganda
PARTY
"POINT"

SECONDARY ACTION

PRIMARY INTERACTION

PRIMARY INTERACTION

LOCALITIES
(FOLLOWING)
Mass Base
Interest Groupings
Dem. and Rep. Societies[1]
Public Opinion

LOCALITIES
(PARTY)
Local Leadership and Cadre
Local Presses
Local Organization[2]
Local Actives

[1] In the period of activity or survival, 1793 to 1795/6.
[2] In development from 1796 to 1805.

lowers. The interaction between central leaders and following, which was so important to intraparty democracy, depended heavily on indirect relationships between leaders at the "point" and the popular following by way of local party units.

Thus understood, Republican party structure was not only more modern and more complex than Federalist structure but also characterized by deeper and more varied foundations, which rested on broader segments of the population as a stable substructure or following. As "a body of men," in Burke's language, the Republicans were remarkably "united," determined to promote "the national interest" in terms of the principles on which they "agreed," and blessed with a degree of "popular confidence" which old-style faction politics could never have provided.

5.

The popular character of the Republican party is related to another aspect of the role of parties in a democracy. This is their potential to redress imbalances of power by counteracting the advantages which social elites or favored interest groups would otherwise enjoy.

The problem is a persisting one. At the constitutional ratifying convention in New York in 1788, Melancton Smith had raised the issue sharply. The general "influence of the great," and their superior opportunities to join together for political purposes, he warned, would give them preponderant power over men of "the poor and middling class." In the Massachusetts convention Amos Singletary touched on the same idea, in a blunt, less-tutored way, when he declaimed against "these lawyers, and men of learning, and moneyed men," who would "get all the power," and "swallow up all us little folks, like the great *Leviathan*." So also did Jefferson in 1791, when he looked toward a greater "agricultural representation" to counter Hamilton's forces, and Madison in 1792 when he called for two parties in "balance."

There are many possible sources of power or influence which men or groups can draw on in politics. Two important ones are wealth and direct economic control over others, with the political ways and means which may follow. Another factor is superior social status or

109

position, which can command deference from lesser members of the population or provide ready access to authority in the political system. Still further possible sources are learning; aptitude at such political skills as associations, legislation, or administration which lawyers so often display; and the quality of leadership that various groups can muster. In addition, consciousness of interests and awareness that these interests can be served through politics may enhance power or influence, as may the opportunity or ability to associate or organize for political action, and the unity or cohesion a group may achieve within its ranks. Moreover, wealth, established status, and education, taken together, tend to compound chances for acquiring leadership experience or ability, and those who hold such resources are also likely to generate strong political consciousness, find ready opportunities for association, and develop substantial unity of purpose and action. Against these sources is a factor for power which is basic to democracy, the superiority of numbers—and yet numbers by no means always prevail.

One after another of these sources of power was touched on directly or by implication in the forebodings of early Republicans. They saw them operating, as a general rule, to the advantage of persons of established privilege, or notables, who could command deference from the populace. Thus, Melancton Smith argued:

If the elections be by plurality . . . it is almost certain none but the great will be chosen, for they easily unite their interests: the common people will divide, and their divisions will be promoted by the others. . . I do not mean to declaim against the great . . . [but] will anyone say that there does not exist in this country the pride of family, of wealth, of talents, and that they do not command influence and respect among the common people?

Without parties, such fears might indeed have been realized in America. Over the years, the advantages of those who enjoyed established property, position, and power were bound to be mitigated by the decline of deference patterns and by the rise of public opinion as an influence on government. Yet Jefferson himself was to find public opinion insufficient, and the discovery convinced him of the necessity of party action. The abstract notion of a popular ma-

110

jority in a pristine conception of democracy was one thing, the exigencies of partical action and results were another.

In the realm of such action, parties may serve as democratic counterforces to advantages in power. Only through time can they affect the economic and social conditions of "the poor and middling class." They can exert a more immediate impact on other factors of power potential, however, if certain minimal conditions obtain in the populace, such as awareness of interests, some propensity for political participation or initiative, and receptivity to association or organization. Parties may offer leaders and leadership; and through their structure they may diffuse knowledge and skill in political tasks, stir the sense of political consciousness and efficacy, promote cohesion in their followings, and develop tools of association or organization. They may also counteract the weakness of "divisions" among "the common people," in Melancton Smith's words, by drawing them together into popular partisan combinations. Thus they may call forth and mobilize the latent strength of numbers. In open party systems, they may also clarify the options presented for decision by numbers in elections. Finally parties, as agents or catalysts for substantial segments of the populace, may effect transfers of power in government by peaceful, democratic means.

The first dozen years of American party politics witnessed such a transfer of power. At the outset the Federalists, with their power-favored components, were dominant. The course of elections from 1792 to 1804, however, showed a steady reduction in the effect of

Figure 6

REVERSAL OF FEDERALIST AND REPUBLICAN
POWER POSITIONS
(Electoral Votes for President, 1792-1804)

	1792	1796	1800	1804
Federalist	77[a]	71	65	14
Republican	55[a]	68	73	162

[a] Electoral vote for vice-president; Republican vote as the total for George Clinton (50), Thomas Jefferson (not a candidate, 4), and Aaron Burr (1).

Taken from Bureau of the Census, *Historical Statistics of the United States, Colonial Times to 1957* (Washington, 1960).

111

their advantages as the Republican party brought its battalions to full strength. Without the development of a popular party or popular parties, such a transfer in government power could hardly have occurred.

The potential of parties for bringing about a balance of power is increased in two-party situations. Where two parties contend, the electorate can choose between readily understood, either-or options of personnel or policy—either Federalists or Republicans, either this policy bent or that, either this set of leaders or the other. Even in relatively free one-party systems, options are likely to be less open and clear than they are in two-party systems. In multifactional or multiparty situations, elections are more likely to be by plurality, with the frustrations for democratic choice Melancton Smith feared, and less likely to be by a majority, as Jefferson would have had it. Two-party systems, on the other hand, strengthen the fulcrum of popular choice on which leverages against imbalances of power may rest.

In any system, however, the ability of party to offset special advantages in power remains a potentiality which is not always realized. Whether it is depends not only on the responsiveness of the populace to parties, but also on the responsiveness of parties to the wishes of their followings. It varies, furthermore, with the significance of the options parties offer in elections and with their ability to carry choices made by the electorate into effect in government. In years to come, in sharply contended struggles, the Republicans were to labor to prove the democratic potentiality of a party in action.

6

The Spirit of 'Ninety-six: Republicans *versus* Federalists

Despite consolidation of Federalist and Republican structures by 1795 or 1796, both parties got off to uncertain starts in the great presidential race of 1796. Before it was over, however, new excitements of party spirit had been fired, and the cleavage of parties had been further clarified.

In part the slow get-away was due to Washington's delay in announcing that he would not accept a third term in office. It was September before he revealed his decision. "At last," Beckley exploded, and then added angrily, "You will readily perceive that the short notice is designed to prevent a fair election, and the consequent choice of Mr. Jefferson." With the retirement effected, the *Aurora* could rejoice "that the name of WASHINGTON from this day ceases to give a currency to political iniquity"—"a new era is now opening . . . for public measures must now stand on their own merits." There was substance in the prediction, despite the partisan cry of "iniquity." The initial age of charisma in America was drawing to its close.

Uncertainties in the race also attended recurrent reluctance in the sensitive Jefferson, who lacked enthusiasm for the role of candidate despite his earlier willingness. He was informally "nominated" for the presidency by a tacit consensus of Republican leaders, but he was not consulted, lest he take the "opportunity of protesting to his friends against being embarked in the contest," as Madison put it. In part Jefferson's reluctance came from the fact

113

that his chief rival would be John Adams, an old friend whom he still respected and against whom he did not want to be pitted openly. The result was that both the Sage of Monticello and the Sage of Quincy sat out the event in bucolic retirement, while their parties ran the race for them.

The Federalists meanwhile experienced an internal fracture in what had been a united political monolith. For years Hamilton had been as wary of Vice-President Adams politically as he was uncongenial with him personally. He despised Adams's temperate stand on issues despite general adherence to Federalist policy, viewed his support of such men as the moderate Elbridge Gerry and the proto-Republican Sam Adams in Massachusetts as verging on party treason, and feared the Vice-President's continued personal friendship with Jefferson. With the prospect that Adams might become president, Hamilton's animosities surfaced and opened a crack in Federalist solidarity.

Division began with an effort to block Adams as Washington's successor. Partly for this purpose, partly in the hope of winning Southern support, Hamilton proposed Thomas Pinckney of South Carolina for a place on the Federalist ticket. Cousin of the Republican Charles Pinckney, and negotiator as envoy to Spain of a favorable treaty which had opened Spanish-American trade and provided for free navigation by Americans of the Mississippi river along the border of Spanish Louisiana, Thomas Pinckney was a popular possibility. The public presumption was that Adams would be the candidate for president, Pinckney his running mate for vice-president. Before long, however, Hamilton was writing privately to Senator Rufus King suggesting that Pinckney be put ahead of Adams. Under the original electoral system each presidential elector cast two votes, and the candidate with the highest number became president, while the runner-up became vice-president. If it could be arranged that one more electoral vote was cast for Pinckney than for Adams, while both bested Jefferson, Pinckney would have the first place. A quasi-caucus of Federalist leaders met and ratified Hamilton's two choices; and then the word was passed among Federalist notables that every effort must be made in the North to win an equal vote for Adams and Pinckney, because the contest with Jefferson would be so close. The scheme looked innocent enough. The hidden strategem was that Pinckney would be supported solidly in the South while Adams would not be, and Pinckney would thereby carry a few more electoral votes than Adams would.

The result of this mining and sapping was a break between two elements within the Federalist party. One was the anti-Adams group shaped by Hamilton, which ultimately merged into a relatively distinct "High Federalist" faction. But Adams also had friends in the party and support in the populace, and a second group primarily concerned for his election formed around him and provided the base for a "Moderate" faction. Between the two elements in 1796 there lay a third seam, composed of men who believed that equal stress must be placed on both Adams and Pinckney. What was developing, in short, was an early version of the intraparty factionalism which was to plague American parties throughout their histories. A faction within a party may be distinguished from a pre-party faction in that it recognizes and works within a party structure, contends for control over party functions such as nominations, electioneering, or management in government, and seeks possession of the emotional resources of established party symbolism and the practical resources of the party as a whole. It was rifts of this sort that Hamilton and his allies set going in their underground maneuvering.

The immediate effect for the Federalists was that they entered the election of 1796 divided and unable to conduct the campaign with as much unity as they had achieved even in earlier struggles.

2.

Despite uncertainties and divisions, both the presidential and the Congressional candidates came to be seen as "defending Federalists" or "challenger Republicans." The total number of states that would participate had been brought to sixteen with the admission of Vermont, Kentucky, and Tennessee. In the eight states (including Pennsylvania and Virginia) where presidential electors were chosen by popular vote, more and more electoral candidates committed themselves to one of the party presidential choices; and in most of the eight that named electors through their legislatures (such as New York and South Carolina), partisan forces dominated the selection.

The great issue was the Jay treaty and related questions of world politics and ideology. The "Spirit of 'Seventy-six" had been a national spirit of independence. The "Spirit of 'Ninety-six" was a distinctively partisan address to the national electorate in terms of contrasting views, perspectives, and positions. Outcries against revolutionary France reached new heights of melodramatic intensity, which were matched by countercharges that the Jay treaty had betrayed America's own revolution and put her in the hands of Albion. The popular talk was all about voting for or against this or that party candidate on the basis of their stands on the treaty, and one observer noted that he "never knew an election so much of *principles*." Circulars, newspapers, and pamphlets cried the issues—and the personalities. The Republican chorus chanted "THOMAS JEFFERSON is a firm REPUBLICAN,—JOHN ADAMS is an avowed MONARCHIST," or cried that Adams was "the declared advocate of ranks and orders in society." In response, Federalists condemned Jefferson as a vacillator and at the same time as the director of a "French faction" which would revolutionize the American system of government.

Clear and avid for Jefferson, Republican leaders and cadremen were less certain in the choice for vice-president. With Clinton ill and in semi-retirement, the most available possibility was Burr. Other names were mentioned, such as Chancellor Robert R. Livingston of New York, Senator John Langdon of New Hampshire, and Pierce Butler of South Carolina. A loose, informal caucus of Republican members of Congress met (reportedly, at least) but was unable to come to agreement. Meanwhile, Beckley informed Madison that Burr had the support of Rittenhouse, Gallatin, and "the whole body of Republicans" in Pennsylvania, and of Chancellor Livingston himself in New York. Virginia, North Carolina, and Georgia were supposed to be "fixed," and Congressional cadremen like John Brown of Kentucky and Blount of North Carolina were deputed to bring in Kentucky and Tennessee. For once, however, Beckley was wrong. The three Southern states were not "fixed," and, although Burr emerged as the presumed Republican vice-presidential candidate, a number of Southern Jeffersonians remained distinctly cool. The Republicans, in fact, had failed to make a clear and binding nomination. They had established themselves as a party, but they had not reached the point where they could quell dissent over a controversial figure like Burr.

Even so, the unquenchable Beckley remained the chief source and guide for co-ordination in the Republican phalanx, and he continued to counsel with leaders, from Burr in New York to Madison in Virginia. The efforts of these and other men achieved a remarkable articulation of state and local units in practical electioneering activity and in appeals to public opinion.

On the assumption that Pennsylvania would decide the outcome, Republican lances were heavily concentrated there. Republican workers made full use of the organization Dallas had begun to shape, and extended it. The effort was formally launched by a joint caucus in Philadelphia of Pennsylvania Republican members of Congress and Republican members of the state assembly. The caucus framed a list or "ticket" of presidential electors, which the voters could deposit at the polls; it also established a central campaign Committee, with Michael Leib of Philadelphia as its chairman. Hoping to win the doubtful middle-area counties as a pivot, Beckley urged General William Irvine to call up his "active republicans in each County," and to "bring the people," in order to flank the Federalist companies in "the little rotten towns." Predicting that nearly all of the North was certain for Adams and the South virtually safe for Jefferson, and that therefore Pennsylvania would be the field of decision, Beckley distributed copies of the "ticket," copies of an "Address to the People," and rousing handbills, in packet after bulky packet. "As the election is to be by the state at large," the "Freemen of Pennsylvania" were warned, "every vote will be of importance; to neglect giving a vote, therefore, under the belief that you are in a minority in any particular district will be a serious evil." In a final effort, the Committee had two of Beckley's friends, with six or eight thousand tickets, ride as a special task force through the middle and lower counties.

Meanwhile, aware that party was more than presidency, Beckley gave attention to Congressional contests. He was determined to "throw out Muhlenberg who gave the casting vote for the British treaty," and replace the old-family defector with the plebeian Blair McClenachan, "who recommended to kick the treaty to hell." He also asked his correspondents for word of Gallatin's prospects, and hoped fervently to hear that the voters had "trimmed the trimmer Gregg, as they did Christie [another of the Jay treaty defectors] in Maryland." Although McClenachan "kicked Muhlenberg to hell," or at least into the limbo of ex-congressmen, Gregg won. But pressure against him and the closeness of his re-election apparently taught him a lesson in party faithfulness. Action against the men who broke ranks on the treaty had paid off.

Among the states, Pennsylvania was undoubtedly in the vanguard again in the degree to which each party achieved articulation. Nevertheless, in other states the "Spirit of 'Ninety-six" was also a strongly partisan spirit, even where it was not exemplified in full co-ordination of activity. Nominating and electioneering processes remained loose in most of New England. Yet in Massachusetts Republican voters were urged to "ROUSE" and "determine whether you will support MONARCHY or REPUBLICANISM," by voting for Sam Adams for Governor and for Republican electors and Republican candidates on a Congressional list—and the Federalists also had their "lists." In Dedham, Nathaniel Ames saw the struggle as clearly a party combat linked with the ideological forces embroiled in world politics, and he hoped 'ninety-six would mark the downfall of "the Prigarchy," while his Federalist or "Prigarch" brother Fisher Ames was deeply "vexed" at Republican stirrings among his neighbors. In Virginia, planning, communication, and co-ordination were to bring triumph over what Beckley called "every exertion of the Aristocracy." In the rest of the South, matters were not so well arranged. In North Carolina there was little evidence of consistent party electioneering, and South Carolina voters were swamped by a flood of nominating lists. The prize for free-style politics remained with New Jersey, however, where no less than forty-six men were listed by one newspaper as having been nominated for the state's five Congressional seats. Nonetheless, particularly in the realm of ideology, the elections were generally viewed by the public and electorate in national party terms.

As the day of decision approached, a new and indiscreet French ambassador added a fillip to the occasion. In 1795 Citizen Pierre Adet had intervened in the controversy over the Jay treaty. His reports had helped persuade the newly established *Directoire* in France that they should declare the Jay compact a breach of the French-American agreements of 1778, suspend diplomatic relations, insist on the withdrawal of Monroe as American minister in Paris, and stiffen French policy toward neutral American shipping. Now in 1796, just before the voting in Pennsylvania, the maladroit Adet filled the American newspapers with announcements to this effect, with the implication that tensions might be eased if a president were elected who would be more sympathetic to France—someone, perhaps, like Jefferson. This bit of open meddling lent weight to Federalist charges that the Republicans were a "French faction," although it apparently did not affect the election significantly either way.

The fact that no one was sure of the outcome—not even the nearly omniscient Beckley—foretold that the race would be close.

3.

As the election approached, it was apparent that groups or individuals were identifying themselves strongly with one party or the other, and that the two parties had acquired distinct followings. Certain broad lines of cleavage persisted. Thus, seaboard and urban areas where mercantile interests were dominant continued to lean toward the Federalists and Western or frontier farming areas toward the Republicans. By 1796, however, a far more complex topography of the party group combinations was apparent. Both parties had achieved areas of strength and the sweeping Federalist program had consolidated a Federalist following. At the same time, there were areas of weakness for the Federalists where shifts were beginning to occur.

If the distribution had been one simply of agricultural against other interests, a "country" party would have had a clear field. All but about 15 per cent of the working population was engaged in agriculture in some form, and not even in New England would a "court" mercantile party have had enough votes to carry a state. It was true that the hard-rock ridges of Federalist strength still consisted of commercial, shipping, shipbuilding, handicraft-manufacturing, export trade, banking, and other investing elements, which also provided the foundations of Federalist extremism in developing factional strife. The connections such groups had with lawyers, the Congregational and Episcopalian clergy, and other professional groups also inclined them toward the Federalist enclosure. All of this tended to give Federalist terrain an urban character, which often, as in shipping and shipbuilding, involved both masters and men. Despite advantages in power, however, such elements alone could not have sustained the Federalist party in a republic which was becoming more and more democratic.

In fact, Federalist success depended also on a strong subsoil of agriculturalists, who also provided the foundations of moderate Federalism in factional divisions. Generally Federalist agricultural support was strongest among the wealthiest planter-slaveholders and among "lesser" agrarian groups in areas where most of the crop was produced for the market, particularly the export market. Thus Federalist rural strength, with some exceptions, ran along New England streams, where many farmers also depended on part-time shipyard employment, or along the coastal plain and the alluvial soils of the river basins in the mid-Atlantic or the Southern states. In some areas, it extended also along important roads which produced a common interest between commercial and exporting-agricultural groups. In terms of its power base, the Federalist party was a "country" as well as an urban-commercial party.

At the beginning, Republican strength largely reversed the Federalist pattern. Its great bedrock was the nation's freehold-farm population, particularly groups engaged in self-sufficient or subsistence farming with few significant connections with national or international markets. The Republicans also enjoyed some support from plantation-slaveholding elements and drew much of their leadership in the South from the modest planter strata or lesser gentry, although even in Virginia most great planters tended at the outset to be wary of Jeffersonian democratic inclinations. Further-more, despite early Federalist predominance in city and town, the Republicans were not without urban strength in New York, Phila-delphia, and certain other centers. They found followers and some leaders and cadremen among town intellectuals, dissenting nota-bles, many small merchants, tradesmen, and craftsmen, and among "sweaty artisans" or laboring groups. In the back country, Baptist, Methodist, and Presbyterian clergy and congregations tended to be Republican, as did Roman Catholics in New York, Philadelphia, and Boston—the "Wild Irish," a Federalist-Congregational con-gressman called them. The alignment of urban outcroppings with the "country" bedrock of Republicanism was suggested in the ad-mission of the states of Kentucky and Tennessee, whose rural reaches would extend from the western Appalachian mountain slopes to the remote Mississippi river banks. Federalists opposed admission as an addition to Republican strength, while Republi-cans, including the egregiously urban Aaron Burr, favored it. As though symbolically, one of the first representatives in Congress to be sent from the New West was a Tennessee youngster named An-drew Jackson, whose name was eventually to epitomize the spirit of *hoi polloi* democracy both rural and urban. Yet it remained true that the Republicans in the 1790's relied mostly on agricultural support.

As the decade wore on, a significant flaw in the Federalist com-bination began to open in their agricultural strata. Certain of Ham-ilton's economic policies and, above all, the Jay treaty opened a crack between the dominant national Federalist leadership on the one side and important portions of their planter support on the other. The movement away from the Federalists in South Carolina was a marked instance of earthslides which also occurred elsewhere in the South, and warned of slippages to come even in the North. Cohesion among disparate elements in the Federalist party com-bination—most broadly, between capitalist and landed property-holders large and small—had rested structurally on mercantile leaders who built the party and on prosperous agriculturalists who joined them. Functionally, unity had depended on brokerage or tacit formulas of agreement which gave some satisfaction to both capitalist and agricultural interests. Cracks between these elements now opened, grew wider, and became almost impossible to bridge. Finally, the Federalists were to lose not only much of their planter support but, more significantly, most of the mass freeholder-agrarian support which had constituted an essential source of votes.

For Federalist strategy, the problem was to hold sufficient agrarian support to maintain a parity in votes against growing Republican strength. As factional fissures opened wider, however, such leaders as Hamilton, other spokesmen of shipping and investing elements with an intense interest in world trade, the New England extremists and their ideological spokesmen like the seaboard "Essex Junto" in Massachusetts or "Pope Dwight" of Yale, and High Federalists generally seemed blinded to the importance of planter or farmer. Self-righteously insistent on their "principles," they obstructed the function of intraparty brokerage, of devising formulas of agreement, of compromise, thereby offending the agricultural strength which Moderate, or Adams, Federalists had hoped to maintain.

In 1796, of course, this was in the future, and despite subterranean rumblings the ultimate crumbing of the Federalist combination was not readily foreseen. The party generally, or Adams as a candidate in particular, maintained sufficient mass-agrarian support to make a strong race against the Republican challengers.

4.

The stability and close rivalry that Federalists and Republicans had finally achieved by the time of the election of 1796 revealed how far they had moved to establish themselves as national political parties, well ahead of modern parties in England or· any European nation. Superficially, it is surprising that a stripling new nation should have achieved such a "first," but some explanation of the event makes it appear less unlikely.

Indeed, the nub of the matter lay in the very differences in development in mother England and in her lusty American offspring. In England in the 1700's politics still operated within restrictions inherited from a feudal past. Even in the long period of the attrition of feudalism, a relatively rigid structure of ranks, classes, and established interests persisted. As a result, political representation was in effect representation of such entities, rather than of individual voters in geographical districts or of diverse interest groups in a fluid, pluralistic pattern. Thus a long-standing, almost "natural" organic representation was built into the system and connected with the king, Lords, and Commons, as agencies of decision-making in government. Furthermore, as another legacy of the feudal past, politics was substantially a game for titled aristocrats, wealthy magnates or notables, and their agents; and political formations were a mixture of "aristocratic" and "notable" factions. Patterns of deference to such leadership had become well established, and they persisted.

Despite its English heritage, American social structure had found a different mode of growth with its own liberal bent. The decades of revolution and reform had gone far to fix the pattern and give America a popular republic as its political expression. The liberal ideology saw individuals as the units of politics—free, atomistic, assertive individuals who settled freely into interests and groups. There were no hierarchical, established estates, no Lords, and therefore no Commons linked in relationships of organic representation. If a society consists of free individuals and boasts no aristocracy or "First" or "Second" Estates, it can hardly have a "Third." Thus the liberal tradition in America could readily take on equalitarian as well as individualistic aspects.

All of these matters of fact and faith brought significant consequences for politics. First, by allowing free play to the discordant, fluid, complex group interests of a developing society, social structure and ideology produced a complex, open conflict of interests and opinions as the standard stuff of politics. Second, if any set of men were to win power and get the business of governing done in such a society, they needed to find some means of political action which would enable them to represent, combine, and mobilize the variety of interests and opinions in the society. Given this fluid, open situation, it remained only for men with political vision and talents to seize the obvious opportunity for power, meet the need, and devise the means—and the means they found were modern parties. In the labors of party building, strenuous as they were,

Americans also were not required to batter down obstacles of the sort they would have faced in England or in other nations with a feudal past. Instead, they could work within a growing consensus which provided freedom of action and association.

These points may be generalized in a statement of conditions for party development applicable to other nations as well as to American experience. Where social structures and ideologies provide an open, individualistic, or pluralistic politics characterized by complex conflicts of interest, needs and opportunities will arise to combine these pluralities of free individuals and interests so as to exercise governmental power; and, in the absence of significant obstacles in limiting social structures, these opportunities will attract men with political ambition and skills, who will develop the necessary means. If these men are inventive, the means they adopt are likely to be modern party action.

There were other significant contrasts between the mother country and the infant American republic. Lacking an Establishment —the Crown, the nobility and the aristocracy, the established Church, and their prerogatives, power, and overtones of prestige— the American political system lacked a ready-made center for "court politics." There was no national center of royal authority and majesty through which men could seek influence almost without regard to the populace, or find hidden or privy roads to power. When John Adams and certain other Federalists sought to approximate such panoplies of "high toned" government, they were frustrated by what contemporaries called the "republican genius" of the American people. The consequence was that leaders or groups seeking political goals had to turn to public opinion or to the electorate for support—in short, to popular foundations of power. This was the path even the elitist Federalists had to walk.

The American republic also produced the earliest instance of extended suffrage in the modern world. Despite limitations, far more men voted in America than in England or in any other country in the 1790's—or, for that matter, for some decades to come. Furthermore, democratic attitudes in the sense of political equalitarianism, notions of popular participation or initiative, and principles of representative government, became more and more central

124

to American ideology. Thus, would-be political leaders found themselves not only denied the private accesses to power available in court politics, but also found themselves face to face with an active popular reserve of power. Again, by a second route, the consequence and opportunity followed: those who would succeed in politics found it necessary, in the face of popular suffrage and general access to political participation, to deal with, mobilize, and shape into a power base the varied elements of a broad, active electorate. In the end, both Federalists and Republicans recognized these facts of political life and turned of necessity to the voters.

These aspects of American party development may also be generalized in a statement which may relate to other societies as well. Where forms of closed or limited politics with special approaches to the centers of power are absent, and established patterns of social deference as sources of power are limited or absent, and where, in contrast, broad suffrage or patterns of participation must be reckoned with in the distribution of power, politically active men or elements in the society will of necessity seek the means of power through appeals to the extended electorate or public. Again, the most efficient means to this end lie in the action of modern political parties.

In sum, the American as contrasted to the English experience in the 1700's suggests that party development in general depends on the particular types of social and ideological conditions stated here, which may—as they did in American experience—accompany processes of political modernization and the emergence of mass or democratic politics.

Later instances of modernization in other societies were to bring new forms of political party structure. In England, and in many other European countries, the development of modern parties came after a long, halting process of the breaking down of patterns of hierarchy, corporatism, virtual representation, "connexions," deference, and the like, and also after a tortuous passage through various mixed or intermediate modes of politics. In later stages of English and European development, new "mass" party models were to appear, based on direct membership in local party units, as in typical Labor or Socialist parties, in a departure from the American type of "cadre" structure and popular following. An even further departure was to come with mass-mobilizing but anti-democratic Communist and Fascist parties.

Later still, new, powerful nationalist formations were to develop in the emerging nations of Asia and Africa in the twentieth century. These also were often militant "mass" parties, created by intellectuals and others to bring their peoples to nationhood and to modernize their new nations on Western models. Unlike American or English parties, these parties were not to grow out of indigenous processes of modernization but rather were to be contrived as broad adaptations of the party structures of other countries, again usually Western. Thus they were often parties which mobilized the masses but were not significantly oriented to popular initiative or participation. Such parties also tended to be keyed to a new elitism of paternal "guidance," and thus to plebiscitarian practices rather than wholly democratic ones, especially where they looked to Russian experience for a guide. Yet it would be naïve to expect that all of today's new nationalist formations could develop as fully democratic or popular parties until modernization, social conditions, and ideology in their own nations provided the necessary foundations. Nor could they be expected to take on a democratic form automatically even then, for the struggle to establish parties in America shows how difficult this process can be.

The various modern parties of Europe and other continents have, however, been associated with processes of political modernization and with democratic or at least mass politics. They have also assumed the basic structure and performed the basic functions of modern parties as these paths were first explored in American party genesis. In short, the American experience as the earliest instance of modern party development exhibited certain generic elements of the process, although it did not fix the only form parties might take.

5.
The contest of 1796 marked the first full opportunity for the electorate in the new American republic to choose between two established, competing parties and their nominees. Though the outcome showed that the parties still had some shaping to do, not-

ably with reference to the vice-presidential contest, the result as a whole revealed how far the Republicans had come toward parity in the party competition.

Victory for the top post went to Adams with 71 electoral votes over Jefferson with 68. A change of two votes would have reversed the result. In no state did either of the two top contenders lose electoral votes to lesser contenders of their own party stripe: in the "Spirit of 'Ninety-six" the vote for both first-place candidates was concentrated in a consistent and partisan way. In the vice-presidential race, however, the results were not so neat. The electors of

Figure 7

ELECTORAL VOTE FOR PRESIDENT AND
VICE-PRESIDENT, 1796

	John Adams	Thomas Pinckney	Thomas Jefferson	Aaron Burr	Others
Vermont	4	4			
New Hampshire*	6				6[a]
Massachusetts*	16	13			3[x]
Rhode Island	4				4[a]
Connecticut	9	4			5[b]
New York	12	12			
New Jersey	7	7			
Pennsylvania*	1	3	14	12	
Delaware	3	3			
Maryland*	7	4	4	3	2[x]
Virginia*	1	1	20	1	19[c]
North Carolina*	1	1	11	6	5[x]
South Carolina		8	8		
Georgia*			4		4[d]
Kentucky*			4	4	
Tennessee			3	3	
	71	59	68	30	48

* States choosing electors by popular vote.
[a] For Oliver Ellsworth (F) of Connecticut.
[b] For John Jay (F) of New York.
[c] One for George Washington, 15 for Samuel Adams (R) of Massachusetts, 3 for George Clinton (R) of New York.
[d] For George Clinton (R) of New York
[x] Scattering: regional or local favorites.
Adapted from Edward Stanwood, A History of the Presidency from 1788 to 1897 (Boston, 1898), 51. Corrected by later data.

South Carolina managed an adroit and self-interested balance, giving eight votes to their native son, Thomas Pinckney, and eight votes to their fellow Southerner, Jefferson. Meanwhile Hamilton's scheme to bring Pinckney in ahead of Adams for president was bilked by Adams supporters in the North, who threw away enough electoral votes on local favorites or stalking horses to leave Pinckney well behind with a total of 59. On the Republican side Burr enjoyed something like full party support only in Pennsylvania, Kentucky, and Tennessee. He was cut heavily in the Southern Republican stronghold of Virginia, which gave him only one electoral tally, and cut totally in Georgia. The clearest evidence of confusion in the vice-presidential race, however, lay in the fact that Burr got a total of only 30 votes, while 38 presumably Republican tallies were thrown to Republican stand-ins or to local or even Federalist names. Had Jefferson been elected president, he would have had not Burr but either Adams or Pinckney as vice-president as the price of uncertainty and division on this question within an infant party. In the event, the Federalist Adams was to have the Republican Jefferson as his understudy.

Promptly Jefferson assured Adams that he would be happy to serve under him, and hoped that there would be no barrier between them. At the same time men like Elbridge Gerry sought to effect a union between Adams and Jefferson, but the High Federalists insisted on rigid proscription of the Republican opposition.

The prediction Beckley had made concerning the balance of votes proved substantially correct. States in the North went overwhelmingly for Adams; with the exception of divided Maryland, states in the South went almost as solidly for Jefferson; and Pennsylvania was very nearly the measure of difference. Yet Pennsylvania's electoral votes for Jefferson were not enough. Furthermore, the outcome in Pennsylvania had been extremely close, with the top elector on the Republican ticket amassing 12,306 votes while the lowest man on the Federalist slate garnered 12,071. In short, the omens were not clear, and Republican calculators looked again to New York, where Jay's election as governor in 1795 (before the storm over his British treaty) had laid the groundwork for an Adams-Pinckney victory in 1796. With Clinton in virtual retirement, Republican hopes turned to Burr, who at the moment was in a bit of a sulk, feeling betrayed by his national party. Soon, however, he again directed his cool eyes to the future and his capable hands to the necessities of political rebuilding.

Farther north, despite Adams's victory and a Congressional outcome which would give the Federalists majorities again in both Senate and House, one of the high priests of the High Federalists was suffering a galloping case of political shivers. In Fisher Ames's dour view, Jefferson's election as vice-president was a calamity: "Party will have a head responsible for nothing, yet deranging and undermining everything, and France [will] have a new magazine of disorganizing influence. . . . I own I am ready to croak when I observe the gathering of the vapors in our horizon!" He might better have given thought to a different gathering of vapors on the horizon of the Federalist future.

The tally counted and announced, the time finally came for the nation's new leaders to take office. Calm and relaxed, carrying a bundle that contained some curious fossilized bones which he wanted to exhibit to the American Philosophical Society in Philadelphia, Thomas Jefferson embarked from Monticello by regular stage. He wanted to find "an opportunity of plunging into the mixed character of my countrymen" on the journey, and "to avoid any formal reception" on his arrival; and he was at least as pleased that he had been chosen president of the Society as he was at his election as vice-president of the nation. He was greeted at Philadelphia, however, by a band, by a banner which read "JEFFERSON, THE FRIEND OF THE PEOPLE," and by the boom of artillery salvos. The call of the people—or of party, politics, and issues—was to prove insistent, and Jefferson soon found himself in active command of the Republican phalanx.

7

The Responsibilities
of Opposition

As he looked toward the day when Adams would take office, Madison mulled over what he saw as a dark future. Since the Federalist election victory, he wrote to Jefferson, "the British party . . . no longer wear the mask." Talk of a war with France and an alliance with Great Britain was widespread among Federalists, and Madison was sure that "a push will be made to screw up the P[resident] to that point." More sanguine as was his wont, Jefferson replied that if Adams could be brought "to relinquish his bias to an English constitution," it might be well "to come to a good understanding with him as to his future elections." He did not believe that Adams wanted war, and he considered that "he is perhaps the only sure barrier against Hamilton's getting in."

Throughout four harrowing years Adams was indeed to feel an unrelenting "push." It came from Hamilton and the High Federalist faction, and extremists in that faction did want all-out hostilities against France. If Hamilton had had his way altogether—"the greatest man that ever lived . . . was Julius Caesar"—the new nation might also have come close to a military dictatorship as a kind of Thermidor to the American liberal Revolution. Despite pressures, however, Adams would not play Hamilton's puppet or take the road to all-out war.

In part, the issue hinged on the political convictions Adams held and on the man he was. His admiration for the English constitution did not make him really a "Monocrat," any more than Madi-

son's or Jefferson's liberal republican views made them "Jacobins."
To Adams the English device which could be generalized for American use was the structure of "mixed government." To him this
meant representation for the aristocracy or the well-to-do in one
house of the legislature, balanced by representation for the many
or the less affluent in another house, with a strong executive keeping both interests or houses in equilibrium. The result would be
that neither of the great segments of society would despoil or op-
press the other. While Adams could plump for much of the panoply of government that would make the executive a center for emotional attachments—essential buttresses to reason in supporting
government, he believed—his ideas also left substantial room for
popular influence. At the center of the whole structure, he placed
a conception of ordered public and private liberty. He was, in sum,
a sceptical, conservative republican. Personally, he was vain, but not
inclined to give himself all the ornaments of pomp he would have
lavished on Washington; bluff and dogged to the point of stubborn-
ness, although he could be tactful when necessary; and subject to
bursts of passion or anger, but fixed to a Puritan sense of duty—
"I must double and redouble my Diligence," he reminded himself
in his diary. He was neither philosophically nor temperamentally
prone to yield to the "push."

Nonetheless, as he assumed the presidency in 1797, the omens
were not auspicious. He continued Washington's cabinet in office,
and the department heads—notably Timothy Pickering of Massachusetts at the State Department, Oliver Wolcott of Connecticut
at the Treasury, and James McHenry of Pennsylvania at the War
Department—were Hamiltonians who were more loyal to "Young
Belcour" than they were to "Old John." The result was dissension
over policy, personal irascibilities, and constant bickering. In the
Senate, where an early Federalist caucus met to assign committee
posts, Hamilton could look to devoted followers who would serve
very nearly as he commanded. The House also had its complement
of old Hamiltonians, together with younger men like the violent,
arrogant extremist, Roger Griswold of Connecticut.

The Republicans meanwhile suffered breaks in their leadership
echelons. In the House, Madison had retired, the slashing Giles

131

was often ill, and the Republicans had to rely largely on John Nicholas of Virginia for oratory. One of the first acts of the Federalists was to oust Beckley from his clerkship by one vote, thus depriving the Republicans of his influence in daily Congressional affairs. Yet Gallatin took over as an effective leader; and before long his Federalist antagonist Theodore Sedgwick was describing the House Republicans, "under the control of the Genevese," as "a well organized and disciplined Corps, never going astray." There was, however, at least some exaggeration in the grudging tribute.

2.

From the outset the Adams Administration was buffeted by the storms of world politics and threats of war with France. As has often been the case with new nations, the United States faced troubles not only with its former imperial master but also from expansive power in other quarters; and it took strenuous effort and wisdom to maintain effective independence and assure the new republic its chance at its own mode of development. All this gave Adams a trying course to steer, but the crossed political winds made it difficult also for the Republicans to decide on the tack they should take.

If a party is to act effectively as an opposition, it must oppose measures of the party in power. It need not oppose recklessly and thus disrupt the nation. A loyal opposition is likely to choose a course consistent with responsibility to the national welfare, if only to avoid the onus of history and, perhaps, political shipwreck in the shoals of popular disapproval. Yet leaders of a popular party in a democratic system are likely to feel additional currents of responsibility: the duty to speak for the groups, interests, and opinions which they represent, and the duty to present alternatives to the policies of the party in power. Furthermore, political necessity generally prompts an opposition to present such alternatives in a way that will bring victory in elections to come. The various currents of responsibility may churn in crossflow, and this was in effect the problem Republican helmsmen faced in the Adams years. There was indeed constant danger of running aground, in view of the fact that the great issues were blown up by tempests in world politics, while at the same time the cause of France with which the Republicans were identified was growing less and less popular. Foreign conflict threatened to drive the Republicans to a position where they could be called unpatriotic.

The storm brewed in a special session of Congress which Adams called early in 1797, and it blew unabated for more than two years. The *Directoire* in France had bluntly refused to accept Adams's new diplomatic envoy, the Federalist Charles Cotesworth Pinckney —brother of Thomas Pinckney and cousin of the Republican Charles Pinckney. The French had begun an interference with American shipping which was to lead to a virtual if undeclared naval war. Although the *Directoire* in fact marked a reaction against the ultra-republican course the French Revolution had taken earlier, and grew increasingly venal, it could still be decried by Federalists as a revolutionary force. Futhermore, it offended much American opinion by an imperious attitude which seemed to scorn the claim of the new American nation to its place among the nations of the world. Determined to avoid war if he could, but pressed also by jingo-minded leaders in his party, Adams requested authorizations, men, ships, and matériel to build up American military potential— which he, at least, wanted so that he could negotiate from strength. He got much of what he asked from Congress in session after session into 1799, but only against strong currents of Republican opposition. To the Republicans, military force and a standing army were at best unwise supplements to negotiation, at worst an ominous threat of war or internal oppression.

Foreign threats intensified domestic party conflict. As early as June 1797, the amiable Jefferson noted the effects of heightened party animosity: "men who have been intimate all their lives, cross the street to avoid meeting, and turn their heads another way, lest they should be obliged to touch their hats." Disappointed in his early hopes for harmony, Jefferson himself now moved into the main channel of party action. He initiated communication with Burr in New York, who, defeated for the vice-presidency and deprived of his Senate seat, was gratified by this display of confidence. Before long the Southern and the Northern leaders were meeting quietly in Philadelphia to scan the political weather and chart courses of action. When Monroe stopped in Philadelphia on his return from France, he, too, conferred with Jefferson, Gallatin, and Burr; and the Republicans arranged a grand testimonial dinner at Oeller's Hotel where they toasted the envoy in a partisan answer to partisan attacks on him. The ultra-Federalist leader Theodore Sedgwick damned Jefferson for being "the very life and soul of the opposition." Within a year of the time Adams had taken office, Jefferson in turn conveyed his conviction to Madison that Adams was only a "stalking horse," and that the Federalist party was "in truth the Hamilton party." By the summer of 1798, the Federalist-dominated Congress had indeed gone on to "repeal" the American treaties with France of 1778 and authorize the seizure of ships flying the *tricouleur*. The undeclared naval war had begun, and all hope of *rapprochement* between Jefferson and Adams had clearly been dashed.

The political waters were further roiled by a diplomatic whirl-wind. The President had at last dispatched a special mission to France consisting of John Marshall, Charles Cotesworth Pinckney, and Elbridge Gerry. Their instructions were to seek a treaty of amity and commerce; but three agents of the *Directoire*—later known as Messieurs X, Y, and Z—proposed an American loan and a munificent bribe as the price of negotiations. When Adams made the XYZ correspondence public in the Spring of 1798, strong patriotic currents built up against the French "insult" to the struggling new nation's pride. These currents carried Adams to unexpected heights of popularity—"Adams and Liberty," the cry ran—and nearly swamped the Republicans, who, from Jefferson down, were condemned by the Federalists as disloyal, as "*Frenchmen* in all their feelings and wishes." The "cause of France," once proclaimed as the "cause of man," now became the cause of near shipwreck for the Republicans. Suspicion raged: High Federalists charged that Republicans were ready to join a French army on American beach-heads, while French tutors in America were eyed mistrustfully as secret agents of the *Directoire*. Immigrants in general and the "Wild Irish" in particular were doubly suspect as potential malignant forces of domestic revolution and disorder. Only the resurgent Federalists—they were once again convinced of their role—

134

could protect the homeland from French domination, from French agents and the "Gallic faction," and from allegedly Gallic excesses of democracy. As the leader of the High Federalist faction in the cabinet, Secretary of State Pickering argued that the time was ripe for an immediate declaration of war. In the wake of the diplomatic disaster, tidal waves of ideological conflict and intolerance rose in new menace.

The impact was felt promptly at the capital. Publication of the XYZ documents "carried over to the war-party most of the waverers in the House," Jefferson lamented, thereby giving a strong working majority to Federalist extremists. Feeling helpless, Giles (ill and nearly broken-hearted), John Nicholas, and two other Virginia Republican congressmen went home, leaving only Gallatin to resist, or "clog the wheels of government" as a Federalist put it: "without him the [Republican] party would be completely scattered." The time was set for a Federalist sally into the troubled waters of world politics and domestic reactions.

3.

In part the new Federalist "Spirit of 'Ninety-eight" was prompted by calculations of political advantage, in part by fear of revolutionary France and democratic ideas, in part by a desire to fence off the troubled and troubling world from American confines—which would then become, presumably, peaceful and Federalist. The spirit was embodied in a series of legislative proposals carried through Congress in the spring and summer of 1798.

The bills were directed against aliens, and against political criticism or alleged sedition. The first lengthened the residence requirement from five to fourteen years for foreigners seeking naturalization as citizens. In the House, the patrician Harrison Gray Otis of Boston, in a swipe at Gallatin across the floor, even wanted to deny naturalized citizens the right to hold public office. A second measure authorized the President to deport any alien considered dangerous to the public peace or suspected of "treasonable or secret" tendencies, but the writ never became practice because Adams never employed it. A third bill imposed fines or imprisonment for sedition on any person who published "any false, scandalous and malicious writing" which might bring government, the president, or Congress into disrepute. The bill was originated in the Senate by the High Federalist General James Lloyd of Maryland, who wrote to Washington on the day of its passage, July 4, that he hoped for a declaration of war, "which I look upon as necessary to enable us to lay our hands on traitors." Though the bill was reworked by Otis, Robert Goodloe Harper of South Carolina, and James A. Bayard in the House, it still opened the way to a substantial docket of prosecutions. A last strenuous effort to block it by Gallatin, Livingston, Macon, and Nicholas, who had returned from his Virginia rest cure, was defeated by the Federalists in a straight party vote. Indeed, "straight party vote" was the battle cry throughout most of the harried, hurried passage of the three measures.

The bills were mainly the product of the High Federalist faction, but they won wide Federalist support. Despite explicit guarantees for freedom of expression and petition in the First Amendment to the Constitution, no Federalist seems to have worried about the constitutionality of the sedition bill. The great jurist-to-be, John Marshall of Virginia, was dubious, but on grounds of expediency. ("I have sometimes been led to think," muttered George Cabot of Beverley, Massachusetts, and of the ultra-Federalist "Essex Junto," the Bank of the United States, and the Senate, "that some of the Virginia Federalists are little better than halfway Jacobins!") Though he had made no recommendations on the subject, Adams had been worked up to a passion by scurrilous attacks on him in the domestic press, and he signed all three bills when they came before him.

In the Federalists' moment of panic and partisan opportunity, the "Spirit of 'Ninety-eight" was pervasive. While it lasted, it was a serious threat to the young nation's experiment as a liberal republic, a threat of the kind that many other infant polities have failed to survive.

Yet action stopped short of the High Federalists' final desires. Despite Pickering's clamor for immediate war, despite still further enlargements of the army, which Adams had refrained from recommending because he considered them unnecessary, Federalist ultras got neither war nor martial law. No call for war came from the

President, and when a motion for a declaration was made in Congress it failed to gather general support. The only policies left appeared to be defense and the Alien, Naturalization, and Sedition Acts.

Defense meant taxes, however. When Hamilton had first broached his "new excise," the doggerel attack on "Young Belcour" had ironically reassured the public: "Untax'd as yet—are Earth and Air." Now the Federalist put a levy on earth, in the form of a direct tax on land, along with a direct tax on houses and slaves, and a stamp tax. As the whiskey excise had stirred a rebellion in western Pennsylvania, so the direct property taxes sparked an uprising in eastern Pennsylvania, where a farmer-soldier named John Fries raised several hundred men against its collection. The insurrection was easily put down by the army, and Fries was convicted of treason but pardoned by Adams. Looking to peaceful processes, Jefferson retained his faith in the people in the face of Francophobia and war fears: "The disease of the imagination will pass over. . . Indeed, the Doctor is now on his way to cure it, in the guise of a tax gatherer." In fact, the direct taxes were to alienate many agricultural sections of New York and Pennsylvania which had been previously Federalist. In the meantime, there was still no levy on air.

The excitements of the Adams years brought a distinct firming of party lines in the House. Men as different as Jefferson and Sedgwick both saw a decline in the number of "wavering characters" (as Jefferson called them) or the "whimsical, kinkish and unaccommodating" (as Sedgwick put it more astringently). At the time of the XYZ Affair, Sedgwick could calculate that votes in the House showed "52 determined and rancorous Jacobins, and 54 who profess attachment to the government, in other words, confidence in the Executive." Despite Federalist factional tensions, the number of those whom Fisher Ames called "Half-Federalist"—men who periodically broke ranks—declined during the Fifth Congress of 1797-1799 and its successor in 1799-1801, as did the number of "Half-Republicans." The ranks of independents and non- or quasi-party moderates were suffering attrition, condemned from both sides.

The trend toward party voting was strong after 1796. By the minimal test suggested by Joseph Charles—by which a member is

137

classed as a "party-voter" if he votes with his party on at least two-thirds of all significant measures, and a "non-party-voter" if he fails to vote with his party as much as two-thirds of the time—non-party voters had never dropped below 20 per cent of all House members until the Jay treaty session brought them down to 7 per cent. In the special session of the Fifth Congress in 1797, however, the number of non-party voters skidded to 4 per cent and remained below 7 per cent thereafter throughout Adams's term, and then fell to none in the first meeting of the new House elected in 1800. In other

Figure 8

PROGRESS OF PARTY-VOTING,* HOUSE OF REPRESENTATIVES,
1797–1802

Congress, Session	Dates of Session	Voting as Federalists	Voting as Republicans	Non-Party
V/1	May–July 1797	49	50	4
V/2	Nov '97–July '98	51	48	6
V/3	Dec '98–Mar '99	50	44	8
VI/1	Dec '99–May 1800	55	46	5
VI/2	Nov 1800–Mar '01	51	52	2
VII/1	Dec '01–May '02	38	64	0

* The criterion of "party-voting" is that the member must have voted with others of the party indicated 66⅔ per cent of the time in the session on measures "of national importance," or involving "some important principle of government," as members saw it.

Adapted from Joseph Charles, *The Origins of the American Party System* (Williamsburg, Virginia, 1956), 93–4. Data computed by Charles from Manning J. Dauer, *The Adams Federalists* (Baltimore, 1953).

words, party-voting on the "two-thirds" basis hovered between 93 and 98 per cent and then rose to 100 per cent. A stricter standard may be raised, classifying a record of voting four to one with party as "party-voting," and a record of less than 80 per cent adherence to party on significant roll-calls as a "Half-Federalist" or a "Half-Republican" course. By this measure, as employed by Manning J. Dauer, the number of "Half-Federalists" fell from fourteen in the special session of the Fifth Congress in 1797 to seven and nine in the succeeding sessions, and then rose slightly to ten and eleven in the two sessions of the Sixth Congress of 1799-1801. The number of "Half-Republicans" fell even more sharply through the same sessions from nine to five to three to one, and then rose to two in the short session of 1800-1801.

Increased cohesion among Republicans was particularly significant in the crucial Middle Atlantic delegations, which had supplied the defectors in the Jay treaty controversy. In the Jay treaty Congress as a whole, Republicans from New York on all significant roll-calls had voted with the bulk of their party 80 per cent of the time, Republicans from Pennsylvania 84 per cent. In the Fifth Congress, the level rose for the New Yorkers to 95 per cent and for the Pennsylvanians to 93 per cent—striking figures, and not all of the deviant votes were on issues where a clear partisan lead was given. Maryland remained a special case because of the ineffable Samuel Smith, merchant-congressman from commercial Baltimore, who in the Fourth Congress voted Federalist oftener than he did Republican, and in the Fifth Congress broke ranks on nearly two votes out of every five. On the other hand, the lone additional Republican from Maryland in 1797-1799 established a record of nearly perfect party regularity.

Thus the "determined and rancorous Jacobins," as Sedgwick called them, were sufficiently cohesive to mark a clear opposition to "the Hamilton party," as Jefferson had put it. In the eyes of the public they presented a clear alternative to Federalist policies.

In the countryside, meanwhile, execution of the Sedition Act and Republican outcries against it brought the issues to full public attention. Suspicion continued to run strong, and Secretary Pickering himself spent mornings in his office persuing Republican newspapers to uncover seditious paragraphs, while foreign affairs presumably had to wait. Some two dozen sedition prosecutions were brought. The managers of the *Aurora* escaped: Bache died of yellow fever in late 1798 before a common law indictment against him could be brought to trial, and his successor Duane was let off by a grand jury after the party reversal of 1800. One of the liveliest cases ran against the Irish-tempered, rough-and-tumble editor-congressman Matthew Lyon of Vermont, called "Spitting Lyon" by Federalists. (He had answered a slight by Roger Griswold on his Revolutionary War record by spitting in Griswold's face on the floor of the House, where, a few days later, Griswold retaliated by belaboring Lyon with a hickory stick.) When Lyon's *Vermont Journal* reprinted a letter recommending that Congress commit Adams to a madhouse, he was convicted under the Sedition Act, fined $1000, and thrown in jail, from where he appealed to his constituents and won overwhelming re-election to Congress in 1798. Prosecutions were also directed against the editors of the New London *Bee* in Connecticut and the important *Independent Chronicle* in Boston, and against the burly, unkempt James Thomson Callender in Richmond for a violent anti-Adams pamphlet, among others. The struggling New York *Time Piece* was put out of business and its Irish-immigrant editor driven to hiding in Virginia. Indeed, several opposition papers suspended temporarily while their editors served time in jail.

Protest against the Federalist acts took various forms. A new forest of "Liberty Poles" sprang up in Massachusetts, carrying long lists of slogans: "Liberty and Equality—No Stamp Act—No Sedition—No Alien Bills—No Land Tax—Downfall to the Tyrants of America." Federalists cried out bitterly at such agitation, and Fisher Ames's brother, Dr. Nathaniel Ames, got himself into a contempt prosecution for his part in the Dedham slogan-writing. In Virginia there were mutterings of impending disunion or secession, and the Old Dominion began to prepare itself as a new haven for the victims of the "repressive acts." In key areas of New York and Pennsylvania, the Alien Act indeed alienated many Irish, German, and French immigrants, or brought them to the voting lists for the first time, bitterly anti-Federalist.

The great partisan counterattack took the form of two resolutions. One was drafted by Jefferson in his study at Monticello and the other was prepared by Madison, with the two men working in close communication. By October, Jefferson's manifesto had been transmitted through Wilson Cary Nicholas to John Breckinridge of Kentucky to put it before the state legislature there, and Madison's draft had gone through Nicholas to John Taylor, who was to sponsor it in the Virginia assembly. The Jefferson-Kentucky manifesto was approved in November 1798, and after a fierce debate the Madison-Virginia resolution was adopted the next month. In each statement the Sedition Act and companion measures were attacked on state-rights grounds as excessive exercises of national power, and as infringements of the liberty of speech and press guaranteed in the First Amendment or violations of other constitutional protections. Yet each state's assembly thought it necessary also to affirm attachment to the Union and to eschew any nullification of the legislation they condemned. A protest had been prepared, although its immediate political effect was somewhat circumscribed by its involvement in new, uncertain, and confusing constitutional questions.

Nonetheless, the Federalist "Spirit of 'Ninety-eight" had been attacked in a public and partisan fashion. The counterattack had evoked the young nation's developing liberal spirit, and it gathered support. It insisted again that a lawful opposition must be permitted to live and act, and this very insistence helped the nation to move from fear of opposition to acceptance of it. It thereby also helped the new polity to survive as a free republic.

Throughout their winter of party discontent in 1798-1799, Republicans were to continue to present the issues as violations of American liberties, and they painted the danger of standing armies, heavy taxation, and the threat of war as contrary to the principles of the American Revolution and the Constitution. Once again the Republican opposition had offered an alternative to the Federalist course, and a democratic public and electorate could make a choice. Indeed, as their impact was felt in the public mind, the Alien and Sedition Acts and the Virginia and Kentucky resolutions became important parts of virtual Federalist and Republican platforms for the presidential contest of 1800.

4.

Yet, despite Liberty Poles, political weather remained unfriendly for the Republicans in the mid-term Congressional elections, most of which were run off before the alien and sedition issues were felt.

In New England, the Federalist clergy and lawyers had intensified their attacks on Jefferson and his party as French sympathizers or radical disrupters. As time passed, indeed, Jefferson was to hear that the Adams taxes were stirring dissatisfaction, and immigration and the growth of Baptist and Methodist congregations foretold some future Republican comfort. In the new Congress which was to meet in 1799, however, Republican representation from New England was limited to the "Spitting Lyon" from Vermont and two lonely members out of fourteen from Massachusetts. Meanwhile the "Essex Junto" of Massachusetts Federalists took new heart in their pro-war, pro-Hamilton course.

In the Middle Atlantic states, signs were more favorable for the Republicans. The New York elections were to reverse a balance of six Federalists and four Republicans in the old Congress to six and four the other way. In Pennsylvania the elections brought Michael Leib from Philadelphia to the House over a Federalist contender with a great Pennsylvania name, Anthony Morris, and returned Gallatin with a comfortable majority. The net result was a Republican gain of one seat in the state's Congressional delegation, and the Republicans also picked up an additional seat in Maryland. Even in "kinkish" New Jersey, gusts of discontent and emerging party action gave the Republicans three representatives out of five where they had had none before.

To the South, however, the prospect was threatening. In North Carolina the Federalists vehemently contested every seat but two, and took half of the total of ten. A late election in South Carolina brought the Republican Charles Pinckney to the Senate, but earlier balloting for the House took two seats from the Republicans. Even more surprisingly, Georgia's two Republican representatives were replaced by Federalists. The great clouds of disaster for the Republicans, however, hung over their old bastion of Virginia, where excitement in late elections ran high, the aging and ailing George Washington rode ten miles to vote Federalist, and riots broke out in Richmond. Gains in the prosperous Tidewater brought four new Federalist members to Congress, for a balance of eight against eleven for the previously supreme Republicans—although one of the latter counted for a host by himself, a brilliant new member named John Randolph who was a master at polemical wit. The chief Federalist victor was John Marshall, who had supported Adams's efforts to find peace with France and had promised to vote for repeal of the Alien and Sedition Acts. In general it was Marshall's Moderate Federalist—though hardly "half-way Jacobin"—

leadership that brought his party a place in the Virginia sun. Below the North-South divide, only frontier Kentucky and Tennessee stood firm for their Republican sponsors.

The Republicans had fought hard, and so had their Federalist antagonists. A Maryland observer noted that "party spirit rages everywhere with great violence," and that "parties are beyond anything ever before known." In the "rage," the Republicans had made no inroads in New England, had gained a shaky seven House seats in the Mid-Atlantic area, and had lost a disastrous dozen in the South.

Yet the Republicans could discern some rays of hope through the clouds. By and large the elections had been decided in the climate of anti-French excitement and suspicion, before the impact of the Alien and Sedition Acts and the protesting resolutions had made their mark, before the direct taxes had produced their full effect. Nonetheless, the Republican leaders planned a cautious course for the new Congress. They would still oppose, but they would minimize contentions on foreign affairs in order to avoid the stigma of being "agents of France."

5.

As a result of the long course of Federalist and Republican development and sharpening partisan rivalry, the American nation was moving toward an "in"-"out," democratic party system. Difficult as it is to build parties as institutions, it is even more difficult to arrive at a going system of competing parties within a moderate spectrum, as other peoples and particularly new nations in the twentieth century were to find. The course on which "parties move to a point between the extremes," as V. O. Key has put it, is indeed "erratic, jerky, disorderly, and accompanied by no little friction and commotion," and wholly understandable only in "its dimension of time." Over the years, Americans had established a pattern in which the parties had provided alternative channels of representation for the variety of interests in the society and alternative opportunities for participation by individuals and groups, and in which the competition of parties had offered options for democratic choice. The American system was a two-party system. Many of its fundamentals, however, were representative of later multi-party patterns of politics as well as two-party patterns.

Indeed, early American experience suggests the basic outlines of plural-party systems in stable democracies generally. The defining characteristic of such systems may be taken as party interaction—a relatively durable relationship between two or more stable parties, in which they regularly compete with one another and must take one another into account in their behavior, their relationships with their followings, their bids for power, and their appeals to the un-committed. Rivalry between parties is concerned with contesting for control or office in government, though it may involve much more than this. Thus, Federalists and Republicans in the first American party system were extraordinarily concerned also with significant issues, or with mobilizing followers behind competing programs, whereas later American parties have not always been so strongly oriented to issues. The relationship between parties may vary with the system or with historical circumstances. Yet it is possible to describe a general model of plural-party systems in terms of four basic criteria.

The first is the existence of continuing conflict between parties. This at once implies, and is in part based on, ideologies or perspectives which emerge in the parties as "we-they" perspectives. These partisan views become involved with a strong desire that the party win power for its own sake, perhaps even more than for the sake of the interests it may represent. In nominations, elections, and appointments to office, a partisan attitude tends to emphasize party loyalty, rather than eminence or ability alone. Where the political situation (and thus the parties) are significantly oriented to issues, partisanship—in the absence of strong counterpressures from local constituencies or factional forces—tends toward the adoption of general party attitudes toward issues rather than singular or "kink-ish" positions. Such attitudes are likely to affect not only party leaders, cadres, and actives but also persons and even groups in the party following. When issues are drawn in this way between parties, the parties themselves tend to rally the pluralism of interests and opinions around their own standards, and thereby moderate plural-istic variety. Many crosscurrents of pluralism may remain, but generally they will not run as strongly as they would in a politics without parties or in faction politics. All of these aspects of party rivalry were observable among Federalists and Republicans in America as they joined in recurring combat with one another. The more the ties of a party become institutionalized, within its structure and with its following, and the further a party moves toward full-scale organization, the stronger the sense of partisanship is likely to become.

Despite conflict, a plural-party system need not tear a society—even a new and untried society—into fragments. Where a social system has arrived at some understandings or achieved consensus concerning political means, parties generally operate and expect to operate within such understandings or such consensus—and this marks a second criterion for a plural-party system in a stable democracy. Strictly considered, this criterion implies commitment to at least two basic propositions: acceptance of the legitimacy of opposition and of opposition parties, and acceptance of freedom of access to government power for the opposition. When deep social conflict is given free play, or when the parties themselves adopt intransigent positions, consensus on these minimal propositions may be threatened and the society may thereby be seriously disturbed or even destroyed. In America many Federalists doubted the legitimacy of opposition, and the Sedition Act at least was a threat to the idea of freedom of political expression for the opposition. Yet the basic values of acceptance of opposition and its access to power triumphed. Furthermore, despite High Federalist pressures, neither party as a whole pushed matters to the extremes of intransigence.

A third criterion is the role of the parties in providing stable links between people and government as the parties contend with one another. The significance of this relationship in terms of political gratification may vary. At a maximum, it may supply effective representation in government for the interests and opinions which are joined in the party following, as both the early Federalists and Republicans in America demonstrated. It may also provide open means of participation in the political process for individuals and groups in the party following, as the Republicans in particular revealed. It may on the other hand involve little more than symbolic or emotional gratification for the sentiments or ideological perspectives which men in the party following share: the rewards of victory may hinge merely on the fact that "our" symbols or rhetoric predominate, that "our" leaders hold office and set the tone. Under certain circumstances party representation may also be constricted within narrow limits of group brokerage concerning relatively insignificant issues.

The effectiveness of parties as links between public and government depends on relationships both within and between the parties. Generally, democracy within a party tends to promote effective representation of significant interests and opinions as well as substantial popular participation. On the other hand, dominance by a few leaders in a party tends to inhibit such popular representation and participation. Despite low levels of intraparty democracy, however, parties in situations where there is conflict on serious issues may, in the very competition for power and votes, differ significantly on these issues and thus offer important options to the electorate. Choice between such options is the fulcrum of interparty democracy—as it was in the interaction of elitist Federalists and popular Republicans in the American experience. Generally, however, intraparty democracy and effective representation promote interparty democracy as popular choice. Furthermore, meaningful choice for the electorate is generally encouraged when there is a significant degree of differentiation on issues between the parties and cohesion on issues within each party—once again, the American Federalists and Republicans are exhibits. Interparty democracy may be frustrated in multiparty systems where parties must make coalitions in order to govern. Similarly, in two-party systems, effective democratic choice is threatened by serious factional divisions within a party in power which may weaken the party's ability to fulfill its general commitments to the electorate. It is particularly endangered when a minority faction of a governing party, dissenting from the basic positions which that party has offered to the voters, works in alliance with a minority party and is thus able to prevent the majority party from carrying out its announced policies. Before long, intraparty factional developments on the American scene were to confuse democratic choice, and such phenomena were to recur throughout American party history. The outbreak of factionalism among Federalists in the Adams years was an omen of chronic (and more serious) difficulties to come.

Finally, if a plural-party system is to survive, each party must have a reasonable chance to win government power. If one giant party dominates the political arena persistently, even though ineffectual opposition parties are permitted to exist, a plural-party system can hardly operate in a meaningful sense as an instrument of democracy as representation and choice. Although the Federalist party was dominant at the beginning, and the Republicans finally became an overwhelmingly dominant party in turn, both parties at the peak of their rivalry enjoyed remarkably equal opportunities to exercise government authority.

The first American party system was in a sense a transitional system. It built on the experience of earlier years, with their essays in the politics of opposition in the colonies and states, and their committees and networks of correspondence in the Revolutionary endeavor. The national party system was in the process of evolution in the 1790's and did not reach its fullest development until 1800, although in the Adams years it went well beyond the personal, factional, nonparty politics of the previous decade. Even at their apogee, however, the parties of Hamilton and Jefferson were still limited in their appeal to voters and in the development of organization, and their lives were comparatively short. In the long sweep of American history, they stood as half-way houses on the road to the fully organized parties of the later Jacksonian era with their expanded mass followings. In its time, nonetheless, the first American party system revealed what parties in an emerging democracy could do.

A system in which parties interact and are balanced can provide a significant instrument for determining democratically who gets what, when, and how in government, and for shaping social and governmental policy. Yet at the same time it entails party contentions of the sort Americans were being treated to in unusually full measure during the Adams regime.

6.

The years 1799 and 1800 marked a sudden quieting of the major storms of international politics. A new climate of peace gradually pervaded the nation. Between parties, however, conflict continued to be sustained and intense, although more in the countryside than in the capital or Congress.

It was the beleaguered Adams himself who finally managed to reduce tensions with France. Hearing from a Republican traveler who had sounded out the *Directoire* that an envoy might at last be welcomed, the President appointed William Vans Murray, a former Federalist congressman from Maryland, as minister to France, soon reported having assurances that Murray would be received, and followed by appointing a commission to aid Murray in negotiations for amity. Having learned to be wary, Adams made the Murray appointment without consulting with Hamilton's pro-war minions in his cabinet, Pickering and McHenry, although Wolcott was informed. Departing in November 1799, the envoys by the fall of 1800 had reached a new agreement with France which superseded the treaties of alliance of 1778. As a result of a change in course by the *Directoire*, and Adams's dogged determination to seize the opportunity for peace, the tempests of Franco-American conflict and their threat of war were quieted at last.

Yet the President's pacific action precipitated new factional furors within the Federalist party. Deprived of their great issue, of their chief weapon against domestic "Jacobins," and of their leverage for a possible British alliance, pro-war High Federalists raged at Adams, and conspired to harass him in the conduct of government and to block his re-election. Aroused to firm action against his factional enemies at last, Adams dismissed Pickering from the cabinet and demanded and got McHenry's resignation, although Wolcott remained. Even while Adams was apparently saving the young nation from a possibly disastrous war, factional animosities reached their ultimate heights in the Federalist formation. In policy, the French mission was a triumph for the Moderates; in political effect, it enraged the extremists.

Party conflict persisted between Federalists and Republicans. More and more leaders, cadre workers, and lesser actives on both sides were taking to heart the cause of party as such, not only in looking upon their party as right and the other as wrong (and issues enough remained), but in an increased determination to obtain political power for their party. Thus the party system became at once a center and an active engine of political conflict. Meanwhile, Jefferson was at last coming to full acceptance of partisanship and party competition as a service to democracy. In 1798 he had conveyed to John Taylor a considered analysis of party functions in a democratic two-party system:

In every free and deliberating society there must, from the nature of man, be opposite parties and violent dissensions and discords; and one of these must for the most part prevail over the other for a longer or shorter time. Perhaps this party division is necessary to induce each to watch and relate to the people the proceedings of the other.

Through difficult days of opposition, in the face of the tempest of world and domestic political discords, the Republicans had indeed related the proceedings of Adams and the Federalists to the public. As Adams's term drew to its close, Jefferson as party leader and director was laboring to give the rest of his philosophy of party effect in combat to come.

8

The Choice of 1800

Major elections under party systems provide prime opportunities for the expression of interests and opinions and for vast popular participation. They are also prime objects of partisan endeavor, for they are the means to the formal sanctions of power and office. Where parties offer significant options on which voters may base meaningful choices as to the men and policies that will govern them, elections may also be the fulcrums of popular decisions in a democracy. Such was the party contest of 1800 in America. Both parties saw the election as an ultimate test between the two great political bodies and their commitments on ideology and policy, and both were determined to rally their followings and seize the victory.

Many signs were favorable for the Federalists, although there were countersigns too. The "in" party had triumphed in the midterm elections, and Adams had finally brought peace with honor. Looking toward the presidential contest, the wary Federalists had even reduced the army to peacetime strength in advance of the settlement with France. Yet many established party leaders were aging or edging toward retirement, and they viewed the new men who had come in with the Congressional victories as dubious replacements. Thus, for example, when Adams named the Moderate spokesman Marshall to succeed Pickering at the State Department, High Federalists were aghast. Furthermore, the impact of the "repressive acts" was beginning to be felt, and sedition prosecutions had led, ironically, to doubling the number of newspapers supporting Jefferson and the "out" party. Finally, in the mood of peace many Americans came to see the Federalists not as brave defenders but as headlong warmongers.

A caucus of Federalist congressmen met in May 1800. "By union," John Marshall warned, "we can scarcely maintain our ground—without it we must sink and with us all sound, correct American principles." Formal nominations were given to Adams and to Charles Cotesworth Pinckney, and the caucus firmly pledged the party's support to both candidates equally.

Yet all was not union underneath. From the moment that Adams had named the mission to France in 1799, Hamilton and his faction had determined to rid themselves of the stubbornly pacific President. Soon Hamilton was touring the Eastern states, working covertly again to spring the same scheme he had planned in 1796. Under the caucus cover of equal support in electoral votes, an edge would actually be given to Charles Cotesworth Pinckney, and Adams would be ditched. The schism soon became public. Deeply offended, and determined to defend himself, Adams passionately denounced Hamilton as the head of a "pro-British faction," and "a bastard, and as much an alien as Gallatin." In reply, drawing on Pickering, McHenry, and Wolcott for inside details, Hamilton circulated a long letter among selected allies, to "prove" that Adams was unfit for office, motivated only by "distempered jealousy," "vanity without bounds," and "ungovernable indiscretion." Still Adams held the support of Marshall, John Jay, and Noah Webster in New York, and Otis and other figures in Massachusetts, as well as most Federalist "leaders of the second class," as Hamilton called them. His moderate course also gave Adams continuing strength with large segments of the electorate. Even so, the scheme still unwound below the surface.

The tensions of world ideological passions and domestic politics had brought Hamilton to a strange metamorphosis. From a party general who marched at the head of a united phalanx, he had become a backstairs factional intriguer against the nominee of that party. He had referred to Washington as his essential "*Aegis*," and the Old Commander had died at the end of 1799 on the eve of the removal of the government to the new capital on the Potomac

151

which glorified his name. Perhaps Washington had been "essential" in more ways than Hamilton knew, standing as he did as a living counsel of moderation and discretion, a fatherly restraint on the more headlong tendencies of "Young Belcour." Yet in another aspect, Hamilton's metamorphosis was not so startling. For a leader who was sure he was right and had never quite accepted dependence on popular judgment, and who now feared that the people would not support his course, perhaps the obvious resort was maneuver among "the wise, the good, and the rich."

2.

The Republicans entered the campaign united and resolute. By 1800 they had made Marache's boarding house in Philadelphia into an informal party command post. Members of Congress as various as Senator Langdon of New Hampshire and Representatives Macon of North Carolina and Randolph of Virginia stayed there. At "Marache's Club," as Randolph liked to call it, some forty-three Republican senators and representatives and several other partisans attended a caucus, also in May 1800, to select the party's nominees. Once again Jefferson was obvious for president, and Gallatin could at last bring word from his father-in-law Commodore James Nicholson that conferences among Clinton, Burr, and other leaders in New York had cleared the way for Burr, who received the caucus nomination for vice-president. The Republicans also committed themselves firmly to an equality of votes, and the New York–Virginia axis at last seemed fixed.

Careful planning characterized Republican efforts throughout. Early in 1799 Jefferson had insisted that for success, "the engine is the press," and had called on "every man [to] lay his purse and pen under contribution." He suited action to his words by personally supervising the distribution of pamphlets and personally soliciting funds, while urging others "to assess their friends also." At Philadelphia he dined or conferred with congressmen who served as a national cadre, and he directed his always voluminous correspondence to the crucial concerns of party strategy.

In several states, new growths of Republican electoral organization developed from the seeds of national party action. Thus, for example, after an early election in New York, Burr traveled through Connecticut and Rhode Island to prepare the ground—labors in New York and Pennsylvania, of course, were already advanced. The Republicans in New Jersey began to organize committees throughout the state; Congressmen Aaron Kitchell arranged for correspondence among "people of information and influence"; and a state meeting at Princeton issued an address exalting Jefferson and the elevation of the common man. The old-style politics which had favored the Federalists was giving way to organized co-ordination. In Virginia, where Monroe was now governor, a legislative caucus named a Republican ticket of electors; a Republican General Committee co-ordinated campaign labors, circulating printed or handwritten tickets which the voters could deposit at the polls; and the Committee also spread addresses to the citizens in the press. Only hesitant shoots of organization were apparent in North Carolina, but the Republicans at last had a newspaper, for Nathaniel Macon had brought Joseph Gales to Raleigh to establish the *Register* there.

Hindered again by the myopia of their notable leaders, the Federalists failed to read the signs. Although they followed Republican methods of organization to some extent in Virginia and Pennsylvania, elsewhere they generally relied on correspondence, occasional public meetings and state gatherings of leaders, national patronage, and press propaganda. This last turned sharply on Jefferson, who was scourged as a Jacobin, the father of mulatto children, an "intellectual voluptuary," a mad scientist whose estate ought to be called "Dog's Misery" because he practiced vivisection there, an atheist whose election would bring on the people of America "the just vengeance of insulted heaven." Voters were asked whether they would choose

GOD—AND A RELIGIOUS PRESIDENT;
or impiously declare for
JEFFERSON—AND NO GOD!!!

Such diatribes, however, did not make up for the Federalist failure to develop open organization comparable to the apparatus Republicans were establishing.

The Republicans also orchestrated a fortissimo propaganda attack. In a public letter-"platform" dispatched to Elbridge Gerry in 1799, Jefferson had taken his stand for "a government rigorously frugal and simple," and "the discharge of the national debt"; for a limited navy and for state militia forces for internal defense, except in case of "actual invasion"; for "free commerce with all nations, political connections with none," and against "joining in the [European] confederacy of kings to war against the principles of liberty"; for "freedom of religion, and . . . freedom of the press," and against "all violations of the constitution" which would silence criticism "by force and not by reason." This summary of Republican "principles" was echoed again and again throughout the campaign, accompanied by specific blasts against the direct taxes and the Alien and Sedition Acts and by repeated praise of Jefferson as "our great Patriot." In addition, the themes of debt, taxes, and war were repeated in emotional reiteration, and popular prejudices were not ignored. A pamphlet called *The Family Compact of Connecticut* sought to expose the political machinations of the Congregational clergy beginning with "Dwight, Timothy—President of Yale, generally called the Pope." In Philadelphia, Beckley prepared several pamphlets for distribution north, south, and east, despite his own illness and the death of his only child.

Often emotional or personal, the Republican electoral appeals were still remarkably oriented to the great issues of the day. In addition, like Hamilton and the Federalists before them, the Republicans had in effect generated a program, a comprehensive set of policies which was patterned on their conception of the national interest and which appealed to broad and varied segments of the public. Only a very sleepy voter could have been oblivious to the choice before him.

3.

The crucial states in the contest turned out to be New York (where Adams had won his margin in 1796), Pennsylvania (which the Republicans had to hold against Federalist maneuvering), and South Carolina (an essential hedge against trouble in Pennsylvania); and Jefferson and other Republican managers watched developments in these states closely. The time and procedures for choosing electors varied from state to state, and thus the struggles in each state were carried on as separate decisive events.

In New York, Burr was the driving force. He carefully arranged a city ticket of eminent men like Clinton, General Horatio Gates, and Brockholst Livingston, to run for the legislature that would name the presidential electors. He himself harangued in the city's taverns, guided an active finance committee, amassed an index of voters and their political histories, organized ward and precinct meetings, and worked at the polls. He also gathered together the forerunner of future partisan-personal machines, composed of cadre-followers who collaborated so efficiently that they became known as the "Myrmidons" or the "Tenth Legion." He cracked the problem of disfranchisement for many city workingmen under the state's property test for suffrage, by arranging for joint land tenancies which made each participant a legal owner. The whole effort found new resources which foreshadowed similar developments elsewhere. Many ambitious lesser merchants and would-be entrepreneurs were beginning to feel that their hopes for advancement were frustrated by Federalists in the interest of a few wealthy magnates. To encourage these disgruntled forces Burr and several associates had formed the Manhattan Company, chartered ostensibly to provide water for the city but granted sufficient powers to enable it to operate as a bank. Haughtily contemptuous of Burr's plebian political tactics, the Federalists now found themselves also threatened by their own brand of politico-financial petard.

In the April elections the Republicans carried all twelve of New York City's state legislative districts over Hamilton's slate of Federalist mediocrities. They also ran well outside the city, and ultimately won a net majority of nineteen in the Senate and Assembly as a whole. Desperate, Hamilton maneuvered to change the rules in the middle of the game. Ignoring the fact that Federalists in 1799 had beaten down a proposal by Burr to name electors by popular vote, arguing bluntly that "in times like these it will not do to be overscrupulous," Hamilton now urged Governor Jay to call a special session of the old Federalist-controlled legislature to authorize a new choice of electors by popular ballot. He hoped thereby to snatch New York from the Republicans after all. Disdaining to answer, Jay noted on Hamilton's letter: "Proposing a measure for party purposes, which I think it would not become me to adopt." The victory in the city had hinged on an average margin of 490 for Republicans over Federalists, but the whole of the Empire State's electoral vote would go to Jefferson—and Burr.

With Pennsylvania in the Republican column, Jefferson had declared, "we can defy the universe"—or at least the Federalists. In 1800 it appeared that the defiance could be effected, as Beckley (as chairman of the Committee of Correspondence for Philadelphia), Dallas, Gallatin, Leib, and others marshalled the Republican organization of committees throughout the state. Following the Republican sweep in 1799, Governor Thomas McKean had removed Federalist officeholders by the score to make room for Republicans. He had commissioned Beckley, for example, as clerk of the Mayor's Court in Philadelphia and provided him with another subsidiary clerkship to pay him what he had drawn in the national House. It was an early version of the party-building "spoils system" which was later to run rampant in American politics, but McKean's patronage platoons marched to battle. There was no doubt that the Republicans had broad popular support also, and a Federalist observer lamented that by 1800 the state was dominated by "United Irishmen, Free Masons, and the most God-provoking Democrats on this side of Hell." Yet the Federalists labored to match Republican organization in Pennsylvania, and also maneuvered to keep the Keystone State from becoming the key to national Republican victory. Utilizing the resources of their holdover control of the Pennsylvania state Senate, they first forced the Republicans to accept a choice of presidential electors by the legislature instead of by popular vote. Next they refused Senate concurrence in a Republican move to choose electors by a joint ballot of both houses of the legislature, in which the Republican preponderance in the more numerous lower house would have enabled them to name all fifteen electors. The Federalists thus compelled a final compromise which gave them seven electors to the Republicans' eight. The result scarcely represented the political balance in the state, as an overwhelming Republican victory in the Congressional elections was to reveal, but it neutralized Pennsylvania in the presidential contest.

As all eyes turned South, the old Federalist bastion of South Carolina was experiencing a new frenzy of electioneering. Taking over active management for Jefferson and Burr, the Republican Charles Pinckney pressed his party's attack against "the Weight of Talent, Wealth, and personal and family interest" which favored the Federalists. He expected to lose Charleston but labored to recruit back-country planters and farmers. Even so, he reported to Jefferson, he was amazed at the Federalist mobilization in the city:

> as much as I am accustomed to Politics and to study mankind this Election in Charleston has opened to me a new view of things. never certainly was such an election in America . . . it is said that several Hundred more voted than paid taxes. the Lame, Crippled, diseased and blind were either led, lifted or brought in carriages to the Poll. the sacred right of ballot was struck at, for at a late hour, when too late to counteract it, in order to know how men [voted] the Novel and Unwarrantable measure was used of Voting with tickets printed on Green and blue and red and yellow paper and Men stationed to watch the votes.

The punctuation in Pinckney's report was archaic and whimsical, but Federalist tactics were indeed "Novel" (if not fraudulent), industrious, and modern—especially against the background of old-style politics in the state.

Yet when the legislature met, Pinckney managed tactics which provided a match for the Federalists. On the evening of the third day, the Republican members caucused and named a committee to prepare a list of electors. Each prospective elector was then interviewed for assurances of loyalty to Jefferson and Burr as well. A few days later the chairman of the caucus learned that a group of Federalists planned to attend a second meeting of the Republicans that night, presumably to propose a bi-partisan ticket of Jefferson and the Federalist Pinckney. A note was promptly posted on the door of the meeting room, stating that no caucus would be held. Meanwhile Charles Pinckney was firming his lines by promises of patronage if Jefferson was elected—promises Jefferson later honored. The day after the Federalist infiltration strategy had been blocked, the legislature named the electors for Jefferson and Burr by a majority of nineteen votes.

The crucial uncertain states of North and South had each gone for Jefferson and Burr by the same legislative margin, and despite a standoff in Pennsylvania the balance had been turned.

4.

The total result was a clear indication of party discipline, although the presidential outcome failed to reflect the full extent of the Republican triumph. The scattering of votes for the vice-presidential post which had occurred in 1796 was entirely eliminated. Every elector who voted for Jefferson in 1800 also voted for Burr, and every Federalist elector but one (in order to assure Adams a lead) gave his votes for both Adams and Pinckney. The final tally showed 73 electoral votes each for Jefferson and Burr, 65 for Adams, and 64 for Pinckney.

The contest had been conducted throughout as a full-scale combat of settled national parties. Clear nominations had been made by parties; the emphasis in the public view had been on national party perspectives, positions, and slates or tickets; intense electioneering had been undertaken by partisan leaders and cadre; followings had been mobilized and groups had been joined together by party. It had become respectable to undertake party electioneering and act in the style of the "firm party man," as Noble Cunningham has put it, whereas in 1790 either might have been perceived as slavish or unpatriotic. To be sure, the presidential results showed continuing sectional biases. All of New England's electoral votes went to the Federalists, and all tallies from the South except four votes from North Carolina were Republican, while once again the vote in the Middle Atlantic states was divided. Yet the Republicans were gathering support even in New England, and were to reduce their sectional dependence and emerge as a truly national party. More and more, parties were coming to act as nationalizing forces.

Even among faction-torn Federalists, partisanship had had a cohesive effect. Despite the determination of High Federalists "to support General Pinckney in good earnest," as Hamilton had put

it, even he eventually had to recognize "a strong personal attachment" to Adams "in the body of the people"; and entirely too many
Moderate Federalists ended up supporting Adams to permit open
execution of the Pinckney scheme. The anti-Adams forces thus had
to rely on the strategem of equal support for both Federalist candidates—and hope. Their final hope had been frustrated by a clear
partisan alignment in South Carolina.

Nonetheless, the results of 1800 were produced, in part, by certain crucial defections from the Federalist cause. They came among
previously Federalist artisan-mechanic groups and even among en-
trepreneurial groups in cities like New York and Philadelphia. More
portentously, previously Federalist farmers in prosperous Northampton, Bucks, and Montgomery counties in Pennsylvania, where
John Fries had raised his rebellion against the land tax, swung
sharply to the Republicans. Similar shifts occurred in many country
areas in New York and New Jersey and in certain parts of New
England. The intransigent, ultra-commercial, pro-war policies of
the High Federalists had finally alienated numerous well-to-do
agrarian conservatives who had once found their natural place in
the Federalist following but who saw no virtue in a war for trade or
in land taxes to pay military bills. In 1800 Adams's moderate appeal
helped hold Federalist lines to some extent in the presidential combat, but the lines broke sharply in the Congressional contests.
When Jefferson as Adams's successor proved that Republicans
could be moderate, too, the Federalists lost still more of their old
"country" support.

Yet the election was more than just party mobilization or group
realignment. It was also a broad appeal to public opinion and to the
electorate, a presentation of remarkably clearly shaped alternatives
for electoral choice, and—in response—a decision as to who should
govern and in what direction. It not only marked the apogee of the
first American competitive party system, but also a profound shift
in political alignments in the young American nation. For a dozen
years Hamiltonians and Federalists had ruled, and now Jeffersonians and Republicans were in time to take over in a democratic
transfer of political power, and keep the power for years to come.
In this sense the election of 1800 was what V. O. Key has called a

"critical election" in that it altered older alignments in the electorate and produced new alignments which were to persist through succeeding elections. Moreover, although presidential electors had been chosen by popular vote in only five states in 1800, sharp party contention in the elections generally had brought voting to approximately 38 per cent of white adult males, a level not generally surpassed for some years to come. Perhaps Jefferson exaggerated when he called the democratic overturn "as real a revolution in the principles of our government as that of 1776 was in form." Nonetheless, most Federalists would have agreed, if wryly and with regret. Few national elections have been as decisive.

When the Congressional results were known, the bent of the electoral decision and the shift in party allegiances were brought home even more sharply. In the contests for the new House, the Republicans won 66 of 106 seats for an unprecedented majority, and also won control of the Senate for the first time by eighteen seats out of 32. In the House elections the Republicans won strong majorities of the seats in every state outside New England except Delaware, which returned its lone Federalist member, and North Carolina and South Carolina, where the two parties broke even. In New England, the Republicans took both of Rhode Island's seats and actually carried six of Massachusett's fourteen places. In keystone Pennsylvania, the Republican candidates for the House carried the total popular vote by almost three to one. The attrition of "wavering," "kinkish," or "half-party" hopefuls had continued, and Republicans could be sure of their control.

There was, however, a curious flaw in the presidential results. The exact equality in electoral votes for Jefferson and Burr meant, under the Constitution as it then stood, that the ultimate selection would be made by the House of Representatives. Furthermore, the issue would go to the old, Federalist-controlled House, not the newly elected one, and constitutionally the House had power to make either Jefferson or Burr president. The Republicans had to face another ordeal before they could enjoy their victory.

Even so, enthusiasm ran high in the moment of popular triumph. Looking out of his window in the village of Dedham, Massachu-

Figure 9

PRESIDENTIAL AND CONGRESSIONAL ELECTION RESULTS, 1800

	Electoral Vote, 1800		Congressional Elections, House	
	Jefferson and Burr	Adams and Pinckney	Republican Members	Federalist Members
New Hampshire		6		4
Vermont		4	1	1
Massachusetts		16	6	8
Rhode Island[a]		4[b]	2	
Connecticut		9		7
New York	12		7	3
New Jersey		7	5	
Pennsylvania	8	7	10[c]	3[c]
Delaware		3		1
Maryland[a]	5	5	5	3
Virginia[a]	21		17	2
North Carolina[a]	8	4	5	5
South Carolina	8		3	3
Georgia	4		2	
Kentucky[a]	4		2	
Tennessee	3		1	
	73	65[b]	66	40

[a] States naming presidential electors by popular vote.

[b] One elector from Rhode Island for Adams and John Jay; thus, Pinckney's total was 64 to Adams's 65.

[c] Before the Seventh Congress met in December 1801, Gallatin resigned to become Secretary of the Treasury and was replaced by a Moderate Federalist.

Adapted from Edward G. Stanwood, *A History of the Presidency from 1788 to 1897* (Boston, 1898), 63, and Manning J. Dauer, *The Adams Federalists* (Baltimore, 1953), 256–8, 328–31.

setts, on the last day of 1800, Dr. Nathaniel Ames waxed apocalyptic. "Here ends the 18th Century," he exclaimed in his diary. "The 19th begins with a fine clear morning wind at S.W.; and the political horizon affords as fine a prospect under Jefferson's administration, with . . . the irresistible propagation of the Rights of Man, the eradication of hierarchy, oppression, superstition and tyranny." It was a large order, but everyone knew that both of the Ameses were a bit extreme.

5.

The electoral campaign and preponderant power in succeeding years brought Republican party structure to its ultimate articulation and to expanding organization. The development of organization was highly uneven, rushing ahead in some states and lagging in others. Nonetheless, the Republicans were developing another party innovation which was as epoch-making for politics as Hamilton's program had been for government.

The key elements of early Republican organization became caucus, convention, and committee. The nominating caucus among members of a party in the legislature was regularized and expanded in its functions. Thus by 1804 in New Hampshire, for example, a Republican caucus formed a state committee on elections and "correspondence," with town committees under it. In the South, the caucus was often virtually the only continuing device of coordinated action. Yet it was subject to suspicion or attack nearly everywhere as an instrument of the arrogance of officeholders or of secret manipulations.

Local conventions marked a more democratic development. The convention, which had also made an early but sporadic appearance, became standard on the county level throughout the Middle Atlantic states. Members or "delegates" were named by local meetings or local committees, although often selection and representation were left loose. The conventions became key agents in making nominations for local and often for Congressional races and in rallying voters. Certain conditions were necessary for their successful construction and maintenance. For example, the Republicans in the Congressional district composed of Northampton, Bucks, and Montgomery counties in Pennsylvania found it necessary to see some chance of victory before conventions and their slates or tickets would be taken seriously. Continued success for conventions also required a significant opposition to make it all worth while. Thus, again in Northampton, Bucks, and Montgomery counties, the convention emerged late but exhibited advanced organization and vigorous action when it did appear to contend against the previously dominant Federalists; and thus, the Republican convention movement in transitional New Jersey came late but then quickly wove a strong net across the state. As organization and conventions spread even into Maryland and Delaware, many Federalists condemned the popular, powerful innovation and even argued that it was illegal.

For the Republicans in the early 1800's, statewide co-ordination depended largely on committees. Proposals were made for state nominating conventions, and new-style New Jersey Republicans soon achieved one. In too many states, however, distance, localism, or inertia still stood in the way. Top leaders, meanwhile, tended to maintain communication face to face, or through correspondence, or in the caucus, and also found their way onto local committees in town or county. The consequence was that state co-ordination tended to fall to informal state cadre groupings or to state committees more or less responsibly established, since these bodies maintained contact and articulation with caucuses in the state capitals on the one hand and with local conventions or campaign committees on the other. Yet state and local committees proved to be effective political engines and even spread into some parts of the South.

In long-hostile New England, Republican structure took on particularly firm lines. In the battle against odds, a strongly centralized organization emerged in which state committees appointed local committees and held them accountable. The committees appealed to young voters, disseminated propaganda, planned rallies and "celebrations" to gather the faithful, and got out the vote. Frightened Federalists railed at such popular mobilization, and burlesqued a Republican celebration in newspaper doggerel:

> They made a most tremendous stir
> Curs'd, swore and quaff'd till half seas oe'r.
> Their skins replete could hold no more—
> Then from their tavern out they sallied
> And under air their forces rallied.

Contrasting stages of development characterized neighboring New York and New Jersey. In the mature politics of the Empire State, the rallying cry of patronage rang out from 1800 on and old

George Clinton's young nephew, DeWitt Clinton, became the generalissimo of political jobs. He sought control over patronage in part as a means to undermine Burr and regain control in the Republican party for Clintonians in alliance with Livingstons—and before long, Jefferson was consulting with the Clintons on appointments, George Clinton was governor again, DeWitt Clinton was briefly senator and then a perennial and able mayor of New York City, Edward Livingston was United States attorney in the state, and Livingston connections and in-laws popped up in post after post. Across the river in New Jersey, by contrast, new Republican organization was remarkably open, issue-oriented, and democratic; and as party competition stiffened, suffrage was extended and party action brought new popular participation. Excitement reached such heights that voters had to be forbidden to appear at the polls with "Weapons of War, or Staves or Bludgeons." Enthusiasm and organization paid off as Republicans moved to dominance in the state.

In Pennsylvania, the Bucks County convention invited general participation on the party Committee. Every voter, the Articles of Association declared, "shall have a right to elect and to be elected," provided only that he "professes to be a Democratic Republican and has supported the character for at least six months." The Committee was to be elected every year, at open polls, with election judges on hand. "Make your Committees a just representation of the Republican interest," a Convention Address of 1803 urged, "and support by your votes the ticket they recommend." Happily, Gallatin could note, the party had indeed won a firm place in the hearts of the electorate. Yet, under McKean's new patronage system, the development of organization brought an increasingly serious threat of party control by men who made careers in political management and who won their rewards in the largesse of office.

To the South, politics exhibited few developments toward stable modern organization, despite progress in the great domain of Virginia and Pinckney's lessons of 1800 in South Carolina. Even so, the party and its followers drew closer together and most Southern voters knew clearly what their party was—Jeffersonian Republican, of course.

164

Everywhere, indeed, ties grew firmer between Republican party structure and individuals and groups in the public. Yet those who occupied the top party positions remained a comparatively small and compact body of men, and as years passed more and more of them followed the Pennsylvania precept, becoming professional politicians primarily concerned with office and power. Before long, the practical intellectuals who had served as the new nation's first party leaders were virtually replaced by such matter-of-fact non- or even anti-intellectual politicians. While some of them also remained concerned with issues or popular wishes as Madison, Jefferson, Beckley, or Gallatin were, not all novitiates of the "new career" found principles, party programs, or intraparty democracy necessary ways of political life. Organization was opening the way to domination by *homo politicus* over the party following. Yet such men did conduct the affairs of party, and thereby sustained parties as potential instruments for popular influence.

As Republican organization developed in Massachusetts, Dr. Ames described his duties as a member of the County Committee for Norfolk in the early 1800's. It was his task, he noted in his diary:

> to communicate with the Central Committee of the State, and town or subcommittees—to watch over the Republican interest both in state and national governments especially as to elections and appointments—convey intelligence—confute false rumors—confirm the wavering in right principles—prevent delusion of weak brethren—and fight that most formidable enemy of civilized men, political ignorance; a task mighty, endless, and insuperable without funds to excite support and disseminate the fruits of patriotic genius—and with the most ample funds will prove a Herculean labor [against] narrow prejudices, wholly actuated by the impulse of the moment.

Although Dr. Ames was an unusually intellectual cadre worker even for Jefferson's time, his job description was a suggestive epitome of the mature Republican party structure and its ties with its following.

6.

The last session of the Federalist Congress met in Washington, the new "Capital City" on the stately Potomac. In fact, it was less city than scraggly village; the streets were less broad avenues than dusty trails in drought and mired paths in rain; and the scattered houses were jerry-built clapboard compared to Philadelphia's neat brick homes. Yet the unfinished capitol building looked to the beckoning West, and the nation looked to the future.

The immediate question was deciding on a president. In the show of party discipline in 1800, Jefferson had assumed that one or two electors would omit to vote for Burr and thus establish the presidential priority, but now the holdover House would have to decide. Although the Federalists had a majority, they controlled delegations from only six of the sixteen states by 1801, while the Republicans by that time could count on eight, and two were divided or uncertain. It would take nine states to elect, and each state would cast one vote, determined by the majority of its representatives voting. Thus the Federalists could block a selection but probably not make one.

Excited rumors chased one another about the village. One reported that some Federalists were planning to name the president of the Senate as a presidential replacement by legislation, perhaps only until new elections could be held—and a few Federalists did toy with this idea. Rumor also had Hamilton conspiring with Burr to make him a captive president by Federalist votes. This time, however, Hamilton eschewed such schemes; he feared Jefferson less than Burr, whom he privately called "truly the Cataline of America." Never exactly chained to principle, Burr was nonetheless not ready to go so far either, and he assured Jefferson that he aspired only to the vice-presidency. Another Washington report had the Pennsylvania Republicans raising an armed band of 1500 to murder any substitute executive—but, in fact, McKean was planning to call the militia only if a failure to name Jefferson brought civil disturbances. Somehow the nation was to survive the rumors as well as the genuine strains of the deadlock.

What most Federalists actually agreed on was to support Burr in order to produce a painfully prolonged standoff. Some thought the prospect of no election would induce frightened Republicans to vote for Burr, whom the Federalists would then control as the Republican party broke up. Deadlock also fitted the strategy Hamilton proposed, which was to secure commitments from Jefferson, and only then to make him president. Some years later, Jefferson remembered calling on Adams and the exchange that ensued, hotly on Adams's side: "Sir, the event of the election is within your own power. You have only to say you will do justice to the public creditors, maintain the navy, and not disturb those holding offices, and the government will instantly be put into your hands." To this, Jefferson recalled replying: "I will not come into the government by capitulation. I will not enter on it, but in perfect freedom to follow the dictates of my own judgment."

To Adams's list Hamilton would have added the rest of his fiscal system and the army, but Gallatin was convinced at the time that Jefferson had "prove[d] decisively that he made no concessions whatever." He had been given election on what amounted to a platform, and he was determined to honor the popular choice.

Everywhere party heads were apprehensive and watchful. Maintaining close intelligence in the House, Gallatin totted up tallies of the probable vote, warned Republican congressmen who were approached by Federalists with Burr-bait against bargains that might shatter "our party," worked through Samuel Smith of Maryland to sound Burr himself, and warned the New Yorker against hoping for any trade on the presidency. In Virginia's capital, Monroe proposed "a chain of expresses" to travel between Washington and Richmond day and night. Meanwhile, Gallatin kept regularly in touch with McKean, Beckley, and Dallas in Pennsylvania, and with Monroe and others elsewhere.

The voting in the House began early in February and continued until February 17, through thirty-five inconclusive roll calls in all. Throughout, the tallies showed every New England state for Burr except Vermont, whose two representatives cancelled one another out; all of the Middle Atlantic states for Jefferson except Delaware (for Burr) and Maryland (evenly divided); and all of the Southern or Southwestern states for Jefferson except South Carolina, whose holdover delegation was Federalist (all for Burr). Over all, Jefferson had only eight states to six for Burr, with the evenly divided votes of Vermont and Maryland not counted. Tension ran high: Nicholson of Maryland (Republican) was brought to the House on his sickbed through a snowstorm to keep his state's tally from going to Burr, and Craik of Maryland (Federalist) was warned by his wife that she would divorce him if he voted for Jefferson. In a last maneuver the Federalist bulk also held firm and so denied Jefferson the essential total of nine states.

Finally the break came. The sole member from little Delaware, James A. Bayard, thought he finally had assurances from Samuel Smith that Jefferson would accede to Hamilton's conditions, and announced his intention to switch—"You can well imagine," he wrote to Hamilton, "the clamor and vehement invective to which I was subjected." Actually, after several desperate Federalist caucuses, a complicated scheme was worked out whereby Bayard and the Federalist representatives from South Carolina, Vermont, and Maryland refrained from voting, thereby allowing Republican votes in the latter two states to add them to the eight Jefferson had held throughout. Thus, on February 17, Jefferson carried ten states to four for Burr, with Delaware and South Carolina now blank. The long agony was ended, and yet no Federalist had to sully his party conscience by casting a ballot for the Republican chief. Within a half-month, Jefferson would be president.

In the final ratification of the popular choice, the new nation had demonstrated its growing political stability. It had for years been making its way to full acceptance of rational or legal patterns of authority in a modernized polity. In the beginning, however, it had depended for legitimacy also on the fatherly charisma of Washington, who in 1801, if he was not like the dying emperors of Rome "about to become a god," was at least revered as the patron saint of the republic. The emerging national censensus had also at the outset been strained by deep suspicion of opposition, and later by the alien and sedition fury. Yet Washington himself had supported the rules of republican conduct, insisting in his Farewell Address that "time and habit" were "necessary to fix the true character of government," and refusing to let his prestige become a passport to perpetual power; and the fear of opposition which had prompted the "Spirit of 'Ninety-eight" had begun to recede. By 1801, the nation was moving away even from its partial dependence on Washington, and toward full acceptance of the rational legitimacy of the

Constitution, and of elections, decision by majority rule, and the counting of votes. The Federalists tried maneuver and bluff against Jefferson's succession to office (even these within the rules), but in the end they abided by the result and simply surrendered power to their opponents. Angered as they were at the outcome, they made no attempt at military resistance and threw up no further obstructions.

It was the first such grand, democratic, peaceful transfer of power in modern politics. It was an example of a procedure which many old as well as many new nations have yet to experience, which many defeated factions or parties have found it difficult or intolerable to accept, but one which 1801 did much to "fix" on the American scene.

Dejected and ill, as was his party, Adams rushed through a series of last-hour appointments. To maintain what partisan influence he could in the judiciary, which Federalist legislation had just enlarged, he signed commissions desperately into the hours of darkness of his last day in office—until midnight, according to legend, but only until nine o'clock, as Jefferson heard it. Early next morning Adams left for New England and home, not staying for the inauguration of his old Revolutionary friend as president. As he rode away from the unkempt capital village, the era of supremacy for the Federalist party vanished with him.

9

The Trials
of Responsibility

It was the policy of Jefferson, John Marshall noted, "to embody himself with the House." As Chief Justice of the United States, a position to which Adams had named him, Marshall was in a position to know. Yet he might have added that it was Jefferson's policy also to embody his purposes in his Administration, the Senate, his party, and the nation. The new President believed that it was up to him to hold Republicans responsible to the mandate of 1800, and that the most efficient means lay in presidential leadership and party action.

His approach was tactful but firm, as though he was the amiable *paterfamilias* of a united clan. In the cabinet, led by such proven scions of the party as Madison at State and Gallatin at the Treasury, Jefferson left departmental matters to the secretaries, who consulted periodically with him, but major matters were discussed among all and generally put to a vote. Thus differences were brought to harmony by "conversing and reasoning," while at the same time Jefferson was always aware that "the power of decision in the President left no object for internal dissension." Bridging the gap between presidency and Congress, Jefferson in addition assumed active leadership in legislative affairs. Here Madison remained generally aloof, and the President worked particularly through Gallatin, whose Washington house was often the scene of informal conferences or even caucuses of Republican leaders or members in Congress. The President himself also maintained informal ties with important figures in the extended Republican family in the legislative halls.

The chief means toward cohesion in Congress were the caucus, the speakership, the committees, and floor leaders. The caucus was regularly employed from 1801 on. Differences were ironed out, the party position on specific measures was shaped in detail, discipline was established—generally at the behest of or in accord with the party's executive leadership. Meanwhile the veteran Republican from North Carolina, Nathaniel Macon, presided as speaker of the House. In consultation with other party leaders, with the caucus, or sometimes with Jefferson himself, Macon appointed staunch Jeffersonians as chairmen of the standing committees which were coming increasingly into use. Thus the young Republican from Virginia, John Randolph, headed the Committee on Ways and Means which handled crucial financial bills; and at the peak of his career as a Jeffersonian leader he was chairman of so many committees that he could scarcely attend all the meetings. The old comrades of Marache's boarding house were later to lapse from the partisan standard, but caucus and committee control remained.

Such formal or semi-formal party connections in the capital were strengthened by informal leadership. Men like Giles and Wilson Cary Nicholas, the latter for a time in the Senate, and Caesar A. Rodney of Delaware after his later election to the House and before he became Attorney General, acted as Republican floor leaders and were generally regarded as Jefferson's personal representatives. The President conferred with them regularly, and they often met with Macon, Joseph Nicholson of Maryland, Randolph, Baldwin of Georgia in the Senate, and others to enjoy Gallatin's genial hospitality and to plan party action. To such men, Jefferson or Gallatin gave outlines of legislation and sometimes detailed drafts. The great function of the floor leaders, however, was to see that party and caucus positions triumphed by making sure that all Republicans "voted as was right." In addition, the very limits of Washington living helped to strengthen political ties. The new Capitol and the Executive Mansion were as yet only partly finished, as was the village itself. Most congressmen were thrown together in a few boarding houses, without access to other society or to entertainments, although a few did drink or gamble; "but the majority drink naught but politics," Gallatin noted, "and by not mixing with men of different sentiments, they influence one another." Thus close personal contact brought additional ties of party unity.

The Jeffersonian endeavor was a remarkable exercise of party management in government and of party connections between executive and legislative branches. It was reminiscent of Hamilton's early leadership, but it was even more thorough in its conduct and effect. The long process of devising new pieces of party machinery, of learning and inventing in the face of necessity, had taken another step forward. Indeed, few successors to Jefferson in the presidency were to prove as apt and determined as he did in party leadership and legislative influence, as successful in party government. Years later, remembering his own early contributions, even the acidulous Randolph recalled this period as a Saturnian age of harmonious Republican ascendancy.

2.

Cohesive action was, nonetheless, only the means to the full measure of Republican party performance. The President and his cohorts believed that the election in 1800 had marked a choice on program as well as personnel, for certain measures as well as certain men; and the question now was keeping faith with the tacit or explicit commitments of ideology and policy they had made. The problem is a perennial one, which has by no means always been answered satisfactorily in American experience. If the crux of democracy in a complex, extended polity is popular choice between parties in elections, such choice is fully meaningful only if the party the voters select is able to put at least the heart of its proclaimed program into effect in government. Here was the basic test of responsibility for the Republicans in power.

Their approach to the problem was foreshadowed in Jefferson's Inaugural Address of March 1801. It was conciliatory and designed to reinforce the fabric of consensus which had been strained by excited contests. It was also designed to assure the moderates whom the Federalists had alienated of Jefferson's own "moderate conduct," as he himself put it, and thereby fix them to the Republican standard—hence his famous declaration, "We are all Republicans, we are all Federalists." At the same time the President made it clear that the Republican party was to govern: the minority had rights which must be respected, but "the will of the majority is in all cases to prevail." He set forth his cardinal political principles: equal justice; peace with all nations, and no entangling alliances; support of state rights; economy in government, and reduction of the national debt; cutbacks in the army and navy; encouragement of agriculture; and protection of individual freedoms. In short, Jefferson remained determined to keep the new American government "essentially republican." His Inaugural program was a virtual replica of his "platform"-letter to Gerry in 1799.

Measure after measure followed in the Republican Congresses of 1801-1802 and after, most of them aimed at a cautious rolling-back or modification of Federalist innovations. They began with a push for stringent economy, underwritten by Gallatin's plan for specific legislative appropriations for government expenditures, and by scrupulous accounting for funds. "Frugality" was a "republican" virtue in itself, and could also serve the next item in Jefferson's program. This was a strenuous and determined effort to pay off the public debt, which Hamilton had seen as a "public blessing" and a major force for hothouse capitalist growth, and which Republicans saw as a public burden in the interests of a few, with its cost falling unduly on agriculture. Net came the repeal of all of the Federalist internal taxes of 1798, which had also jibed with Hamilton's conception of the use of the taxing power as part of his promotional scheme. Finally, large reductions were effected in the army and navy, not only to avoid the threat of military despotism by a "handful of ragamuffins" (as Randolph put it), but also for the sake of economy. In the area of personal liberties, the Republicans sought to eliminate the "despotic" legislation of 1798—as Jefferson called it in his Inaugural Address—by permitting the limited term of the Alien and Sedition Acts to run out without enforcing these; by repealing the naturalization law and replacing it with its more liberal earlier version; and by executive pardons and Congressional remission of fines for victims of the sedition statute. They repealed the Judiciary Act of 1801, which had enlarged the court system and opened the way for Adams's late appointments, and which Republicans saw (with some justice) as adding new tentacles of "controul" by prejudiced Federalist judges over "life and property," and over the power of the states. The Federalist statute was replaced by a new judiciary law. The Republicans also sought to eliminate bias by Federalist judges, by impeaching such examples as the wildly intemperate John Pickering on the Federal court in New Hampshire and the vitriolic Samuel Chase on the Supreme Court—who in a four-hour tirade before a grand jury had charged that the Republicans would bring on "a mobocracy, the worst of all possible governments." Although Pickering was removed, the lack of a tenable legal case against Chase led to his acquittal in the Senate. In consequence, however, other Federalist judges moderated their behavior.

An innovation came with a policy to encourage agriculture and western settlement by reducing the prices of the public lands in the Northwest Territory, halving the minimum number of acres required for purchase, and extending credit to settlers. By 1803 population increases in the old "Western Reserve" area had made possible the admission of the new state of Ohio, and Republican land policy was to provide a further spur to settlement.

Such measures hardly constituted the millennium Dr. Ames had envisioned in his Dedham study, but in terms of the actual concerns and issues of the day they added up to a substantial list of accomplishment.

One part of Hamilton's handiwork, the Bank of the United States, was a source of deep trial and long discussion for Jefferson and Gallatin. To the President the bank's monopoly was "certainly an evil," which had supplanted "the precious metals by a paper circulation." With its local branches "it multiplied an influence" which could be used against the government or against democratic processes, and it was, Jefferson argued, essential to subordinate this potential "powerful enemy"—"no government [is] safe which is under the vassalage of any self-constituted authorities." To the business-like Secretary of the Treasury the national bank was a secure depository for government funds and a convenience to government fiscal operations, and Gallatin in any case did not fully share his chief's agrarian distaste for Hamilton's capitalist innovation. In addition, certain mercantile or other business elements who were more and more filtering into the Republican ranks were sympathetic to the bank, although other elements opposed it as a competitor of local enterprises.

Perhaps most important, Jefferson felt that his hands were tied. The bank's original legal charter ran for twenty years, to 1811. Presumably it could not legally be cancelled out of existence, any more than Hamilton's original funding and assumption of the debt could be struck down at a blow. In the course of the ordeal a frustrated Jefferson confided in his friend Pierre du Pont de Nemours, a French Physiocratic philosopher who had recently moved to America where his son was to found a dynasty. The Republicans could pay off Hamilton's debt in fifteen years, the President declared, "but we can never get rid of his financial system. It mortifies me to be strengthening principles which I deem radically vicious, but this vice is entailed on us by the first error." Every effort would be made "by degrees to introduce sound principles and make them habitual," but, meanwhile, "what is practicable must often controul what is pure theory." As an alternative means to handle the government's fiscal affairs and limit the scope of the bank's power Jefferson projected an independent treasury system in which the government would hold its own funds. This proposal failed to impress Gallatin, however, and the bank remained.

Out of the travail a policy finally emerged. Careful not to push his steadfast, invaluable Secretary of the Treasury too far, Jefferson accepted continuation with certain modifications. Government funds would be deposited in other banks as well to reduce the "monopoly" bank's power and stimulate competition; the national bank was pressed by Gallatin to establish branches at Washington and other points for the convenience of the government; and the removal of the government from Philadelphia helped to reduce the number of congressmen on the bank's directorate. Furthermore, Jefferson agreed with Gallatin that "it is material to the safety of Republicanism to detach the mercantile interests from its enemies," and Gallatin's bank policies assisted in the detaching.

The only dramatic Republican achievement came with a windfall, but one whose fruits the Administration quickly seized. Political realignments in Europe had brought a transfer from Spain to France of the huge American area between the Mississippi river and the Rocky Mountains, known as Louisiana. Fearing that Napoleon, who now ruled France as First Consul, might close the port of New Orleans to Western trade at the mouth of the Mississippi and turn Louisiana into an imperial threat to the United States, Jefferson instructed Robert R. Livingston in Paris to negotiate for an American base on the lower Mississippi and later sent James Monroe to join him. Then, suddenly, word came that Napoleon would sell all of Louisiana for $15,000,000. It was a large sum, a sixth of the total national debt; the Constitution provided no explicit authority to purchase territory from a foreign nation; and Federalists condemned the whole idea when they heard of it. In short, the opportunity posed a series of difficult questions. At first Jefferson suggested a constitutional amendment to provide the necessary power and worried about the money, but he went ahead boldly when he learned that delay might lead Napoleon to withdraw the offer. In the Fall of 1803, with all party resources mustered, the Senate approved a treaty of purchase by a vote of 24 to 7, and the House provided the funds by an overwhelming majority of 90 to 25 and added enabling acts. The purchase votes reflected solid Republican gains in the enlarged House elected in 1802—"the federalists spoke & voted against it," Jefferson wrote Livingston in Paris, "but they are now so reduced in their numbers as to be nothing." The territory of the United States had been doubled, and broad fertile reaches had been opened to settlement. Meanwhile, with true Republican care, Gallatin managed to service the purchase bonds without raising taxes. Despite acquisition of the vast new territory, the Republicans went on chipping away at Hamilton's debt and by 1811 had cut it in half.

The picture of Jefferson in office has been painted as an irony, in terms of a contrast between the utopian hopes of the Republicans as an opposition party and the harsh realities of power. In fact the exigencies of power generally impose some limits on the fulfillment of promises, but any portrayal of the Jeffersonian tenure as ironical must rest on certain expectations or assume certain standards of measurement, which have often remained largely unexamined.

The Republicans in office were conciliatory and moderate, and effected no sweeping constructive measures short of the Louisiana windfall. It is easy to seize on these facts and conclude that the Republicans thereby betrayed the popular faith or somehow failed. Yet, in fact, Jefferson and his party had never promised social revolution or intransigent policies, and it is an overdramatization to characterize them in their years of opposition as though they were virtually an American branch of world-revolutionary Jacobinism, committed to basic social reconstruction. Moreover, to call any administration a failure that does not put positive social legislation onto the books is to apply standards of later times which were quite foreign to Jefferson and his colleagues. The Republicans in opposition had not proposed any sweeping system of positive legislation even of the sort that Hamilton engineered, much less any commitment to positive government of the sort that later twentieth-century reform movements were to produce. They had from the beginning believed that a frugal, limited government, which would intervene little in the economy or daily life, was the best protection for a predominantly agrarian *status quo*, republican simplicity, and individual freedom. Fidelity and responsibility to their actual purposes and program called for little more than negative action to eliminate or modify certain aspects of the "energetic," positive-government Federalist system. In this, they were largely successful.

More cogently, it has been argued that the irony of the Jeffersonians in power was in a failure to hold to certain specifics in their earlier position. Thus, the argument runs, Jefferson and the Republicans had stood for a strict construction of the Constitution and against Hamilton's latitudinarian interpretation of its grants of power; for legislative preponderance and against a broad scope for executive influence or action; for an agrarian Arcadia and therefore, presumably, against the claims of commerce or national expansion; for economy and the reduction of the debt and against large expenditures; or even for action by government only on the basis of public mandates and against policy initiative in government itself. Yet, this version of the Republican irony runs, the actions of Jefferson and his party in power were inconsistent with all of these commitments, particularly on the fresh issue of the Louisiana Purchase.

Once again, the premises of the argument are overstated. The Republicans did strain their constitutional and fiscal scruples in the Louisiana opportunity, and did act without a mandate. Even Hamilton, however, had remarked that Jefferson did not in fact believe in a weak presidency or necessarily in a restricted use of executive authority; a Republican Congress voted overwhelmingly for the treaty and the appropriations and, despite the purchase, the Republicans continued to reduce the debt; and there was hardly time to secure a mandate even though Jefferson at first hoped for an authorizing amendment. The acquisition did serve the interests of commerce among others, as did the Administration's vigorous action against depredations on American shipping by pirates off the Barbary coast of North Africa, and Louisiana did expand the nation to virtually twice its original size, as Jefferson's later proposal to acquire West Florida would have expanded it also. Yet Jefferson and the bulk of Republicans had not in fact opposed commerce as such, but only its domination of agriculture or excessive power for commercial interests in government. Similarly, Jefferson and most of his colleagues had from the outset been nationalists, at least in the sense of envisioning a broad America and in their patriotic concern. Furthermore, even the Louisiana Purchase was consistent with the most basic of the Jeffersonian commitments: their popular-agrarian perspective and its national fulfillment. On other issues where the Republicans did have a mandate, their measures were remarkably faithful to it, although some discrepancy was introduced by the trends and conditions Republicans inherited, or from the devices Jefferson had found "entailed on us," such as the national bank. Taken over-all, however, the Republicans' first years in power revealed a remarkable fruition of party responsibility. The true irony was to come later.

Meanwhile, the Republicans as a party could approach the elections of 1804 with popular confidence in their moderate course and with winning issues—notably the tax and debt reductions, the cutbacks in the army and the navy and the savings they effected, and the acquisition of Louisiana.

3.

Looking from the capital to the country, Jefferson sought to use patronage to solidify his party and at the same time assure efficient government. It was a trying business, as the cry for office went up from men as diverse as the Clintons in New York, the energetic Giles in Virginia, Duane and Leib in Pennsylvania, and Samuel Smith in Maryland. Although Jefferson knew that the rewards of office could divide, he also knew that they could provide essential cement for his party, and he labored accordingly.

In his initial cabinet appointments, three New Englanders got posts in an effort to strengthen the Republican position in their section: Levi Lincoln of Massachusetts (Attorney General), Henry Dearborn of the District of Maine (Secretary of War), and Gideon Granger of Connecticut (Postmaster General). The Navy portfolio went to Samuel Smith's brother Robert Smith, a prosperous, ambitious admiralty lawyer of moderate abilities, who was not Jefferson's first choice. The faithful Beckley was re-elected as Clerk of the House and also named director of the newly established Library of Congress, but he no longer took active leadership in politics.

For lesser posts, Jefferson evolved a cautious but effective policy. He scrutinized prospective appointees carefully to ensure able personnel: "The merit as well as reputation of an administration depends as much on that as on its measures." For marshal in western Virginia, for example, he sought a man "most respectable & unexceptionable," as well as "especially . . . republican." Yet party counted also: when Freneau in New Jersey proposed a nominee, Jefferson wondered that the poet-editor said nothing of the man's politics. Still, although the government offices were filled with Federalists, Jefferson would dismiss only for "malversation," or for "open, active and virulent abuse of official influence in opposition." He was, however, determined to eliminate Adams's last-ditch partisan appointees except for those named to life posts. The whole process was extremely painful, and Jefferson commented on the lack of vacancies during his early months in office: "Those by death are few; by resignation, none." Yet Jefferson himself sometimes retained or appointed strategically placed Federalists in order to win over Federalist waverers, and at least in North Carolina this policy was influential in consolidating Republican power. On the whole, office was expected to serve partisan welfare, but it was not thrown open in an unlimited spoils game.

Nonetheless, Madison remarked that removals and appointments were a trial to the executive branch, and he himself experienced a comic embarrassment. An office seeker asked him first for a territorial governorship, then for a collectorship, then for a post office job. When Madison refused all on the grounds that the applicant was unfit, the petitioner fell back to a final plea: did the Secretary of State have any old clothes he could spare?

Currents of politics and patronage brought dramatic developments in New York. Denied all but the barest recognition by the Administration, Burr decided to reinstate himself by running for governor in 1804. At the same time, Timothy Pickering and a few other Essex Junto extremists, sure that the Louisiana Purchase implied endless Republican rule, began to hatch a scheme for the secession of New England from the Union. Knowing that Burr would need Federalist support against the Clinton forces in New York, the Pickering plotters approached Burr to bring his state into their new Northern Confederacy in return for election aid, and thought that they had at least his tacit agreement. During the New York campaign Hamilton, who had rebuffed the Essex Junto plan, was reported to have said that Burr was "a dangerous man, and one who ought not to be trusted with the reins of government." The upshot was that Burr challenged Hamilton to a duel; and in July 1804, on the dreary New Jersey flats across from Manhattan, Burr fatally wounded his old antagonist. At the time Hamilton had been devising plans to revive the Federalist party by an elaborate pattern of national, state, and local organization, and a later observer commented that "Burr's pistol blew the brains out of the Federal party." The duel certainly contributed to a final disastrous defeat for Burr in New York. Before long he was involved in a shadowy, allegedly secessionist conspiracy in the West which brought an action for treason at Jefferson's hands. Acquitted under Chief Justice Marshall's strict interpretation of the law, Burr lived out the final thirty years of his long life in clouded obscurity. Meanwhile, the scheme for a Northern Confederacy had collapsed utterly.

Developments in Pennsylvania were also threatening although less dramatic. Both Gallatin at the Treasury and McKean at the statehouse practically ignored Duane's demands for patronage and favored the Dallas group in the state. Thereupon Duane in the *Aurora* ticked off clerks in the Treasury and the statehouse as "Picaroon," "Nothingarian," and "Nincompoop," and soon made an ally of Leib, whose following among Philadelphia workingmen lent strength. Truce talks at Gallatin's Washington home foundered, Gallatin failed in a later attempt to break the alliance between Duane and Leib, and even Jefferson's efforts to mollify Duane were of little effect.

Meanwhile, Republicans were slowly filling the federal offices. There had been only six Republicans on the rolls at the end of Adams's term, and Jefferson thought these were "chiefly half-breeds." Of some 316 posts subject to presidential appointment excluding judicial and military positions, Jefferson calculated, he had removed only 15 by the summer of 1803; but by that time only 130 places were still held by Federalists and the rest had gone to Republicans—a net total, apparently, of 186. Numerous lesser appointments made by other officials also went presumably, to Republican "stalwarts."

As elections approached, Jefferson as party leader turned his eyes to general politics. In Delaware, for example, dissension was stirring even as Republican hopes rose, and early in 1802 Jefferson urged Caesar A. Rodney to stand for Congress as "the only person who can unite the greatest portion of the republican votes"—a hope Rodney was to fulfill, although not until two years later. Again, in the spring of 1804, the President helped Thomas Ritchie to establish his *Enquirer* in Richmond, Virginia, to counterbalance the Federalist press there. Thus Jefferson watched development in state after state and gave aid where he could.

The elections of 1804 were little more than an approving referendum on the course the Republicans had taken. General support for their policies, the payoff in their program for agricultural and other groups, the appeal of Jefferson himself, party organization and the influence of patronage, and the disarray of the Federalist party all gave the Republicans a position of strength. An amendment to the Constitution had provided for separate electoral ballots for president and vice-president. A formal Republican caucus nominated Jefferson for president and George Clinton of New York for vice-president, while a conference of Federalist notables put up C. C. Pinckney for president and named Rufus King of New York as his running mate. The electoral tally was 162 for Jefferson and

Figure 10

FEDERALIST-REPUBLICAN RIVALRY, TRANSFER OF POWER,
FEDERALIST DECLINE
(Presidential Election Results and Seats in Congress, 1792–1818)

	Presidential Electors		Members, House		Members, Senate	
	Fed	Rep	Fed	Rep	Fed	Rep
1792	77[a]	55[a]	54[b]	52[b]	17	13
1794			48	57[b]	19	13
1796	71	68	58	48	20	12
1798			63	43	19	13
1800	65	73	41	65	14	18
1802			39	102	9	25
1804	14	162	25	116	7	27
1806			24	118	6	28
1808	47	122	48	94	6	28
1810			36	108	6	30
1812	[c]	128	68	112	9	27
1814			65	117	11	25
1816	34	183	42	141	10	32
1818			27[d]	156	7[d]	35

Italic numerals indicate victorious or majority party. Discrepancies between presidential and congressional columns are due to scattering of votes in some presidential contests, seats in Congress given to states between regular elections, or vacancies in Congressional seats.

[a] Electoral vote for vice-president; with votes for George Clinton (50), Jefferson (not a candidate, 4) and Burr (1) as "Republican."

[b] Because party connections were loose and uncertain before 1793 or 1795, designations for 1792 might better be listed as "Administration" and "Opposition," and the "Republican" designation for 1794 as "Opposition."

[c] Fusion of De Witt Clinton Republican faction and Federalists: 89.

[d] From local remnants of national party, nominally Federalists.

Adapted from Bureau of the Census, *Historical Statistics of the United States, Colonial Times to 1957* (Washington, 1960), with corrections from later data, where available.

Clinton compared to a mere 14 for Pinckney and King, and the Republicans again increased their preponderance in the Senate and the House. The triumph of the party appeared to be complete. Although the Federalists were to experience brief stirrings of revival in later years, the trend toward their eventual extinction was apparent.

4.

Renewed power brought new trials of responsibility, however, and soon also brought Jefferson to the irony of his tenure. Although he rated Jefferson's first Administration as "brilliant," Monroe voiced a common reaction when he argued that the second Administration had floundered badly. There was perhaps some envious exaggeration in the comment, but the second term never enjoyed the harmonious fulfillment of the first.

Early signs of trial came with dissension at the head of the national party. Its origins lay as much in personalities and ruffled egos as in issues, but the precipitating event was controversy over the so-called Yazoo lands. In the 1790's the Georgia legislature, under questionable circumstances, had arranged to sell large tracts of the state's western land holdings to four land companies. Cries of fraud had gone up and a later legislature rescinded the sale, but meanwhile the companies had sold off parcels to individuals who bought the land in good faith. When Georgia ceded its western lands to the national government, the whole mess was put up to a special commission composed of Madison, Gallatin, and Lincoln, who recommended a settlement in 1804.which gave partial recognition to the claims of individual purchasers. The purist-Republican Randolph, who had had his doubts about the Louisiana Purchase too, promptly turned all of his waspish invective on the "Yazoo conspirators," attacking Madison in particular, although Randolph's erstwhile friend Gallatin was chiefly responsible for the commission's proposed solution. Anyone who did not wholly reject all Yazoo claims, Randolph insisted, was party to the "fraud." Appalled at this sudden turn, Gallatin appealed to a mutual friend: "For God's sake, try and find what is the matter with him." The matter was Randolph's purist-Republican conscience and the erratic, stubborn

183

strain in his character, and it was beyond curing. He was soon pouring out his bitterness to Macon, Nicholson, and others.

Other issues complicated the situation. When Jefferson requested funds for an abortive plan to acquire West Florida from Spain in 1806, Randolph cried out again. He would not be mollified, despite Gallatin's efforts in private conversations and in a personal plea to Randolph before his Ways and Means Committee met to consider the matter. Soon Randolph had broken with Gallatin as well as with Madison, and was looking to Monroe as a presidential candidate for 1808 to block Madison's probable succession to Jefferson. He began to think that the Administration was showing too much attention to Northern, mercantile, and industrial interests, and talked of "more union and decision among real friends of freedom"—limited, presumably, to strait-laced Virginia agrarians. Also in 1806, as the Napoleonic wars resumed and Great Britain launched new depredations of American shipping, Randolph opposed a retaliatory Administration measure which had been introduced by his friend Nicholson to restrict British imports. The same year he published a pamphlet under the pseudonym "Decius," attacking several members of Congress and their presidential "idol," Jefferson, who saw the pamphlet as a declaration of "perpetual opposition." On the floor of the House Randolph gave the veil of philosophy to a threat. "Ours is not a government of confidence," he cried, "it is a government of diffidence and suspicion, and it is only by being suspicious that it can remain a free government."

The first national intraparty faction in the Republican body was at hand, and it was soon known as the "Tertium Quids" or simply Quids. Its foundation lay in Virginia, but it also won some support elsewhere and for a time could count Nathaniel Macon in its number, as well as such men as John Taylor and Littleton Tazewell of Virginia. The adherence of the eminent Macon added temporary strength, but his allegiances were divided. The Quids remained a small band throughout, scarcely more than a clique. They were a threat because of the influential positions many of them held and their noisy volubility—"all tongue," Jefferson called them at one juncture.

Coolly and with determination, Jefferson moved to isolate the fever of faction before it spread. He labored to win Macon back from Randolph, proclaiming his continued confidence, proposing a long evening of talk when he would be free from interruptions, hoping to assuage Macon's own purist-Republican conscience, holding out the lure of an appointment as Postmaster General. He sought to seal off Monroe by reminding him that the main body of his friends were "among the firmest adherents to the administration," men who would have no converse with Randolph—"you must not commit yourself to him." When Macon nonetheless continued his Quid course, he was given the speakership again by a margin of only three votes in 1805, and Jefferson carefully worked around both Macon and Randolph on his Florida proposal in 1806. The next phase of the treatment was a resolution to deprive the speaker of the power to name committees; and, although it was not passed, Macon felt constrained to replace Randolph on Ways and Means with Joseph Clay of Pennsylvania—not without sleepless nights over what he now called "the disagreeable seat of Speaker." Yet Clay also soon revealed an opposition complexion despite Jefferson's early hopes, and in 1807 the Administration forces finally took the speakership from Macon and gave it to Joseph Varnum of Massachusetts, who promptly appointed a party man as chairman of Ways and Means. Through Jefferson's careful physic and under party pressure, Randolph had been cut off and factionalism had been isolated. Soon Macon, who had absented himself for a month at the beginning of the session in 1807, rejoined the main body of Republicans.

Throughout the factional ague, Jefferson had remained sanguine. Vote after vote in the House saw the Republican bulk overwhelm the Quids by ten to one or better, thereby demonstrating, Jefferson thought, "which side retains its orthodoxy." Yet Jefferson recognized that the new Congress in 1807 would lack figures of "talents & standing," to replace the lost leaders Macon and Randolph. In this situation he urged Wilson Cary Nicholas to run for the House in the late Virginia elections, in order to provide a "rallying point." Nicholas did so, and undertook the service Jefferson pressed on him.

185

Factional divisions also opened in some of the states, most notably in Pennsylvania. The old contention between Duane-Leib and McKean-Dallas groups had run to what Jefferson called "bloody schism" as the decline of the Federalists removed the threat of opposition. Intraparty quarrels broke out mainly around state issues, but even so the Duane-Leib "radicals" followed Randolph's lead for a time at least, and Gallatin remained identified with the McKean-Dallas "conservative" group. Regretfully, Jefferson noted the break between what he called "High Flyers" and "Moderates," and predicted similar schisms elsewhere, "as soon as the Republicans shall be so strong as to fear no other enemy." Divisions and animosities indeed appeared in some other states, and Jefferson remarked that "such a spirit of intolerance" among members of the same party was "a poor presage of future tranquility." Although for the moment factionalism was kept in bounds, his successors were to feel its full force.

On the national scene, meanwhile, issues of foreign policy brought Jefferson and his party to their most agonizing trial of power. As the tempests of world politics had beat furiously about Adams in his four years as president, so they blew up again to harass Jefferson in his last years in office, as war was renewed in Europe and England resumed an aggressive policy. From early 1806 to the end of his tenure early in 1809, the President struggled to avoid war and win peace and at the same time to maintain American rights and prestige. Try as he would, however, it seemed impossible to devise a workable solution.

An early endeavor in diplomacy brought no results. After prolonged negotiations, James Monroe and William Pinkney of Maryland sent a treaty back from London in 1807 which violated their instructions from Jefferson and Madison and failed to resolve the issues of restrictions on American trade, ship seizures, and the impressment of American seamen onto British vessels. It was so weak that Jefferson decided not to send it to the Senate for ratification. Although Monroe thought the instructions too harsh and suspected Madison of a plan to damage his reputation, even Samuel Smith (now in the Senate) was soon convinced that the treaty would be rejected if it were submitted.

186

In the face of continued intransigence in London, Jefferson turned to economic sanctions. The Nicholson Act of 1806 banning importation from England of a long list of articles was enforced after a period of disuse, but it failed to budge the British. The President then pressed for a general ban on commerce with foreign nations, not just with Great Britain, and a general Embargo Act was passed in 1808 against bitter Federalist opposition in a vote which saw some Eastern Republicans break ranks. Yet the effect on Great Britain was negligible, as smuggling was undertaken both by sea and by land through Canada, and before long the Embargo was replaced by a less stringent Non-Intercourse Act. On the domestic scene meanwhile, the Embargo stirred violent resistance. Although it encouraged domestic industry, it seemed to men in the carrying trade to portend disaster. In the areas affected, newspapers, petitions, and cartoons protested against the "cursed Ograbme"— "embargo" in reverse spelling, pictured as an incubus on trade. Altogether sanctions had proved not much more successful than diplomacy had been.

For the first time since Jefferson took office, really strong pressures beat against the Republican party. The cautious Gallatin urged an alternative policy, in part because he thought the Embargo would lose New England and perhaps New York for the Republicans. A subdued Macon supported the measure even though it would hurt him as a tobacco grower, as he knew it would hurt exporting rice and cotton planters in the South and wheat growers in the central and western areas; and he feared imminent war—but Macon noted that he, "as much out of fashion as our grandmothers' ruffle cuffs," was not consulted by anyone about anything. In New England and New York, in the commercial reaches of Maryland, in parts of Virginia, and in the commercial-exporting areas of North Carolina, Federalists enjoyed a brief upsurge, and found that many mercantile-minded Republicans would join with them at least against the "Ograbme." As the election approached, anti-Embargo Republicans turned to Clinton, the universal cork of early American politics, as a possible presidential candidate.

In the face of world tempests and domestic squalls, Jefferson looked forward to final retirement to Monticello. He had foresworn more than two terms in office, and he could look back on the two he had served with substantial pride despite turmoil at the end. Throughout he had labored ably at the task of effective party leadership, and his first years in Washington had been attended by resounding successes. Even the later years had marked his continued attempts to deal with new problems which arose in accord with democratic party responsibility. His policies of diplomacy, neutrality tinged with wariness toward England, sanctions to maintain America's national position despite hardship to commerce as compared with self-sufficient agriculture, and continued efforts for peace, were all in accord with historic Republican perspectives. Sanctions might indeed have worked even against England's power. Diplomacy failing, they were in any case the only apparent course which was consistent with Republican aims.

In another sense, however, the trials of responsibility had ended ironically for the Republican *paterfamilias*: an administration begun in high hopes of harmony with all nations and of domestic tranquility was doomed to depart battered by foreign conflict and domestic discord. Yet the ultimate irony, war with England, was reserved for a later day.

5.

A party in which one man has long been both dominant and revered is likely to face problems in establishing a succession, and this was the case with the Republicans as Jefferson neared retirement. The issue was marked in 1808 by a hurly-burly of infighting within the party. When the dust had cleared, nonetheless, it had emerged victorious once again.

The heir-apparent was Madison, but not everyone was ready to accept him. Such leaders as Nicholas and Giles stepped forth as the informal managers of his candidacy, but Randolph and his remaining Quids still pressed for Monroe, who had a following in Virginia and elsewhere. Early in 1808, Jefferson also noted that his "old friend Clinton [was] estranging himself from me"—and "old" was descriptive, for the septuagenarian veteran was growing feeble and virtually incapable of presiding over the Senate, where an observer remarked that he often forgot or mistook the question, "not infrequently declares a vote before it is taken," and had "no mind—no intellect—no memory." Even so he was played up as a putative anti-Embargo candidate in New York, parts of Pennsylvania, and parts of Maryland. The situation was further complicated by the fact that both Monroe and Clinton had some early Federalist support. Even Randolph was ready to turn to Clinton in tacit fusion with Federalists, if it proved necessary in order to stop Madison.

When the national Republican caucus was called to order in January, Monroe and Clinton supporters carefully absented themselves. The caucus nominated Madison by 83 votes out of 89, and sought to "balance" the ticket by naming the wavering, doddering Clinton for vice-president again. The caucus also adopted a motion by Nicholas for a national campaign committee of correspondence to consist of one member from each state. Promptly Randolph sought to unify the enemies of Madison by a protesting "Address to the People," signed by sixteen caucus absentees including members of the Duane-Leib faction in Pennsylvania and several New Yorkers. Individually, Clinton also condemned the "illtimed and corruptly managed" caucus, and objections came from Samuel Smith of Maryland. Soon, however, an uncertain Duane dropped his early equivocal support for Clinton and came out for Madison, and Clinton decided not to withdraw his name for the vice-presidential nomination.

A turn in Federalist strategy further buttressed the Republican alignment for Madison. Hope for Monroe's dissident candidacy had depended on the likelihood that the Federalists generally would prefer him to Madison. In the late fall, however, the Federalists decided to put in their own candidates instead, and a last-minute secret conference of Federalist leaders representing eight states met in New York to nominate C. C. Pinckney and Rufus King again. In the face of revived interparty rivalry, the Republicans moved to at least quasi-unity behind Madison.

The result was a clear victory, another step on the party's path to dominance. The Republicans carried twelve of the seventeen states, and Madison had 122 electoral votes to Pinckney's 47, while New York gave six presidential votes to Clinton, who was also elected vice-president over King. In comparison with 1804, Madison had

189

lost 40 electoral votes, and the Federalists had regained all of New England except Vermont. Outside of New England, however, Pinckney and King carried only Delaware and a minority splintering of five votes from Maryland and North Carolina. The anti-Embargo resurgence of the Federalists was also reflected in the Congressional results, which marked a Republican loss of 24 seats in the House. Still, the Republicans would have a majority of 94 against the Federalists' 48. The ultimate strength for Monroe was perhaps best revealed in Virginia, where a popular election of electors returned a Madison ticket over a Monroe ticket by a four-to-one margin.

The Republicans had been returned to power and Jefferson could retire to the peace of Monticello. Peace, however, was hardly to be the lot of his successor.

Epilogue

Disintegration
and Re-establishment

The Federalists under Hamilton had marked the trail to party development, and the Republicans under Madison and Jefferson had followed it, hacking out on their own additional paths toward a popular party. In their rivalry the parties had cut the clearings for a two-party system, and had substantially completed the work within a quarter-century of the time the new American nation had declared its independence.

Yet the original American party system was not to endure. The Federalists, unable to make headway with an agrarian-democratic electorate and torn by factional dissension, fell away after the year of Jefferson's triumph. Before long the Republicans were also entangled in thickets of factionalism, and within a decade of Jefferson's retirement they had all but disappeared. New men were faced with the task of cutting paths for new parties, although they were able to benefit from the work of their predecessors.

While failure may bring failure in party interaction, as it had for the Federalists, success does not always bring success. The very triumph of the Republicans, their position as a dominant party, the fact that their dominance drew around them an increasingly broad combination of interests and segments of opinion, the variety of leaders they attracted—all contributed to the outbreak within the party of what Madison years before had called "the violence of faction." In the post-Jefferson era the rivalries of politics—rivalry for power and between personalities, rivalry of interests trying to win recognition for their demands in public policy, rivalry for office and patronage—occurred more and more within the Republican party, rather than between Republicans and Federalists. Thus intraparty struggle and contention came to replace interparty competition on the high road of political conflict. As the old two-party system gave way, the successful Republicans were beset by difficulties of a sort which often threaten a single supreme party.

The ironic consequence was that the party Madison had helped to found was to be torn apart on the harsh thorns of faction, and it was Madison's role to head the party as it neared its destruction.

2.

Intimations of trouble came as the President-elect planned his cabinet in 1809. Although the able and experienced Gallatin seemed the obvious choice for secretary of state, resistance to his appointment soon appeared. It began with a clique gathered around the influential Smith brothers of Maryland—Samuel, in the Senate, and Robert, Jefferson's former Secretary of the Navy—and their Virginia kinfolk including Wilson Cary Nicholas, together with other allies. The movement also drew support from some of the associates of George Clinton in New York and from many of the Pennsylvanians who had personal or patronage quarrels with Gallatin, including Duane and Leib, who was now in the national Senate. The Smith clique and the anti-Gallatin "Invisibles," as they came to be called, advanced Robert Smith for the State Department post. As a strong party- and presidential-leader, Jefferson had moved adroitly to contain or divert such factional forces. The question now was, what would Madison as the new party leader do?

Unfortunately for the Republican party's future, he capitulated. He appointed the mediocrity, Smith, and granted patronage to the Smith clique and the Invisibles, thereby offending the friends of Gallatin. Yet two years later, Madison was forced to remove Smith and replace him with Monroe, this time offending those he had previously gratified and confirming them in opposition. Soon insiders were commenting on the conflict between Madison's "Cabinet" group and the Invisibles as intraparty factions. Meanwhile, the faithful Gallatin remained at the Treasury.

The whole futile episode was symptomatic of Madison's address to such party problems. Always hoping for harmony, he proved re-luctant to fight, surprisingly inept in handling appointments and patronage to strengthen party cohesion, and often irresolute; once an able Congressional party leader, he seemed increasingly lost in the problems of party as he became more and more absorbed in the trying problems of state. Thus he lost the direction of affairs at the capital and even within his Administration itself. By 1811 Washington Irving was commenting, "Poor Jemmy! . . . [he is] a with-ered little apple-John." In the same year John Randolph com-mented more acidly, "He is President de jure only; who exercises the office de facto I do not know."

The harassments of clique maneuvering were soon followed by open, forest-fire factionalism. The Republican combination had been stretched again and again to encompass the variety of interests in the nation, and it had been further enlarged with the settlement of the New West beyond the Allegheny Mountains. From Kentucky and Tennessee, and from frontier areas of New York, South Caro-lina, and Georgia, came increasingly strident expansionist demands for American acquisition of Canada and Spanish Florida. Angered by new blows to American interests in British-instigated Indian raids on the frontiers and with one eye on recurring British depreda-tion of American commerce on the high seas, extreme nationalists from the West pressed for war against Great Britain. Meanwhile, partly in reaction to such forces, the Congressional elections of 1810 had swept 63 of the 142 members of the previous House of Representatives out of office, most of them Republicans. Many were replaced by Republicans of a new generation, who were expan-sive, untameable, and aggressive in their views and style, particu-larly when they came fresh from frontier districts. When Congress convened in 1811 these new members found their leader in the adroit, magnetic Henry Clay of Kentucky, gambler, political man-ager, and orator, whom they elected Speaker in his first term of office —an unprecedented tribute. Old "Invisibles" were thus replaced by "Young Republicans" in the forefront of faction. Such men as Peter B. Porter of western New York and the brilliant John C. Calhoun of the Piedmont area of South Carolina soon joined Clay as factional leaders.

No country bumpkins in politics, the Young Republicans moved promptly to consolidate their power in the House. They breathed new life into the Congressional caucus and generally controlled it. They also encouraged the development of standing committees, knowing that Clay as speaker would appoint their chairmen; and by 1814 the committee system had become the dominant force in the chamber. Thus effective power was exercised not by the President, as had been the case with Jefferson, but by factional Congressional leaders working through the speakership, the caucus, and the committees. The Young Republicans had less influence in the slower-to-change Senate, but even there they had allies and sympathizers led by the imposing William H. Crawford of Georgia. A distinct Congressional as opposed to presidential wing of the Republican party had emerged, and it intended to have its own way.

The new men continued to press their extreme nationalist demands. In the House, John A. Harper of New Hampshire reiterated the call for American acquisition of Florida as the intent of "the Author of Nature," and in the Senate Crawford of Georgia banged his desk and demanded Canada. By the spring of 1812 the most extreme of the Young Republicans were so stridently demanding war against Great Britain that Randolph's epithet for them was appropriate—"War Hawks," he dubbed them. In domestic affairs Clay and his allies pressed for what Clay grandiosely called the "American System," a program which ultimately came to include high protective tariffs, internal improvements at Federal expense in roads and canals (particularly in the West), a national bank, and a continuing public debt. This system was entirely too neo-Hamiltonian, too bluntly aimed at developing the nation and particularly the New West on a capitalist basis, to be anything but anathema to purist, seaboard "Old Republicans." Yet it was more than just Hamilton over again, for in the period of Madison's Administration this earlier version of a "people's capitalism" appealed to far broader segments of the population than Hamilton's original program had. All told, the policies of the Young Republicans gave their forest-fire faction great resources of power.

Once again, Madison's stance was uncertain. Trying to find wise roads of policy, he nonetheless felt unduly pressed and was inclined to accommodate the Young Republicans as far as he could. Moved by other issues and the failure of other policies as well as by War Hawk pressures, he finally called for a declaration of hostilities against Great Britain and thus undertook the War of 1812. The year before, while the President had remained silent, Congress had refused to recharter Hamilton's bank, but in 1816, faced indeed by new conditions as well as new pressures, Madison signed a bill which Congress sent to him establishing a second Bank of the United States. Clique, factional, and group pressures had produced sharp intraparty divisions in the roll-call. From 1812 to 1815 the war served as an effective barrier to imports into the United States and thus vastly encouraged the development of domestic manufactures, but in 1816 the first set of protective tariff duties were enacted, and more were to come in 1818 and again in 1824. In the roll-call on the tariff of 1816, which Madison opposed without much resolution, Republicans in the House voted 63 yea and 31 nay, revealing another intraparty division which reflected local and factional currents and also gave a preponderance of votes against the President. Pressures for internal improvements were only partially contained by vetoes on constitutional grounds from the Executive Mansion, some by Madison and some by his successor. With the war, of course, the public debt rose to new heights and was to be kept there for some time to come. Thus, for the man who had fought Hamilton, the irony of factional strife was compounded by the irony of neo-Hamiltonian measures in Republican dress. Meanwhile, John Marshall on the Supreme Court was on the way to fixing Hamiltonian conceptions in the corpus of broad constitutional interpretations by the judiciary.

The Young Republicans had become the effective driving force in politics. Yet they were only an intraparty faction contending with other factions, and not a party. They lacked the formal control of the executive which would have enabled the voters to hold them fully responsible for the conduct of government, and they could not present options to the electorate as a party. The United States had come almost, but not quite, to a stage of one-party government accompanied by intraparty factionalism. The Republicans were virtually unassailable in positions of power despite Federalist residues; the party was the nearly universal vehicle for the representation of interests and for political participation; most of the important conflicts of national or sectional interest groups were more and more fought out within its boundaries; and the great issues were shaped and settled mostly by men who carried its name. In this sense, the Republican formation exhibited certain parallels with later dominant parties in new nations of the twentieth century. More than one faction fought within its ranks, and the party as a whole and its presidential leadership were unable to subdue or control factional forces. Yet in this situation, the Young Republicans were the major innovative element within a loose and divided party, but not a controlling one.

Thus, other factional surges had appeared in the election of 1812, and the trials of Madison-Job seemed without limit. The Young Republicans supported Madison in a late Congressional caucus in 1812 only after they were convinced that he would call for war. Yet many "Old Republicans," the Smithites and others in the Middle Atlantic and New England states, and the mercantile and shipping elements who had found their way into the extended Republican coalition, all opposed what came to be called "Mr. Madison's War." The consequence, again fostered by local and personal motivations as well as by national conflicts, was a movement for young DeWitt Clinton of New York as a presidential candidate, and the top Clintonian leaders joined in a secret conference with certain Federalist leaders to effect a tacit fusion for the election. "Poor Jemmy" was beleagured on both sides in 1812, by Young Republicans crying up the war, and by seaboard and mercantile forces crying it down—nearly all of them working under the name Republican! As a result, democratic choice for the voters was confused. Suggesting opposition to the war in some areas and support for it in others, the carefully ambiguous Clinton carried all of the New England states except Vermont, along with New York and New Jersey and five of Maryland's eleven electoral votes. The original Clintonian strategy had been to hold these bastions and to strike for Pennsylvania's twenty-five electoral votes; and if fusion had succeeded in Pennsylvania, he would have won the day. As it was,

Madison pulled through only by the margin of his victory in the Keystone State.

In the long run, however, the often discouraging war had also stirred patriotic sentiments. Finally the hostilities seemed to end in a blaze of glory when frontier troops under Andrew Jackson of Tennessee smashed British regulars led by Lord Pakenham at New Orleans. The outbursts of joy and patriotic hallelujahs swept the nation. One result was immense popularity for the "Old Hero" or "Old Hickory," as Jackson was soon known. Another was an additional setback for the Federalist party, many of whose leaders had opposed the war, while some in New England had even verged on treason. The Republican star climbed higher, and despite a factional struggle in an ill-attended Congressional nominating caucus in which Monroe barely won over Crawford, it continued to shine benignly in the presidential election of 1816. In consequence, Monroe bested Rufus King by an electoral count of 183 to 34. Events, however, were to show that his triumph was not in fact a gain for party.

3.

Beginning his term with a three-month state procession up the seaboard to New England and west to Detroit, Monroe indeed deprecated the very idea of party. Believing that partisan distinctions could be ended, anxious "to bring the whole"—including Federalists—"into the republican fold as quick as possible," he argued that party action and partisanship were not necessary in a free government. In the Executive Mansion he sought a status above party as a kind of republican constitutional monarch. He thus soon found himself on an irreversible course of "reign without rule," which ultimately led the nation to a second experience in non-party factional strife. Because of the decline of Federalist-Republican rivalry, the Monroe period has been referred to as an "Era of Good Feelings." In terms of the conflict of interests and factions, however, it was actually more an intraparty "war of every man against every man," in Hobbes's phrase.

Action in office—or the lack of it—was suited to Monroe's newly announced convictions. Grandly, he gave the ex-Federalist John Quincy Adams and ambitious leaders like Crawford and Calhoun places in what he hoped would be a non-political cabinet. Grandly again, he distributed patronage with little or no regard to support for the partly edifice, and he made no effort to recruit leaders in Congress for his Administration despite willing hands. Meanwhile, the old unifying connections of party were stretched further as still more former Federalists moved into the hospitable Monroe-Republican house.

The result was soon demonstrated. It was a further weakening of party structure under the impact of group and sectional demands, personal rivalries, and internal torpor. At the same time Monroe revealed even less concern and offered even less flair for party leadership than Madison had done, and made even less of an effort to counter destructive forces. Early in 1817 Crawford sounded a warning in a letter to Gallatin:

It is certain that the great depression of the Federal party, and their apparent disposition to lose themselves for a time in the council of the nation by uniting in the measures of the Executive, cannot fail to relax the bonds by which the Republican party has been hitherto kept together. Should they pursue this course until the schism shall be completed, it is not easy to foresee the consequences to the Republican party.

Two years later, Crawford noted that "notwithstanding the ostensible popularity of the Administration, the materials of a most formidable opposition may easily be discovered." A few more years and the young Senator from New York, Martin Van Buren—who saw clearly the need for party—was pleading for action to rebuild what was left of the Republican edifice. Yet Monroe pursued his original above-the-battle course throughout his eight years in office.

The process of party collapse was marked by a series of crucial events. In 1819 controversy raged over the admission of far-western, slaveholding Missouri as a state. The conflict turned around the sensitive question of slavery and the balance of slaveholding and free states in the union, and thus the Missouri issue became the great national question. Though he had opinions, Monroe offered no guide for action and in effect waited for Congress to send up bills. At the critical juncture, however, Clay was absent and minor sectional spokesmen stepped forth to try to fill the gap, but ended by filling the Congressional air with inflammatory oratory. Despite overwhelming formal Republican majorities, the nearly endless votes on the Missouri question were sectional or factional rather than party votes. Finally in 1820 a basic compromise was evolved which admitted Missouri as a slave state and Maine as a free state, and a subsidiary compromise was worked out by a reactivated Clay a year later. While the Missouri controversy raged, the nation was also beset in1819-1821 by its first really severe economic panic and depression. Farm prices fell, mortgages were foreclosed, businesses failed, unsound state banks exploded, and woe was the cry across the land, accented by demands for relief. Various proposals for relieving the depression were forthcoming at the capital as well as in the states, and Monroe himself had an idea or two but did not press them. Nor did any proposal stand as party measures, as policies in the years of Hamilton's or Jefferson's management had done—in short, party played no significant role. Finally, the ultimate breakdown of party was revealed in the election of 1820. No formal party nominating caucus met and a poorly attended informal gathering decided against any action, for indeed there was no significant objection to Monroe's succession to Monroe as *roi fainéant*. Even the old-Federalist John Adams served as a Monroe elector in Massachusetts—after all, his son John Quincy Adams was Secretary of State in Monroe's cabinet. Despite sectional conflict over slavery in the Missouri controversy, despite economic crisis and depression, neither the President nor his "party" were held responsible. The President was returned to office in a meaningless plebiscite which revealed more national indifference than anything else, with only one electoral vote in opposition.

Within two years, even Monroe was complaining to Madison that Congress and the Republican party were a shambles. Personal conflicts raged and every man was striking out for himself:

Never have I known such a state of things as has existed here during the last session. . . While there is an open contest with a foreign enemy, or with an internal party, in which you are supported by just principles, the course is plain, and you have something to cheer and animate you to action, but we are now blessed with peace, and the success of the late war has overwhelmed the federal party, so that there is no division of that kind to rally any persons together in support of the administration.

To this lament of "mortification," Monroe added a grievance of "embarrassment." The big three of his cabinet were all looking toward the presidency for themselves in 1824, in an undignified personal scramble.

In the absence of any serious effort to subdue them, the forces of party destruction had done their work. What had happened, beginning with the strains of factionalism under Madison and continuing with a weakening and slipping of all joists under Monroe, was the disintegration of the Republican national party structure. The name remained as the label practically every man in politics assumed, and here and there in the states something like local party structure remained also; but nationally the Republican party had ceased to exist as a formation which undertook party functions in a party fashion. It had long since given up the effective management of government and had suffered a virtual breakdown of communications between executive and legislative branches. It was no longer an effective force in shaping national opinion, and it had funked the tasks of nominating and electioneering. Intraparty brokerage had given way to a helter-skelter scramble of groups and related factions, who made *ad hoc* alliances as they found them expedient. In short, with the collapse or falling apart of the once stately Republican mansion, intraparty factionalism had become nonparty factionalism again, on a national scale.

The disintegration of the party was painfully apparent in the presidential election of 1824. Factional confusion was everywhere. Not only Adams, Crawford, and Calhoun were ambitious, but so was Henry Clay from his place in the House. Innumerable independent candidates outside of the capital arena were hopeful also, and soon the commanding, ramrod figure of Andrew Jackson of Tennessee emerged as the most prominent outside contender. Eventually Calhoun decided to settle for the vice-presidency, leaving the big race to be run by Adams, Crawford, Clay, and Jackson.

200

A last, abortive Congressional caucus gave a rump "nomination" to Crawford, who turned to Van Buren as his chief manager; and the names of other candidates were thrown in by state legislatures or conventions. Each man drew what elements he could around him, on a personal basis, in terms of more or less contrived conjunctions of interests, or on sectional grounds. There were "coalitions of every description without the least regard to principle," Gallatin observed. "I see nothing but . . . the fulfillment of personal views and passions."

Inevitably, meaningful choice for the voters was confused by the multiplicity of candidates and their varied appeals. These ranged from Clay's relatively clear stand for the "American System" to the increasingly charismatic, "Old-Hero" attraction of Jackson. It was the first election in which most of the states—eighteen out of the twenty-four which now composed the Union—named presidential electors by popular vote, but in the face of the confusing multiplicity of candidates and issues, the turnout of voters was light. As democratic choice was blurred in the pluralistic swirl of the new faction politics, democratic participation declined. Although "Old Hickory" Jackson led in both the popular and the electoral vote, no candidate had a majority. Under the Constitution the selection was thrown into the House, where each state delegation cast one vote; and an Adams-Clay coalition made John Quincy Adams president by a margin of one state. Cries of protest went up from the Jacksonians, who proclaimed that Adams had made a "corrupt bargain" with Clay to win his support. The charge was false, but it was in accord with a substantial reaction of disgust to a partyless election which had dissipated the elements of democratic decision. The grandiloquent Senator from Missouri, Thomas Hart Benton, thought the action of the House was a disgraceful "violation of the *demos krateo* principle." As the years passed, Adams was not allowed to forget either charge.

Not quite half a century after the new American nation had declared its independence, the strains of factionalism had brought the Republicans to their concluding irony and the nation to a party vacuum.

4.

If American experience is symptomatic, any major party in a complex society—particularly a party which has become dominant in a two-party system, or a governing party in a one-party system— is likely to contain within itself forces which threaten factional division and even disintegration. It may or may not generate counter forces which will act as checks on faction or as preventives of disintegration.

Disruptive strains are inherent in major parties in a pluralistic society. The first such force lies in the tensions engendered by conflicting interests or bodies of opinion which may gather in the party combination, and in the possibility of increasing intensity of conflict among such groups at critical junctures of the party's history. The greater the success a party has in winning power and achieving a position of dominance, the greater the effect of this disruptive force is likely to be, as more and more disparate elements find their way into the party's structure and power base. A second weakening force may lie in a tendency, as a party encompasses a wider and wider variety of loosely attached elements, toward lessened intensity of unifying, distinctively partisan faiths, loyalties, or commitments among leaders or cadremen. Sense of identification or even loyalty to the party label may remain among thousands of voters in the party following, as they did with innumerable Americans who continued to call themselves Republicans even as the party was disintegrating. Yet, particularly when a party finds that its original mission is largely completed or that it is no longer compelled to distinguish itself sharply from a threatening rival, firm emotional attachments to the party may decline among its crucial leaders and cadre workers, who will no longer place party welfare so high on the scale of values against other claims. Meanwhile, concerns with particular interests, personalities, groups, or sections may come to the fore. This was clearly the case with the factional Republican leaders of the Madison and Monroe years. Thus, even as habitual ties to party persist, the sense of stake in party as such may weaken, the strong feeling that "we" must maintain our strength and identity because "they" threaten us may decline, and the sense of drive or *élan* within the party may grow flaccid. The further a party has progressed with the passage of time toward status as an institution and toward organization, the less likely it is that such a loss of unifying party spirit will occur or wreak severe damage, but the Republicans had hardly reached this stage of development. A third possible divisive force is the development among the party's leaders, cadremen, and actives of sharp rivalries for the prime goods of political careers, such as office, power, patronage, and prestige. Again, the greater the success or dominance of a party and the richer the prizes it offers, the greater the strength of this disruptive force is likely to be. Where one or more of the disintegrating forces operate strongly, the party corpus is threatened. If all of them ran unchecked, the party would surely be doomed.

The operation of possible cohesive forces is not inherent in parties, but depends heavily on the endeavors of party leaders and cadres. Indeed, the first such force comes with the action of party leaders, who can be effective in a variety of ways. Able and energetic spokesmen may supply a continuing stimulus to loyalty and hard work by party cadremen and actives. Adroit or determined leaders may also devise workable compromises or formulas of agreement which will keep the various elements in the party and its following reasonably well satisfied, or evoke strong responses in the public and electorate. Indeed, in situations of stress, strongly innovative or charismatic leadership may even produce new opinions or new alignments of interests on issues, which transcend or subdue old conflicts and thereby generate new unifying partisan perspectives or *élan*. The second and third possible integrating forces are linked, and may sustain leadership as they also depend upon it. They are the development of high degrees of co-ordination or organization in the party, and a reasonably efficacious use of patronage as a means of party sustenance. Organization, as a regularized pattern of division of labor and co-ordination of functions with intrinsic psychic or material rewards for the men who conduct it, may provide mechanisms to ease the resolution of conflict and promote party discipline. Organization may also bring into being a group within the party whose interests are separable from those of groups in the following, and whose great stake is perpetuation of the party structure and its vote-getting facilities—thus, the men who manage party organization may also constitute an interest group in themselves. Patronage, if it is linked to continuing co-ordination in the party structure or to the development of organization, may be utilized as a means to reward the faithful, recruit the hopeful, and punish the unfaithful. Thus leadership, organization, and patronage may serve toward unifying or maintaining a party.

A final integrating force, in itself one index of cohesion, is intra-party concordance on ideology or policy. Concordance may on occasion develop almost naturally from similarities of interests and views among the groups which come to constitute the party combination. Ordinarily, however, concordance must be painstakingly built by devising formulas of agreement or patterns of compromise, so that satisfaction is maximized and conflict is minimized among such groups, or by arousing new ideological drives or policy commitments which large numbers of men in the party and its following can take up with enthusiasm. As parties mature in a complex society, internal concordance is more often an artificial than a natural product.

The question for any major party is the dynamic balance or equilibrium of integrating and disintegrating forces in the party. In their infancy, particularly in the bloom of Hamilton's brilliant early leadership and of the happy concordance of interests within the party and its following, the Federalists scored high in all of the integrating forces and were remarkably fortunate in the minimum impact of disruptive elements. From the time of the Jay treaty controversy and the election of 1796, however, the balance of forces among the Federalists tended to shift away from cohesion and toward threatening disruption. The Federalists' failure to come to terms with the agrarian-democratic bent of the electorate remained their great weakness, but this failure was compounded by division and strains within the party which also contributed directly to its decline.

The Republican formation presents a more complex life history. After an early gestation period, it discovered itself as a party in the unifying and invigorating experience of the Jay treaty combat, and was able to maintain itself for a decade as a cohesive political body. Integrating forces ran strong, and the party was little threatened

by disruptive tensions. With the loss of Jefferson's leadership, ever, and the ineptitude of Madison and the fecklessness of Mc in the face of new threats, the Republican party suffered fror unfavorable balance of forces—despite, or in part because o continuing success with the electorate. In consequence, it b out first in a disruptive rash of multiple factionalism, and then fered disintegration and ultimate death. Although toward the signs of its fate were detected even by Monroe, the time for ac had passed.

The tragedy for the Republicans and their founder-philoso who presided at the beginnings of party disintegration lay in fact that the cohesive forces which may preserve a party are c potential. All of them depend upon the wisdom, purpose, and ergy of men, and when the years of trial came neither Madison his colleagues were able to find sufficient reserves of these qualit

5.

The decline of the Federalists and the disintegration of t Republicans marked confused meanderings in the course of Am ican party development. As John Quincy Adams took office, and a John Adams and his old friend and rival Thomas Jefferson di on the same July 4, fifty years after they had signed the Declarati of Independence in 1776, the nation found itself again in the bra bles of faction politics. It appeared that the party building labors Hamilton, Madison, and Jefferson had all gone for naught. T reverse was only temporary, however, and new parties and a stron party system soon emerged.

The first of the new formations cut its road to party standing opposition to the second Adams. Its obvious unifying figure Jackson, who now carried not only the glory of New Orleans also the sympathy of thousands of Americans who felt that democratic process had been negated by the selection of Adam the House. Thus reactions to that event helped to "re-estab . . . parties upon the basis of principle," as Benton put it; "it d anew party lines, then almost obliterated under the fusion of ties" and by the effort of leaders to make "personal parties" themselves. Furthermore, the depression of 1819-1821 had prodt

205

a delayed reaction of resentment across the country, a feeling that somehow government had got away from the true Jeffersonian commitment to the service of common men and their concerns. Much of this feeling also turned to Jackson as the stern and resolute hero who would somehow set things right. Finally, as Adams out-Clayed Clay in furthering the "American System," especially in internal improvements, it seemed to many Americans that Hamilton and his basic policies did indeed live again and that another Jeffersonian rebuke was in order. Moving on parallel paths with all these forces were the ambitions of men like Calhoun, Martin Van Buren of New York, and Jackson himself, ambitious for political advancement and power or the chance to direct government policy in terms of interests they represented.

In this situation Van Buren stepped forward as party surveyor and architect. Building on the work he had done for Crawford in 1824, he now labored to assemble the old Crawford, Calhoun, and Jackson factions and other elements around "Old Hickory" as a candidate who could defeat Adams in 1828. He put his New York masons and joiners to work to rebuild a national party around the New York–Virginia alliance which had been the crossbeam of the Jeffersonian structure, and linked his own Albany *Argus* with the Richmond *Enquirer* in a jerry-built information office. The epitome of the practicing politician-manager, shrewd, tactful, and genial, Van Buren was aided by other adept managers in the states who emerged more and more as highly professional politicians. In the great Mississippi Valley, Benton won masses of voters by his agrarian-democratic appeals and showed himself a redoubtable party builder in his state. Finally, Van Buren and others worked to seal off the Adams and Clay factions from the new political edifice.

The result was a victory for the new forces in the crucial election of 1828. A hurrah campaign for Jackson brought out a popular vote more than twice that of 1824, and the "Jackson men" triumphed by a wide margin over the hapless Adams. As Jackson began his dramatic career in office, the elements around him were soon joined as the Democratic party. New issues were drawn by his Administration and its Congressional spokesmen. In a surge of equalitarian democracy, a broad range of group interests found representation,

206

popular participation in politics increased, and meaningful options were put before the public. A new popular party-of-politicians was at hand, reaching even more broadly and deeply into the *hoi polloi* masses than Jefferson and the Republicans had done. The Democratic party, like its predecessors, experienced the strains of internal factionalism, and it was temporarily torn asunder when the slavery controversy eventually broke into Civil War. Yet it managed to call up the forces of stability and survive.

Conflicts of interest and cleavage over policy inevitably produced opposition, which was also expressed through popular parties. For a time the old Adams-Clay coalition continued as a loose National Republican formation. By 1834, however, these elements, certain Southern leaders who followed Calhoun out of the Democratic ranks, other dissident conservative Democrats, and units from a short-lived "Anti-Masonic" third force were reassembled in a powerful Whig party. For years the Whigs stood as the major rival to the Democrats in renewed two-party competition, and men like Clay, the oratorical Daniel Webster of Massachusetts, and the adroit Thurlow Weed of New York emerged as effective leaders and managers. The Whigs also suffered vicissitudes, losing the Calhoun faction back to the Democrats and undergoing additional internal dissensions. Finally, in the slavery conflict of the 1850's, they fell apart in a process of disintegration similar to the one that had destroyed the Republicans in the era of Madison and Monroe. Their last wanderings, however, were accompanied by the joining together of still another major national party, which assumed the old name Republican for their new coalition. Thus opposition was taken up again in a new competition of Democrats and latter-day Republicans. Despite third-party challenges and periods of near one-party dominance, this two-party system was to persist through the years.

The original labor of cutting party ways in the new American republic had been a labor of Hercules, and the results did not endure. Yet when a later generation took up the task again, they had the trails that had been marked by their predecessors to guide them, and the task was made that much lighter.

There were in fact constructive contrasts between the first and the second American endeavors in establishing a party system. In

207

the first, in the 1790's, party founders had no model to go by. They were not even conscious at the beginning that they were shaping parties, or of the efficacy of party; and, indeed, they had doubts of the legitimacy of parties even as they took the first steps toward their development. In consequence, party development was erratic and marked by much groping, *ad hoc* invention, and uncertainty. The nation's second party builders, however, knew what modern parties and a party system could be. They had before them the clear models that Hamilton, Madison, and Jefferson had finally contrived, and they had no doubt of the virtue of party. Moreover, the original leaders of the American Revolutionary era had done their work well, and the new American nation had proved that it could survive and "promote the general welfare" as a stable, modernized democracy in the liberal tradition. Perhaps at the outset the new republic could not have sustained the animosities and frictions which would have arisen in a wholly open politics dominated by the rivalry of full-scale popular parties. By the age of Jackson, Van Buren, and the later Clay, however, new men could work in the open tradition of a liberal spirit which had proved itself.

The shapers of the American nation had provided profound lessons for a second generation of party leaders. They had shown what parties could be, and had marked the way toward a renewed American party system which could sustain broad representation, mass participation, and popular choice in a functioning political democracy. Perhaps their achievement may have an even wider application and offer some useable guidelines for the new nations of today, as they find their own ways toward political modernization and development.

A Summary
of Sources

More and more materials on American party history are appearing, yet even most of the recent materials are not concerned with analysis. Any attempt to treat party development within a framework which goes beyond mere narrative requires piecing together data, interpretations, and suggestions from many sources, in a general reworking. In consequence, this summary focuses on studies which have proved of greatest use in a wide variety of ways. In addition, it is cumulative: that is to say, a source cited for early use may also have been drawn upon at later stages of the discussion. Usually the title of the study will reveal whether it was relevant at only one phase of the essay, or at more than one point.

There are few general histories of American parties of any significant value. They include Charles A. Beard, *The American Party Battle* (New York, 1928), which is brief but expresses its author's influential economic analysis; Wilfred E. Binkley, *American Political Parties: Their Natural History*, Fourth Edition (New York, 1962), which applies much of Beard's approach and is currently the leading work in the field, although among other faults it lacks conceptual clarity; M. Ostrogorski, *Democracy and the Organization of Political Parties* (New York, 1902), still a classic despite its bias against parties and its historical errors or lapses; and Edgar E. Robinson, *The Evolution of American Political Parties: A Sketch of Party Development* (New York, 1924), which remains a remarkably suggestive interpretation and offers greater clarity concerning

209

the nature of party than Binkley's work does. See also Herbert Agar, *The Price of Union* (Boston, 1950). Tangential but helpful for the study of party history is Eugene H. Roseboom, *A History of Presidential Elections* (New York, 1957); and useful data not readily found elsewhere is available in the older treatment by Edward Stanwood, *A History of the Presidency from 1788 to 1897* (Boston, 1898). Election and other relevant data are also to be found in Bureau of the Census, *Historical Statistics of the United States, Colonial Times to 1957* (Washington, 1960). The extraordinarily well-edited compendium, Richard B. Morris, *Encyclopedia of American History* (New York, 1953, 1961), is also perennially valuable.

Two useful monographs on the genesis of American parties are Joseph Charles, *The Origins of the American Party System* (Williamsburg, 1956), which is brilliant if sometimes overstrained or biased in its interpretation, and Noble E. Cunningham, Jr., *The Jeffersonian Republicans: The Formation of Party Organization, 1789-1801* (Chapel Hill, 1957), which compensates in meticulous thoroughness for its limited range of analytical concern. Useful for general historical interpretation for the early American period are Edmund S. Morgan, *The Birth of the Republic: 1763-1789* (Chicago, 1956), John C. Miller, *The Federalist Era: 1789-1801* (New York, 1960), and Marcus Cunliffe, *The Nation Takes Shape: 1789-1837* (Chicago, 1959). Much of my general approach has drawn on the stimulating innovative treatise concerning the nature of the American experience by Louis Hartz, *The Liberal Tradition in America* (New York, 1955), and I have also found Richard Hofstadter, *The American Political Tradition and the Men Who Made It* (New York, 1951) suggestive, although I have in effect quarreled with it in my treatment of Jefferson in power. As this essay was in the last stages of revision, I had an opportunity to look at the unpublished manuscript by Seymour Martin Lipset, "The United States—The First New Nation," 1962, in which I found not only many ideas parallel to my own but also useful additional insights. Valuable for the background of the early American years are Merrill Jensen, *The New Nation: A History of the United States During the Confederacy, 1781-1789* (New York, 1950), and the incisive essay by Benjamin Fletcher Wright, *Consensus and Continuity, 1776-1787* (Boston, 1958).

For the approach to party and party politics in general, Maurice Duverger, *Political Parties: Their Organization and Activity in the Modern State* (New York, 1955); V. O. Key, Jr., *Politics, Parties, and Pressure Groups,* Fourth Edition (New York, 1958); Avery Leiserson, *Parties and Politics: An Institutional and Behavioral Approach* (New York, 1958); Robert Michels, *Political Parties: A Sociological Study of the Oligarchical Tendencies of Modern Democracy* (New York, 1915); and Max Weber, "Politics as a Vocation," in H. H. Gerth and C. Wright Mills, eds., *From Max Weber: Essays in Sociology* (New York, 1946) have all proved valuable in various ways, as has the brief summary by Neil A. McDonald, *The Study of Political Parties* (New York, 1955). The discussion of party in Edmund Burke, *Thoughts on the Cause of the Present Discontents,* ed. F. G. Selby (London, 1902) is suggestive for the treatment of party origins, particularly because, in action as well as in his essay of 1770, Burke stood as a transitional figure, familiar with old-style "connexions," but straining toward the broader modern connections of party. In addition, various analytical questions relating to party or democratic politics are treated in David B. Truman, *The Governmental Process* (New York, 1951), and in Seymour Martin Lipset, *Political Man: The Social Bases of Politics* (Garden City, 1960), and I have drawn on formulations from both. For historical explanation, Patrick Gardiner, *The Nature of Historical Explanation* (London, 1952), William Dray, *Laws and Explanation in History* (London, 1957), Carl Hempel, "The Function of General Laws in History," *Journal of Philosophy,* XXXIX (1942), 35-48, and Maurice Mandelbaum, "Historical Explanation: The Problem of 'Covering Laws,' " *History and Theory,* I (1961), 229-42 have proved particularly suggestive in contrasting ways. Numerous other works have contributed less directly to the theoretical framework of this essay.

A variety of materials have provided information concerning American pre-party or faction politics in the 1770's and 1780's, notably Elisha P. Douglass, *Rebels and Democrats: The Struggle for Equal Political Rights and Majority Rule During the American*

Revolution (Chapel Hill, 1955); Frederick W. Dallinger, *Nominations for Elective Office in the United States* (New York, 1903); Ralph Volney Harlow, *The History of Legislative Methods in the Period before 1825* (New Haven, 1917); George D. Luetscher, *Early Political Machinery in the United States* (Philadelphia, 1903); Allan Nevins, *The American States During and After the Revolution* (New York, 1924); E. Wilder Spaulding, *His Excellency George Clinton* (New York, 1938); Charles S. Sydnor, *Gentlemen Freeholders: Political Practices in Washington's Virginia* (Chapel Hill, 1952); Jackson T. Main, "Sections and Politics in Virginia, 1781-1787," *William and Mary Quarterly*, XII (January, 1955), 96-112; Henry McGilbert Wagstaff, "State Rights and Political Parties in North Carolina, 1776-1861," *Johns Hopkins University Studies in Historical and Political Science*, XXIV (Baltimore, 1906); and Ulrich B. Phillips, "The South Carolina Federalists," *American Historical Review*, XIV (April, July, 1909), 529-44, 731-44. In particular, Dallinger, Harlow, and Luetscher were also useful for later discussions of political practices. The pioneer economic analysis of the conflict over the Constitution of 1789, Charles A. Beard, *An Economic Interpretation of the Constitution of the United States* (New York, 1913), is brilliantly and devastatingly criticized by Forrest McDonald, *We the People: The Economic Origins of the Constitution* (Chicago, 1958), which also contains a wealth of well-organized data concerning politics in each of the thirteen states for the period. Unfortunately Jackson T. Main, *The Anti-Federalists: Critics of the Constitution, 1781-1788* (Chapel Hill, 1961) appeared too late for me to make use of it. The early study by Charles Oscar Paullin, "The First Elections Under the Constitution," *Iowa Journal of History and Politics*, II (January, 1904), 3-33 is still useful, and I have drawn also on Richard P. McCormick, "New Perspectives on Jacksonian Politics," *American Historical Review*, LXV (January, 1960), 288-301, as well as other sources, for the analysis of voting participation in the Jeffersonian and Jacksonian eras.

Valuable traces of early Federalist and Republican development may be found in *The Journal of William Maclay* (New York, 1927) if it is read constructively, for its revelations of behavior more than for its polemic. Useful information concerning various aspects of party growth (and particularly the emerging Republican opposition) may be found also in Henry Jones Ford, *Washington and His Colleagues: A Chronicle of the Rise and Fall of Federalism* (New Haven, 1918); Charles A. Beard, *Economic Origins of Jeffersonian Democracy* (New York, 1915); Stuart Gerry Brown, *The First Republicans: Political Philosophy and Public Policy in the Party of Jefferson and Madison* (Syracuse, 1954); and Eugene Perry Link, *Democratic-Republican Societies, 1790-1800* (New York, 1942). Although its title suggests far more than it covers, Margaret Woodbury, *Public Opinion in Philadelphia: 1789-1801* (Durham, North Carolina, 1919) provided some useable material.

Much of the story of early party formation lies in the histories of major political leaders, whose careers have been traced by scholars, although usually without clear or rigorous attention to party or their party labors. The convenient one-volume study by Marcus Cunliffe, *George Washington: Man and Monument* (Boston, 1958), does treat important aspects of the Revolutionary hero's symbolic and political role. For Hamilton I have consulted Louis M. Hacker, *Alexander Hamilton in the American Tradition* (New York, 1957), John C. Miller, *Alexander Hamilton: Portrait in Paradox* (New York, 1959), and Nathan Schachner, *Alexander Hamilton* (New York, 1946); unfortunately the second Hamilton volume by Broadus Mitchell, *Alexander Hamilton: The National Adventure, 1788-1804* (New York, 1962), appeared too late for use in this study. For Madison, Irving Brant, *James Madison: Father of the Constitution, 1787-1800* (New York, 1950), is eulogistic and journalistic, but nearly exhaustive; also useful, for Madison's own utterances, are *Letters and Other Writings of James Madison: Fourth President of the United States . . . Published by Order of Congress*, 4 vols. (Philadelphia, 1865), and Gaillard Hunt, ed., *The Writings of James Madison: Comprising His Public Papers and His Private Correspondence, Including Numerous Letters and Documents Now For the First Time Printed*, 9 vols. (New York and London, 1900-1910). For Jefferson the most valuable materials are the brief and evocative volume by Gilbert Chinard, *Thomas Jefferson: The Apostle of Americanism* (Boston, 1929), the more thorough Dumas Malone, *Jefferson and the Rights of Man* (Boston, 1951), which brings the story down to 1793, and Jefferson's own writings in Paul Leicester Ford, ed., *The Works of Thomas Jefferson*, 12 vols., (New York, 1904-1905); Dumas Malone, *Jefferson and the Ordeal of Liberty* (Boston, 1962), for 1793-1800, appeared too late for use here, and the definitive collection, Julian Boyd, ed., *The Papers of Thomas Jefferson* (Princeton, 1950-1961), had barely reached 1790 at the time of this writing. The important but little-known Beckley is treated in Philip M. Marsh, "John Beckley, Mystery Man of the Early Jeffersonians," *Pennsylvania Magazine of History and Biography*, 72 (1948), 54-69, and in Noble E. Cunningham, Jr., "John Beckley: An Early American Party Manager," *William and Mary Quarterly*, XIII (January, 1956), 40-52, as well as in Cunningham's monograph on the Republicans, cited above. Other personalities are presented in Dice Robins Anderson, *William Branch Giles: A Study in the Politics of Virginia and the Nation from 1790 to 1830* (Menasha, Wisconsin, 1914); Samuel E. Forman, "The Political Activities of Philip Freneau," in *Johns Hopkins University Studies in Historical and Political Science* (Baltimore, 1902); Lewis Leary, *That Rascal Freneau: A Study in Literary Failure* (Rutgers University Press, 1941); and Philip M. Marsh, "Philip Freneau and His Circle," *Pennsylvania Magazine of History and Biography*, 63 (January, 1939), 37-59; Nathan Schachner, *Aaron Burr* (New York, 1937); William B. Hatcher, *Edward Livingston* (University, Louisiana, 1940); Raymond Walters, Jr., *Alexander James Dallas: Lawyer-Politician-Financier, 1759-1817* (Philadelphia, 1943); W. P. Cresson, *James Monroe* (Chapel Hill, 1946); and William E. Dodd, *The Life of Nathaniel Macon* (Raleigh, North Carolina, 1903). The article by Russell J. Ferguson, "Albert Gallatin, Western Pennsylvania Politician," *Western Pennsylvania Historical Magazine*, 16 (August, 1933), 183-95, is a useful summary of Gallatin's early political career. Provocative interpretations of Washington, Hamilton, Jefferson, Adams, and other figures appear in the monograph by Charles, cited earlier.

Local facets of the halting Republican development are touched on by Leland D. Baldwin, *Whiskey Rebels: The Story of a Frontier Uprising* (Pittsburgh, 1939); William Miller, "The Democratic Societies and the Whiskey Insurrection," *Pennsylvania Magazine of History and Biography*, 62 (July, 1938), 324-349; Harry Marlin Tinkcom, *The Republicans and Federalists in Pennsylvania, 1790-*

1801: A Study in National Stimulus and Local Response (Harrisburg, 1950), which is particularly detailed, thorough, and useful; William Miller, "First Fruits of Republican Organization: Political Aspects of the Congressional Election of 1794," *Pennsylvania Magazine of History and Biography*, 63 (April, 1939), 118-143; and John Harold Wolfe, *Jeffersonian Democracy in South Carolina* (Chapel Hill, 1940).

Various aspects of Republican party consolidation or ideology, nationally or locally, are dealt with in Charles Henry Ambler, *Sectionalism in Virginia from 1776 to 1861* (Chicago, 1910), supplemented and corrected by Harry Ammon, "The Formation of the Republican Party in Virginia, 1789-1796," *Journal of Southern History*, XIX (August, 1953), 283-310; Samuel Flagg Bemis, *Jay's Treaty: A Study in Commerce and Diplomacy* (New York, 1923), which deals distressingly little with domestic politics; Charles Biddle, *Autobiography of Charles Biddle, 1745-1821* (Philadelphia, 1883); Bernard Fay, "Early Party Machinery in the United States: Pennsylvania in the Election of 1796," *Pennsylvania Magazine of History and Biography*, 60 (October, 1936), 375-90; Russell J. Ferguson, *Early Western Pennsylvania Politics* (Pittsburgh, 1938); Sanford W. Higginbotham, *The Keystone in the Democratic Arch: Pennsylvania Politics 1800-1816* (Harrisburg, 1952); Paul A. W. Wallace, *The Muhlenbergs of Pennsylvania* (Philadelphia, 1950); Walter R. Fee, *The Transition from Aristocracy to Democracy in New Jersey 1789-1829* (Somerville, 1933); Delbert Harold Gilpatrick, *Jeffersonian Democracy in North Carolina, 1789-1816* (New York, 1931); Samuel Eliot Morison, "Squire Ames and Doctor Ames," *The New England Quarterly*, I (January, 1928), 5-31; Charles Warren, *Jacobin and Junto: or Early American Politics as Viewed in the Diary of Dr. Nathaniel Ames 1758-1822* (Cambridge, 1931), which offers valuable insights into doctrinaire Republican ideology as Ames represented it; Howard Lee McBain, "DeWitt Clinton and the Origin of the Spoils System in New York," *Columbia University Studies in History, Economics and Public Law*, XXVIII (New York, 1907); William A. Robinson, *Jeffersonian Democracy in New England* (New Haven, 1916); and Charles Page Smith, *James Wilson: Founding Father 1742-1798* (Chapel Hill, 1956). For Gallatin in his years of party leadership,

Raymond Walters, Jr., *Albert Gallatin: Jeffersonian Financier and Diplomat* (New York, 1957) is useful although not as thorough as on might wish, as is the collection by Henry Adams, ed., *The Writings of Albert Gallatin*, 3 vols. (Philadelphia, 1879). More sophisticated studies of state party developments, a penetrating biography of Gallatin, and an adequate edition of his writings are badly needed.

For the conflict of Federalists and Republicans in the Adams years and the maturing of the first American party system, the leading monograph is unquestionably Manning J. Dauer, *The Adams Federalists* (Baltimore, 1953), which covers and analyzes much more than its title indicates. For Adams himself and events of the period, see also Stephen G. Kurtz, *The Presidency of John Adams: The Collapse of Federalism 1795-1800* (Philadelphia, 1957). For the Alien and Sedition Acts and reactions to them, I have used John C. Miller, *Crisis in Freedom* (Boston, 1951); James Morton Smith, *Freedom's Fetters: The Alien and Sedition Laws and American Civil Liberties* (Ithaca, New York, 1956); Adrienne Koch and Harry Ammon, "The Virginia and Kentucky Resolutions: An Episode in Jefferson's and Madison's Defense of Civil Liberties," *William and Mary Quarterly*, Third Series, V (April, 1948), 145-76; and John C. Livingston, "Alexander Hamilton and the American Tradition," *Midwest Journal of Political Science*, I (November, 1957), 209-24. See also Leonard W. Levy, *Legacy of Suppression: Freedom of Speech and Press in Early American History* (Cambridge, Massachusetts, 1960), for the background of the problem in America. Other aspects of party development and action in the late 1790's and for 1800, or their significance, are treated in Anson Ely Morse, *The Federalist Party in Massachusetts to the Year 1800* (Princeton, 1909); Richard P. McCormick, *The History of Voting in New Jersey: A Study of the Development of Election Machinery 1664-1911* (New Brunswick, New Jersey, 1953); Edgar E. Robinson, "The Place of Party in the Political History of the United States," *Annual Reports of the American Historical Association for the Years 1927 and 1928* (Washington, 1929); and Charles O. Lerche, Jr., "Jefferson and the Election of 1800: A Case Study of the Political Smear," *William and Mary Quarterly*, Third Series, V (October, 1948), 467-91; as well as in many of the works cited above. The recent volume by Frank van der Linden, *The Turning Point: Jefferson's Battle for the Presidency* (Washington, 1962) is colorful but little more.

Problems of the Republican ascendency and the Federalist decline during the Jefferson Administration are treated or touched on in Henry Jones Ford, *The Rise and Growth of American Politics: A Sketch of Constitutional Development* (New York, 1898); Norman J. Small, "Some Presidential Interpretations of the Presidency," *Johns Hopkins University Studies in Historical and Political Science* (Baltimore, 1932); Bray Hammond, *Banks and Politics in America—From the Revolution to the Civil War* (Princeton, 1957); Irving Brant, *James Madison: Secretary of State, 1800-1809* (New York, 1953); William Cabell Bruce, *John Randolph of Roanoke 1773-1833*, 2 vols. (New York, 1922); Charles Henry Ambler, *Thomas Ritchie: A Study in Virginia Politics* (Richmond, 1913); Stanislaus Hamilton, ed., *The Writings of James Monroe: Including a Collection of His Public and Private Papers and Correspondence Now For the First Time Printed*, 7 vols., (New York, 1898-1903); Jack L. Cross, "John Marshall on the French Revolution and American Politics," *William and Mary Quarterly*, Third Series, XII (October, 1955), 631-49; Anson D. Morse, "Causes and Consequences of the Party Revolution of 1800," *Annual Report of the American Historical Association* (1894), 531-40; and Dixon Ryan Fox, "The Decline of Aristocracy in the Politics of New York," *Columbia University Studies in History, Economics and Public Law*, LXXXVI (New York, 1919). A modern, definitive study of the Jeffersonian Republicans in power has, at this writing, yet to appear, although a study by Noble E. Cunningham, Jr., is promised for 1963.

In addition to many of the works cited above, materials concerning the disintegration of parties may be found in George Dangerfield, *The Era of Good Feelings* (New York, 1952) and also in the older history by Frederick Jackson Turner, *Rise of the New West 1819-1829* (New York and London, 1906). Although it offers little data, I found some suggestive ideas for this problem in Anson D. Morse, *Parties and Party Leaders* (Boston, 1923). For Madison himself in this period, the final two volumes by Irving Brant, *James Madison: The President, 1809-1812* (Indianapolis and New York,

217

1956) and *James Madison: Commander in Chief, 1812-1836* (New York, 1961) are valuable although defensive. For the important role of Clay, I have drawn on Bernard Mayo, *Henry Clay: Spokesman of the New West* (Boston, 1937), Glyndon Van Deusen, *The Life of Henry Clay* (Boston, 1937); Clement Eaton, *Henry Clay and the Art of American Politics* (Boston, 1957), and John D. Hopkins, ed., *The Papers of Henry Clay* (Lexington, 1959, 1961). See also J. E. D. Shipp, *Giant Days, or the Life and Times of William H. Crawford* (Americus, Georgia, 1909)—unfortunately, no adequate study of Crawford or collection of his papers exists. Useful monographs and articles include Julius W. Pratt, *Expansionists of 1812* (Gloucester, Massachusetts, 1957); Everett S. Brown, *The Missouri Compromise and Presidential Politics: 1820-1825* (St. Louis, 1926); Glover Moore, *The Missouri Controversy, 1819-1821* (Lexington, 1953); Samuel Rezneck, "The Depression of 1819-1822," *American Historical Review*, XXXIX (October, 1933), 28-47; Lynn W. Turner, "The Electoral Vote Against Monroe in 1820—An American Legend," *Mississippi Valley Historical Review*, XLII (September, 1955), 250-73; James A. Kehl, *Ill Feeling in the Era of Good Feeling: Western Pennsylvania Political Battles, 1815-1825* (Pittsburgh, 1956); and Philip Shriver Klein, *Pennsylvania Politics 1817-1832: A Game Without Rules* (Philadelphia, 1940). Other representative figures and the shape of politics at the end of the period of disintegration are treated in Charles M. Wiltse, *John C. Calhoun: Nationalist, 1782-1828* (Indianapolis, 1944), Marquis James, *The Life of Andrew Jackson* (Indianapolis, 1938), William Nisbet Chambers, *Old Bullion Benton: Senator from the New West, 1782-1858* (Boston, 1956), and Robert V. Remini, *Martin Van Buren and the Making of the Democratic Party* (New York, 1959). The recent volume by Shaw Livermore, Jr., *The Twilight of Federalism: The Disintegration of the Federalist Party, 1815-1830* (Princeton, 1962) came into my hands too late for use in this study. Finally, some suggestive ideas for the Republican story are contained in Charles S. Sydnor, "The One-Party Period of American History," *American Historical Review*, LI (April, 1946), 439-51.

The re-establishment of parties and the development of the second American party system, barely foreshadowed in this essay, is a subject in itself and requires a bibliography in itself.

Index

Index

Index

Du Pont de Nemours, Pierre, 175
Dwight, Timothy, 56, 122, 154

Education: role in democracy, 14, 99, 110; educational background of early U.S. leadership, 69–70; in early America, 100–101
Elections, conduct of, 4, 22–3, 31; *see also* Congressional elections; Federalist party; Presidential elections; Republican party
Embargo Act of 1808, 186
England, 130; personal politics in, 3, 5; and war with France, 42, 77; and Jay treaty, 78; tense relations with U.S. in 1800's, 184–7; and War of 1812, 188
English political tradition, 2–3, 8–9, 92, 97, 122–4
Enquirer (Richmond), 181, 206
Episcopalians, 40, 120
Equalitarianism, 18, 55, 56, 101, 123–5, 206–7
"Era of Good Feelings," 197
Essex Junto, 122, 136, 142, 180

Faction politics (nonparty), 43–4, 95, 96; in South Carolina, 13, 25; characteristic of early American politics, 17, 21, 23; "country" and "court," 18; in New York, 20, 25, 83–4; in state legislatures, 25–6; types of, 26; consequences for democratic functioning, 26–7, 32, 50, 201; and ratification, 27–9; and elections of 1788–1789, 30, 31; in Congress in 1789, 38; distinguished from party politics, 45–50, 86; in America from 1824 to 1828, 205; *see also* Caucus; Cliques; Factions; Juntos
Factionalism, intraparty, 50, 89, 115, 146–7, 191, 195–6; *see also* Democratic party; Federalist party; Republican party
Factions: Hamilton's capital faction, 38–9, 58; Madison's capital faction, 53–7, 60, 68; High Federalists, 115, 122, 128–30, 134–6, 145, 148, 150, 158–9; Moderate or Adams Federalists, 115, 142–3, 148, 150, 159; "Tertium Quids," 184–5, 188; Smith clique, 192; Young Republicans and War Hawks, 193–7; under Monroe, 197–8, 199–200; in election of 1824, 200–201
Federal system, 11, 12
Federalist, The, 6
Federalist party, 46, 66, 71, 111, 112, 124, 139, 153; Hamilton, founder of, 1, 6, 36, 53, 74; as capital faction, 6, 39–40, 46, 49, 54, 58; capital opposition to, 6, 51–2, 65–6; organization, 12, 44, 49, 147, 153; as prototype of American parties, 16, 191; economic policies of, 36–8, 102–3; cadre, 40, 41, 49; following, 40–41, 49–50, 106, 119–20, 121–2; functions, 40, 49, 50, 121; mercantile interests in, 40, 119, 120, 121–2, 155, 159; as "party of notables," 40, 41, 44, 153; planter interests in, 40, 120; South Carolina, strength in, 40, 41, 121, 157–8, 167; structure, 40, 41, 49, 84–5, 106, 121; agrarian interests in, 41, 44, 120, 121–2, 159, 204; electioneering by, 41, 49; use of press, 41–2, 49; French Revolution and, 42–3; George Washington as symbol of unity in, 42, 43, 48, 94; ideology, 42–3, 48, 49, 50, 102; elitism in, 44, 106, 107; as modern party, 49, 125; party voting in Congress, 50, 88, 90, 137–9; popular opposition to, 61–5, 66; attitude toward opposition, 65–6, 97, 145; youthful leadership of, 67–8, 69; Pennsylvania, strength in, 71, 81, 156, 159, 162, 186; New York, strength in, 72; nominations and elections—of 1792, 72–3, 111; —of 1794, 74; —of 1796, 111, 113–22, 126–9, 204; —of 1798, 141–3; —of 1800, 111, 151, 153, 154, 156, 157–9, 160, 169; —of 1804, 111, 182; —of 1808, 189; —of 1812, 196; and Jay treaty, 78–80, 86–8, 204; New England,

222

Index

Gregg, Andrew, 89, 118
Grenville, Lord, 76; see also Jay treaty
Griswold, Roger, 139–40

Hamilton, Alexander, 46, 84, 95, 109, 147; founder of Federalist party, 1, 2, 6, 9, 16, 36, 53, 66, 208; and program for economic development, 1, 11, 36, 37–8, 51, 53–6, 72, 90–91, 102–3, 121, 162, 176; attitude toward party and opposition, 5, 43–4, 61, 65, 97; author of *The Federalist*, 6; conflict with Jefferson, 6, 57, 58–9, 130, 178; relations with Madison, 11, 55, 58, 76, 195; in New York state politics, 20, 71–2; and ratification, 28; and elections of 1788–1789, 30; personality, 34–5, 58, 59, 151–2; political philosophy, 34, 35, 36–7, 45, 58, 101, 102, 177; quoted on political leadership, 34, 93; quoted on foundations of government, 35; relations with Washington, 36, 42, 57, 151–2; forms a Congressional faction, 38; forms a capital faction, 39, 58; establishes *Gazette of the U.S.*, 41; attitude toward the masses, 45, 58; as "Belcour" in popular criticism, 53, 131, 137; Congressional opposition to, 56, 105; and John Taylor, 64; and Whiskey Rebellion, 64; age, 68; education, 69; and elections of 1792, 72; resigns as Secretary of the Treasury, 74; and Mrs. Reynolds, 82, 83; and Jay treaty, 86, 87; election of 1796, 114, 127; relation with John Adams, 114–15, 131, 151; as party leader, 122, 172, 191, 199, 204; and pro-war policy in Adams's administration, 130, 148; and elections of 1800, 151, 155–6, 158–9; and Jefferson-Burr contest for the presidency, 166–8; duel with Burr, 180; policies compared with Clay's "American System," 194, 206
Hamiltonians, 20
Hampton, Wade, 79, 105

Harper, John A., 194
Harper, Robert Goodloe, 40, 136
Hartz, Louis, 97
Harvard University, 56, 69, 70
Henry, Patrick, 25–6, 28, 30, 31, 61, 104, 105
High Federalists, 115, 122, 128, 129, 130, 134, 135, 136, 145, 148, 150, 158, 159; see also Factions; Federalist party, factionalism in
Hobbes, Thomas, 58, 197
Hutchinson, James, 62, 81

Ideology, in America: "Anglomen" and "Gallomen," 43; France and Britain, policy toward, 76, 78, 134–5; "Spirit of 'Seventy-six," 78, 116; "Spirit of 'Ninety-six," 113–29; democratic, 124–5; "Spirit of 'Ninety-eight," 135–6, 141, 168; see also Federalist party; Parties, political, ideology; Republican party
Impressment, 77, 186
Independent Chronicle (Boston), 140
Intellectuals: in new nations, 67, 100; in American politics, 69–70, 165
Interests and interest groups, 2, 6, 11, 15, 46, 109, 123; see also Democracy *and specific interests*
"Invisibles," 192, 193
Irish in U.S. politics, 76, 121, 139, 156
Irvine, William, 117
Irving, Washington, 193

Jackson, Andrew, 18, 33, 49, 121, 147, 197, 201, 205–6, 208
Jarvis, Charles, 78
Jay, John: cadreman for Federalist party, 40; age, 68; education, 69; candidate for Governor of New York, 71–2, 104; as author of Jay treaty, 75, 77, 78, 80, 86; elected Governor in 1795, 128; as Moderate Federalist, 151; and elections of 1800, 155–6; see also Jay treaty
Jay treaty, 90, 98, 128; Madison quoted on, 75, 77–8; content of, 76–7; Washington's support of, 76–8, 86–7; defense of, 78; popular op-

224

Index

Lyon, Matthew, and *Vermont Journal*,
139–40, 142

McClenachan, Blair, 62, 71, 78, 118
McHenry, James, 131, 148, 151
McKean, Thomas, 156, 164, 166, 167,
180, 186
Maclay, "Billy," 38, 39, 56, 70, 104
Macon, Nathaniel, 56, 68, 69, 73, 136,
153, 171, 184–5, 187
Madison, James, 84, 95, 165, 199;
founder of Republican party, 2, 9,
82, 83, 208; as Congressional candidate, 4; collaboration with Jefferson,
6, 57–8, 60, 64, 71, 114, 130; forms
Congressional opposition to Federalists, 6, 53, 54, 56–7, 60, 68; personality, 6, 54, 69; relations with Hamilton, 11, 58, 76; relations with
Washington, 11, 57; election of
1788, 30; and Hamilton's economic
policies, 54, 55, 195; attitude toward John Adams, 56; establishes
National Gazette, 57, 60, 104–5;
and Democratic and Republican Societies, 63; and Taylor's attack on
Federalists, 64; and Whiskey Rebellion, 64; attitude toward political
parties, 66, 70, 92, 93; political philosophy, 66, 97, 104, 109, 130–31;
age, 68; education, 69; and elections
of 1792, 73–4; and Jay treaty, 75,
77–8, 86–8; and Republican party
in Virginia, 84; quoted on differences between Federalists and Republicans, 91–2; and election of
1796, 113, 116–17, 130; retires from
Congress, 131; author of Virginia
Resolution, 140; as Secretary of
State, 170, 180, 186; and Yazoo
lands, 183; and "Tertium Quids,"
184; and election of 1808, 188–9;
quoted on faction, 191; as President,
192–7; responsibility for Republican
factionalism, 192–7, 200, 202, 205,
207; and War of 1812, 193–5, 196,
197; Washington Irving quoted on,
193; election of 1812, 196–7

Maine, admission of, 199
Manhattan Company, 155
Marache's boarding house, 152, 171
Marshall, John, 40, 68, 69, 136, 142–
3, 150, 151, 170, 180, 195
Marx, Karl, 101
Maryland, politics in: nonparty, factional politics in, 19; planter control of the legislature, 1780's, 25;
and ratification, 28; and elections of
1788–1789, 30–31; Congressional
delegation of, 39; Federalist strength
in, 40; agrarian discontent in, 64;
delegation splits on Jay treaty, 88,
89; elections of 1796, 128; Republican delegation and party loyalty,
139; elections of 1798, 142; Republican organization in, 163; and Jefferson-Burr contest for presidency,
167, 168; and Embargo Act of
1806, 187; and election of 1808,
189, 190; and election of 1812, 196
Mason, George, 104
Massachusetts, politics in: nonparty
conflicts in, 19; and Shays's Rebellion,
19; and Boston caucus, 25; and ratification, 28, 39; elections of 1788–
1789, 30; Federalist party strength
in, 40, 41, 142; and Jay treaty, 80;
Republican following in, 80; and
elections of 1796, 118; reaction to
Alien and Sedition Acts in, 140; and
elections of 1800, 160; Republican
organization in, 165
Methodists, 121, 141–2
Middle Atlantic states, politics in, 21,
40, 139, 142, 143, 158, 167
Mifflin, Thomas, 19, 70–71, 81, 82
Missouri, admission of, 198–9
Moderate Federalists, 115, 142–3,
148, 150, 159
Modernization, economic, 37–8, 55–6,
96, 99
Modernization, political: defined, 14–
15; party functions in, 16, 49, 208;
obstacles to, 81; in American experience, 95–6, 99, 168–9; in England,
125–6; social and economic requi-
sites for, 125–6

226

Index

North Carolina, politics in: and ratification, 28; agrarian discontent in, 64; elections of 1792, 73; reaction to Jay treaty, 79; elections of 1796, 116, 118; elections of 1798, 142; elections of 1800, 153, 158, 160; Republican strength in, 179–80; and Embargo Act of 1806, 187; and election of 1808, 190

Northern Confederacy, 180–81

Notables in politics, 40, 41, 44

Ohio, 174

Opposition, 12; legitimacy of, 5, 7, 63, 145, 168; and liberal tradition, 9, 10; responsible, 14, 99, 132–49; Hamilton's attitude toward, 44; Federalist attitude toward, 57, 65

Otis, Harrison Gray, 135, 136, 151

Paine, Thomas, 17, 57–8, 60

Pakenham, Lord, 197

Panic of 1819–1821, 199, 205–6

Parties, political: Jefferson's attitude toward, 5–7, 59, 67, 93, 110, 149; Washington's attitude toward, 6–7; as artifacts, 10, 49; as cohesive force in fragmented governmental system, 11, 14, 17, 23; democratic function, 12–13, 27, 47, 50, 51, 107, 109–12, 126, 143–7, 149, 150, 172, 201, 208; popular, 13, 15, 95–112 *passim*; in loyal opposition, 14, 99, 132–49; role in nation building, 14, 158; modern parties, 15, 103, 123–5; and role in political modernization, 15, 16, 49, 208; role in pluralistic society, 21, 46-7, 144; functions, 29–30, 45–7, 106, 122, 126, 158, 200, 203; and voting participation, 33, 160, 201; Hamilton's attitude toward, 43–4; distinguished from factions, 45–50, 96, 106; following, 45, 47, 106, 144, 147, 158; organization, 45, 111, 203; structure, 45, 85–6, 106, 111, 158; electioneering, 46, 103, 158; nominations, 46, 158; programs of, 46–7; ideology, 48, 106, 144, 158, 202,

204; cadre parties, 51, 106, 126; mass parties, 51, 125–6; Madison's attitude toward, 66, 70, 92; cohesion in, 89–90; democracy within, 107, 109, 146; plebiscitarian, 126; destructive and cohesive forces in, 202–5; leadership in, 202, 203; patronage in, 203, 204

Party system, 2, 12, 15; one-party, 13, 15, 51, 202; two-party, 13, 14, 47, 50, 51, 66, 112, 143–7, 192, 202, 207; in Pennsylvania, 19; multi-party, 112, 146; plural-party, 143–7

"Patriots" in the American Revolution, 8, 17–18, 80

Pendleton, Edmund, 84

Pennsylvania, politics in, 6; earliest state parties in, 19–20, 21, 23, 70; poor communications in, 24; factions in 1780's, 25; and ratification, 28, 104; and elections of 1788–1789, 30, 32; Congressional delegation from, 39, 88, 89, 139, 166; popular opposition to Federalist party in, 61; Democratic and Republican Societies in, 62; and Whiskey Rebellion, 64, 104, 137; youthful political leadership in, 68; Republican strength in, 70–71, 81–2, 85, 162, 164, 165; Federalist strength in, 71, 81, 156, 159, 162; and elections of 1792, 73–4; and elections of 1794, 74; electoral vote of, 83; and Fries Uprising, 98, 137, 159; election of 1796, 115–19, 127, 128; and Alien and Sedition Acts, 140; and elections of 1798, 142; and elections of 1800, 153, 154, 156–7, 160; Republican patronage squabbles, 180, 192; Republican factionalism in, 186; and election of 1808, 189; and election of 1812, 196–7

Philadelphia, 24, 53, 75, 78, 89, 129; as capital of U.S., 36, 166, 175; Federalist strength in, 40; and elections of 1794, 74; opposition to Jay treaty in, 78; center of Republican organization, 81, 82, 86, 117, 133; and elections of 1800, 152, 154

Pickering, John, 174
Pickering, Timothy, 131, 135, 136, 139, 148, 150, 151, 180–81
Pinckney, Charles, 13, 79, 80, 105, 114, 133, 142, 157
Pinckney, Charles Cotesworth, 133, 151, 157–8, 182, 189
Pinckney, Thomas, 114–15, 127, 133
Pinkney, William, 186
Planter interest, 2, 19, 21, 24, 25, 27, 28, 31, 40, 41, 55, 76, 79, 81
Pluralism, in American society, 2–3, 11, 19, 101; parties and, 14, 15, 24–5, 46, 144; produces factional politics, 19–21; and ratification, 27–8; and elections of 1788–1789, 33
Politicians, professional, 20, 84, 95, 101, 165, 206, 207
Populism, 18, 29, 62
Porter, Peter B., 193
Presbyterians, 121
Presidential elections—of 1788–1789, 29–33; —of 1792, 111; —of 1796, 6, 111, 113–22, 126–9, 204; —of 1800, 111, 141, 150–69; —of 1804, 111, 178, 181–3, 189–90; —of 1808, 188–90; —of 1812, 196–7; —of 1816, 197; —of 1820, 199; —of 1824, 32, 200–201; —of 1828, 32, 33; —of 1832, 32; —of 1836, 32; —of 1840, 32, 33
Princeton University (College of New Jersey), 54, 69
Propaganda, 15, 23, 41–2; see also Newspapers
Public opinion, 4, 6, 42, 45, 106, 110

Randolph, John, 142, 171, 172, 183–5, 186, 188, 189, 193, 194
Ratification of Constitution, conflict over, 27, 28–9, 103–6
Register (Raleigh), 153
Republican party (of Thomas Jefferson), 112; Jefferson as leader of, 1, 6; organization, 12, 147, 153, 162, 182; as popular party, 13, 65–6, 103, 106–7, 125, 207; as prototype for American parties, 16, 103, 191; and popular opposition to Federal-

ists, 53, 54, 61–7; as Congressional faction, 54–7; economic policy, 55–6, 101–2, 103, 173, 177; Congressional leadership in early years, 56, 82–3; as capital faction, 58, 66; Jefferson as rallying point of opposition, 59–60; patronage, 60, 156, 157, 163–4, 179, 181, 182, 192, 198; use of newspapers, 60–61, 83, 117, 152, 154; ideology, 61, 64–5, 76, 89–93, 97, 102, 154, 172, 177, 178, 188; agrarian support of, 65, 119, 120–21, 173, 181; following, 65, 76, 103, 106, 107, 109, 191, 193; as opposition party, 66, 91, 130–49; leadership, 68–9, 131–2; cadre formation—in Pennsylvania, 70–71; —in New York, 71–2; —in Philadelphia, 80; —nationally, 82–5, 107; interstate co-ordination, 70, 82; Pennsylvania, strength in, 70–71, 73–4, 81–2, 117, 156, 159, 162, 164; New York, strength in, 71–2, 73–4, 83–4, 159, 163–4; Virginia, strength in, 72, 73, 83, 84–5; New York–Virginia axis in, 73; nominations and elections—of 1792, 73–4; —of 1794, 74; —of 1796, 111, 113–22, 126–9; —of 1798, 141–3; —of 1800, 111, 152, 154; —of 1804, 111, 178, 181–3; —of 1808, 188–90; —of 1812, 196–7; —of 1816, 197; —of 1820, 199; —of 1824, 200–201; movement becomes a party, 76; structure, 76, 84–5, 91, 106, 109, 162–5, 198; and Citizen Genêt, 77; and Jay treaty, 77–80, 86–93, 204; Congressional caucus of, 87, 103, 116, 152, 170, 194; standing committees in Congress, use of, 87, 194; Middle Atlantic states, strength in, 88, 158; party voting in Congress, 88, 90, 137–9, 170, 195; philosophical antecedents, 92; distinguished from Federalist party, 98, 106, 119; antecedents in American politics, 103–6; as "party of politicians," 106; tripodal structure of, 107–9; artisan support, 121; planter sup-

Index

Republican party (*continued*)
port, 121; urban support, 121; and French crisis of 1797, 134; and Alien and Sedition Acts, 136, 139, 140–41; in two-party rivalry in U.S., 144, 145–8, 159; party program of, 154, 172, 173–4; factionalism—in New York, 164, 180–81; —in Pennsylvania, 181, 186; —of "Tertium Quids," 184–5, 188; —in Madison's administration, 191–7, 202, 205; —nationally, 191, 204; —of Young Republicans, 193–7; —in Monroe's administration, 197–200, 202, 205; and Jefferson-Burr contest for presidency, 166–8; in Jefferson administration, 170–90; and Louisiana Purchase, 178; and Yazoo lands, 183–4; as dominant party, 191–2, 196; disintegration of, 191, 200–201, 202, 204, 207; and War of 1812, 196–7; and Federalist demise, 198; and Missouri compromise, 199; and panic of 1819–1821, 199; integrating and disintegrating factors in, 204–5

Republican Societies; *see* Democratic and Republican Societies
Revolution, 7–8, 98; *see also particular revolutions*
Reynolds, Mrs. James, 82, 83
Rhode Island, politics in, 19, 25, 28, 153, 160
Ritchie, Thomas, 181
Rittenhouse, David, 81, 116
Rodney, Caesar A., 62, 76–7, 171, 181
Rush, Benjamin, 62, 70, 73, 81
Russell, Benjamin, 41
Russia, 9, 126

Schuyler, Philip, 34, 71
Schuyler family (New York), 20
Sedgwick, Theodore, 40, 68, 69, 86, 132, 134, 137, 139
Sedition Act; *see* Alien, Naturalization, and Sedition Acts
Shays's Rebellion (Daniel Shays), 19, 98; Shaysites, 25
Singletary, Amos, 34, 109

Smith, Melancton, 13, 62, 73, 104, 109, 110, 111
Smith, Robert, 179, 192
Smith, Samuel, 89, 139, 167, 168, 179, 186, 189, 192
Smith, William Loughton, 58, 86
Smith clique, 192
Society of the Cincinnati, 40, 63
Society for the Preservation of Liberty, 23
Sons of Liberty, 17, 21
South Carolina: reaction to Jay treaty, 79–80, 87; Republican strength in, 154, 157–8, 159, 160, 164; and Jefferson-Burr contest for presidency, 167, 168; expansionist demands in Madison's administration, 193
South Carolina, politics in: faction politics in, 13, 19; planter domination in, 25; and ratification, 28, 105; elections of 1788–1789, 30; Federalist strength in, 40, 41, 121; and debt assumption, 42; agrarian discontent in, 64; elections of 1796, 116, 118, 127–8; elections of 1798, 142; elections of 1800, 154, 157–60
Southern states, politics in: nonparty nominations in, 21, 22; deference patterns in, 24, 81; Federalist strength in, 40, 121; and Jay treaty, 79–80, 86; Republican strength in, 83, 120–21, 162, 164; elections of 1796, 115, 128; elections of 1798, 142–3; elections of 1800, 157–8; and Jefferson-Burr contest for presidency, 167
Speaker of the House of Representatives, 171, 193, 194
Spoils system; *see* Patronage
Suffrage, 3–4, 18, 24, 32, 81, 124, 125, 164; *see also* Democracy
Sumter, Thomas, 79, 105

Tammany Society, 84
Tariffs, 101, 195
Taylor, John (Caroline Co., Va.), 64, 65, 82, 84, 140, 149, 184
Tazewell, Littleton, 184

230

Tennessee, politics in, 115, 116, 121, 127, 143, 193
"Tertium Quids," Republican faction, 184–5, 188
Time Piece (New York), 140
Tocqueville, Alexis de, 98
Truman, David B., 47

Urban politics; *see specific cities*
Urbanization, 99, 100

Van Buren, Martin, 198, 201, 206, 208
Van Cortlandt, Pierre, 89
Van Cortlandt family (New York), 20, 89, 104
Varnum, Joseph, 185
Vermont, politics in, 80, 87, 115, 167, 168, 190, 196
Vermont Journal, 140
Virginia, politics in, 1, 4, 6; Jefferson as governor, 19; electioneering in 1780's, 23; notable politics in 1780's, 25; and ratification, 28, 104; elections of 1788–1789, 30; Federalist strength in, 40; capital on border of, 54; and assumption policy, 55; Republican party leadership in, 57; popular opposition to Federalist party in, 61; Republican strength in, 72, 73, 83, 84–5, 120–21, 164; and elections of 1792, 73; and Jay treaty, 79, 85; and elections of 1796, 115, 116, 118, 127; reactions to Alien and Sedition Acts, 140, 141; and elections of 1798, 142–3; and elections of 1800, 153; and "Tertium Quids," 184, 185; and Embargo Act of 1806, 187; and election of 1808, 190
Virginia and Kentucky Resolutions of 1798, 140–41, 143
Voting participation, 32–3, 160, 201

War of 1812, 188, 193–5, 196, 197
"War Hawks," 194
Washington, George, 2, 72, 81, 98, 131, 136; and Federalist party, 2, 9, 11, 50, 57; candidate for House of Burgesses, 4; attitude toward opposition, 5, 97; as charismatic figure, 5, 35–6, 42, 43, 65, 94, 95, 168; attitude toward political parties, 6–7; as President, 6, 57, 59; as symbol of national unity, 9, 11; elections of 1788–1789, 31; personality, 35; relations with Hamilton, 36, 42, 151–2; symbol of Federalist party unity, 42, 43, 48; neutrality policy, 43, 61, 79, 84; quoted on Freneau, 57; on Democratic and Republican Societies, 63; and Whiskey Rebellion, 64; age, 67–8; and Jay treaty, 76, 78, 86, 87; Beckley on, 82, 113; Republican attacks on, 83; and election of 1796, 113; and elections of 1798, 142; farewell address, 168
Washington, D.C., 151–2, 166, 169, 171–2, 175
Ways and Means Committee, 87, 171, 184, 185
Weber, Max, 44, 45, 106
Webster, Daniel, 207
Webster, Noah, 42, 151
Weed, Thurlow, 207
Whig party in America, 33, 207
Whigs, in England, 4, 5
Whiskey Rebellion, 63–4, 66, 98, 137
William and Mary, College of, 59, 69
Wilson, James, 19
Wolcott, Oliver, 131, 148, 151
Wythe, George, 79, 104

XYZ Affair, 134–5, 137

Yale University, 56, 69, 122, 154
Yates, Robert, 30
Yazoo lands, 183
"Young Republicans," 193–7

231